Robert Lowell and Irish Poetry

Robert Lowell and Irish Poetry

Edited by Eve Cobain and Philip Coleman

Afterword by Marie Heaney

PETER LANG

Oxford • Bern • Berlin • Bruxelles • New York • Wien

Bibliographic information published by Die Deutsche Nationalbibliothek.
Die Deutsche Nationalbibliothek lists this publication in the Deutsche National-
bibliografie; detailed bibliographic data is available on the Internet at
http://dnb.d-nb.de.

A catalogue record for this book is available from the British Library.

Cover photo: Copyright 2010, Ivana Lowell, used by permission of The Wylie
Agency (UK) Limited.
Cover design: Peter Lang.

ISBN 978-1-78874-509-3 (print) • ISBN 978-1-78874-510-9 (ePDF)
ISBN 978-1-78874-511-6 (ePub) • ISBN 978-1-78874-512-3 (mobi)

© Peter Lang AG 2020

Published by Peter Lang Ltd, International Academic Publishers,
52 St Giles, Oxford, OX1 3LU, United Kingdom
oxford@peterlang.com, www.peterlang.com

Eve Cobain and Philip Coleman have asserted their right under the Copyright,
Designs and Patents Act, 1988, to be identified as Editors of this Work.
© the editors and contributors 2019

All rights reserved.
All parts of this publication are protected by copyright.
Any utilisation outside the strict limits of the copyright law, without
the permission of the publisher, is forbidden and liable to prosecution.
This applies in particular to reproductions, translations, microfilming,
and storage and processing in electronic retrieval systems.

This publication has been peer reviewed.

Contents

Acknowledgements — ix

PHILIP COLEMAN AND EVE COBAIN
Introduction — 1

ANNA CHAHOUD
The Orator and the Poet: J.V. Luce on Robert Lowell — 7

JOHN VICTOR LUCE
Oration on the Conferral of an Honorary DLitt Degree on Robert Lowell by the University of Dublin, Trinity College, 31 May 1976 — 17

PAUL MULDOON
Robert Lowell at Castletown House — 21

STEVEN GOULD AXELROD
Robert Lowell in Dark Times — 23

FRANK J. KEARFUL
Names and Naming: Robert Lowell and the Boston Irish — 49

ALEX RUNCHMAN
Weaving the Great Clan: Robert Lowell, Robert Kennedy and Martin Luther King — 67

ADAM BEARDSWORTH

From Terrible Beauty to Stale and Small: W.B. Yeats's Influence on Robert Lowell's Political Poetry 83

CALISTA MCRAE

Robert Lowell and Louis MacNeice: Reading Likeness through Elegy 107

KARL O'HANLON

Rebels in Formal Dress: Robert Lowell, Denis Devlin and their Transatlantic Literary Network 123

STEPHEN GRACE

'thudding in a big sea': The Oceanic Ecologies of Robert Lowell and Seamus Heaney 147

GERALD DAWE

Waiting for the New Life: Reading Robert Lowell in Bangor, Co. Down, in the 1970s 167

MICHAEL HINDS

Name and Shame: 'Identification in Belfast' 177

LUCY COLLINS

Lost Connections: Reading Family in the Poetry of Eavan Boland and Robert Lowell 193

ELLEN DILLON

Radical Tensions: Robert Lowell, Charles Altieri and Catherine Walsh 211

Contents

EVE COBAIN
'The way we are living': Robert Lowell and Leontia Flynn 229

JULIE O'CALLAGHAN
Seamus Heaney Introducing Robert Lowell in Kilkenny, 1975 249

SEAMUS HEANEY
Introduction to Robert Lowell Reading at Kilkenny Arts Week,
Kytler's Inn, Kilkenny, 28 August 1975 251

MARIE HEANEY
Afterword 253

Notes on Contributors 257

Index 263

Acknowledgements

This volume of essays on Robert Lowell and Irish poetry is based on a symposium held in Trinity College Dublin, Ireland, in March 2017 to celebrate the centenary of the poet's birth. The 'Robert Lowell and Ireland' symposium was supported by the School of English, the Faculty of Arts, Humanities and Social Sciences, and the Trinity Long Room Hub, Trinity College Dublin. Financial support was also provided by the Irish Association for American Studies, the Office of Public Works (Ireland), and Poetry Ireland. The publication of this volume has been made possible by the Trinity Trust and Foundation.

Permission to include a previously unpublished piece of writing by Seamus Heaney in this volume has been granted by the Estate of Seamus Heaney and Faber and Faber Ltd. The editors and publisher gratefully acknowledge the assistance of Marie Heaney and Catherine Heaney in making it possible to include Seamus Heaney's work in this book. Thanks are also due to Hannah Styles of Faber and Faber's Permissions Department for her assistance.

The editors also wish to acknowledge Ivana Lowell and the Estate of Robert Lowell for granting permission to use an image of Robert Lowell and Caroline Blackwood on the cover of this volume. Thanks are also due to Isla Forrester of The Wylie Agency for assistance in relation to this.

Permission to reproduce excerpts from unpublished correspondence by Robert Lowell in Karl O'Hanlon's essay in this volume has been granted by Farrar, Straus and Giroux on behalf of the Estate of Robert Lowell. The editors thank Victoria Fox of Farrar, Straus and Giroux for her assistance.

Paul Muldoon has given permission for his poem 'Robert Lowell at Castletown House' to be included in this volume.

This volume brings together a number of those who contributed to the 'Robert Lowell and Ireland' symposium and participated in conversations about Lowell throughout the weekend of 3–5 March 2017. However, the success of that event was due to the assistance and input of many individuals without whom it would not have been possible. The editors are pleased to acknowledge these people here who, in various capacities, helped to make the symposium such a success or assisted with the preparation of this book: Thomas Austenfeld, Rise Axelrod, Emily Bourke, Christine Casey, Jonathan Creasy, Peter Crooks, Caitríona Curtis, Dorothea Depner, Aileen Douglas, Kevina Dunne, Sarah Dunne, Feena Flanagan, Eugene Foster, Daniel Geary, Mary Heffernan, Emily Johnston, Darryl Jones, Benjamin Keatinge, Maureen Kennelly, Grzegorz Kość, Caitríona Leahy, Stephen Matterson, Paula Murphy, Eiléan Ní Chuilleanáin, Niamh NicGhabhann, Julie O'Callaghan, Kristina Odlum, Jane Ohlmeyer, Michael O'Loughlin, Diederik Oostdijk, Suzanne Richmond, Diane Sadler, Muireann Sheahan, Valerie Smith, Moya Thompson, Tom Walker.

Finally, the editors wish to thank Christabel Scaife, who gave great advice when the initial pitch for this volume was made, and the following people at Peter Lang who saw the book through its various stages of production: Natasha Collin, Philip Dunshea, Anthony Mason, Simon Phillimore and Jonathan Smith. Thanks are also due to the anonymous readers, whose input is greatly appreciated.

Eve Cobain and Philip Coleman
Trinity College Dublin, November 2019

PHILIP COLEMAN AND EVE COBAIN

Introduction

On 13 September 1977, *The New York Times* reported that Robert Lowell had passed away the day before: 'Mr. Lowell, who was 60 years old, was stricken while riding in a taxicab on his way to Manhattan from Kennedy International Airport. He was returning from Ireland where he had been visiting his wife and son.'[1] Lowell had been visiting Caroline Blackwood, his third wife, and their son Sheridan, at Castletown House, Co Kildare. The week before, Lowell and Blackwood visited Seamus and Marie Heaney at their home in Sandymount in Dublin, but the Heaneys sensed that all was not right. Ten days later, as Marie Heaney writes in the moving recollection that appears as an Afterword to the present volume, Seamus Heaney composed 'Elegy' in Robert Lowell's memory.[2]

If that last meeting with the Heaneys ended on a somewhat sombre note, with the imminent dissolution of Lowell's marriage to Blackwood hanging heavy in the air, Lowell and Blackwood were very much a part of Irish literary and cultural life during their time spent in Ireland in the mid-1970s. Lowell gave a reading at the Kilkenny Arts Festival in August 1975, introduced by Seamus Heaney, with several younger poets in attendance, including Derek Mahon, Julie O'Callaghan and Dennis O'Driscoll. In the summer of 1976, Lowell was awarded an Honorary DLitt degree from the University of Dublin, Trinity College. During this time, in other words, Lowell was recognized in Ireland – and by Irish poets – as a major figure. For J.V. Luce, who wrote and delivered the public oration in Lowell's honour in Trinity College Dublin in 1976 – brilliantly contextualized here by Anna Chahoud – Lowell was presented to an Irish audience as a poet

[1] 'Robert Lowell, Pulitzer Prize Poet, Is Dead at 60', 13 September 1977: 1; available online at: <https://www.nytimes.com/1977/09/13/archives/robert-lowell-pulitzer-prize-poet-is-dead-at-60-robert-lowell.html> (accessed 13 May 2019).
[2] See Seamus Heaney, 'Elegy' in *Field Work* (London: Faber and Faber, 1979), 25–27.

whose work is characterized by formal 'compression and energy' as well as one who has critiqued 'cruelty [...] greed, and [...] the barbarities of war'.³ It is hardly surprising, then, that Lowell should have struck a chord with Irish poets in the 1970s, and especially poets such as Heaney and Mahon, for whom the challenge of how best to engage with the unfolding catastrophe of the Troubles in Northern Ireland was such a central concern during this period.

While he may have been regarded as 'a prophetic, public poet and a courageous pacifist' in the 1970s, as Tom Paulin has put it, Lowell was also seen by many at the time as something of a celebrity.⁴ Indeed, a few weeks before they visited the Heaneys in September 1977, a 'Late News' column in *The Irish Times* reported that:

> A number of people were arrested and drugs were seized when gardaí [*sic*] raided Castletown House, in Celbridge, Co Kildare, this morning where a party was being held for a rock singer, Phil Lynott of the Thin Lizzy group. Several hundred people were attending the party in the stately Georgian mansion, including many who had 'gate-crashed'.⁵

It is tempting to suggest that Lowell and Blackwood attended this party, though they may have de-camped to Dublin on the night in question. Whether they were there or not, however, they were closely connected to a literary and cultural scene in Ireland at the time that was itself caught up in a maelstrom of social change. Reflecting on that 'Late News' piece from 1977 in 2019, Una Mullally wrote that 'the story captured the hedonism

---

3   See J.V. Luce, 'Oration on the Conferral of an Honorary DLitt Degree on Robert Lowell by the University of Dublin, Trinity College, 31 May 1976' in this volume. An excerpt from Luce's oration was also printed in *The Irish Times* (1 June 1976): 7.
4   Tom Paulin, 'The voice of America', rev. of Robert Lowell, *Collected Poems*, eds Frank Bidart and David Gewanter (London: Faber and Faber, 2003), available online at: <https://www.theguardian.com/books/2003/aug/03/poetry.robertlowell> (accessed 13 May 2019).
5   See Una Mullaly, 'The summer of 1977 was the moment when rock music tipped over in Ireland' in *The Irish Times* (30 March 2019), available online at: <https://www.irishtimes.com/culture/heritage/the-summer-of-1977-was-the-moment-rock-music-tipped-over-in-ireland-1.3834024> (accessed 13 May 2019).

(for some) of that era – police raids, rock stars, stately mansions and drugs. The summer of 1977 was the moment rock music tipped over in Ireland, laying the foundations for what we now call festival season.'[6] If the summer of 1977 was Ireland's 'Summer of Love' – though that is probably overstating it – Lowell was very much a part of it, promoting a sense of poetry as something that could help to effect real change in the public sphere.

It is clear that Lowell's work has been an important example for many Irish poets from the 1940s to the present and the heyday of his influence may have been in the 1970s. However, as Paulin has put it: 'You don't need to have been young in the Sixties to appreciate this Faustian poet.'[7] The purpose of this volume, then, is to explore some of the ways in which Irish poets have engaged with Lowell since the 1940s, when his first books started to appear. This is an important theme not least because so many Irish poets have responded to Lowell in interesting and various ways – only a relatively small but representative number of them are considered here – but also because the topic seems to have been neglected in critical studies to date. While there are scattered references to Middle Generation US American poets such as John Berryman, Allen Ginsberg, and Sylvia Plath in Jefferson Holdridge and Brian Ó Conchubhair's important volume *Post-Ireland? Essays on Contemporary Irish Poetry* (2017), for example, Lowell does not feature anywhere in the collection. Does this mean that Lowell does not matter to contemporary Irish poets? The essays in the present volume, which explore a wide range of Irish poets from various backgrounds, suggest otherwise.

In his seminal study *Yeats and American Poetry* (1983), Terence Diggory downplays the importance of W.B. Yeats in Lowell's development, suggesting that Allen Tate was a much more significant early influence. In Thomas Austenfeld's edited collection *Robert Lowell in a New Century: European and American Perspectives* (2019), however, a broader sense of Lowell's importance to contemporary and earlier poets writing in Europe is given, suggesting that a lot more remains to be said about both

6   Ibid.
7   Paulin, 'The voice of America'.

Lowell's appreciation for – and his poetic reception in – the Old World. Steven Gould Axelrod and Adam Beardsworth reassess aspects of Lowell's engagement with Yeats in their essays in the present volume, but others explore the many ways that Irish poets have been reading and thinking about Lowell over many decades. Notwithstanding the central role played by Seamus Heaney, in particular, in that discussion, a picture emerges in these essays of Lowell as a poet whose work has mattered to Irish poets who are not often considered alongside each other because of a critical insistence on the hard borders of generational, regional and other kinds of perceived cultural affiliation. While it may not come as a surprise to learn that Lowell's early work was reviewed in positive terms by the great Irish formalist Austin Clarke, for example, the sense of connection that Lucy Collins discerns in the younger Eavan Boland's engagements with Lowell is an important recognition of the US American poet's example for Irish poets of the 1970s who sought to turn their attention to the domestic sphere. Lowell's work has mattered to Irish poets across generations, from Clarke to Boland and beyond, often for very different reasons. Moreover, his influence is acknowledged here in essays that look at examples from both sides of the Northern Irish border, including poets such as Boland, Gerald Dawe, Denis Devlin, Seamus Heaney, Leontia Flynn, Louis MacNeice and Catherine Walsh. The radical eclecticism of that list reveals a constellation of poets for whom Lowell was, and still is, a poet of signal, if not central, importance.

Seamus Heaney's previously unpublished introduction to Lowell's reading in Kilkenny in 1975 provides a marvellous insight into the Northern Irish poet's sense of the American's importance here, but the perspectives of the next generation, as it were, are given in the poetic and biographical reflections of Paul Muldoon and Gerald Dawe in their contributions to the volume. Between them, Muldoon and Dawe speak to the complexity of the Lowellian inheritance for (Northern) Irish poets, which is in turn tackled as a subject of real critical difficulty in Calista McRae's reading of Louis MacNeice's affinities with Lowell and Karl O'Hanlon's probing account of Lowell and Denis Devlin within the contexts of transatlantic late modernism and Catholicism. The Irish-American contexts of Lowell's work are also examined here in very different ways by Frank J. Kearful and

Alex Runchman, while Lowell's importance to contemporary poets such as Catherine Walsh and Leontia Flynn is considered in the contributions, respectively, of Ellen Dillon and Eve Cobain. A strong sense of context – historical and critical – informs these essays but they are all closely attentive to the intricacies of formal procedure that have made Lowell's work so rewarding, and challenging, from the beginning. At the same time, many of the essays included here challenge us to think of Lowell in new ways precisely because of the way that Irish poets have engaged with him. In his consideration of what he terms the 'oceanic ecologies' of Lowell and Heaney, for example, Stephen Grace opens up a new sense of the shared ground between the poets. Michael Hinds, meanwhile, asks what is at stake when Lowell gets it wrong in his representation of Irish history, as he appears to do in his sonnet 'Identification in Belfast'.

Writing in August 2003, a few months after the US American-led invasion of Iraq, Tom Paulin wrote in a review of Lowell's *Collected Poems*:

> Rereading his lines now, on the heels of another unjust, small war, I see that Lowell is drawing on Shelley's *Prometheus Unbound* (that sweet volcanic cone) and adapting Marvell's octosyllabic couplets and stanza form allusively to reinforce his public stance. He knows the heart of darkness in the American imperial sublime, as his fascination with Melville shows.[8]

Nearly two decades later, the horrible irony of the phrase 'small war' has given way to the age of Trump, a truly dark time in which, as Steven Gould Axelrod argues in the opening essay in this collection, the world needs poets of Lowell's searing honesty more than ever. Axelrod's essay, which was delivered as the H.O. White Memorial Lecture in Trinity College Dublin in 2017, reinforces the view articulated by J.V. Luce in his public oration on the occasion of the award of an honorary DLitt degree to Lowell in 1976, but all of the essays collected in this volume share this sense of Lowell's importance to the contemporary cultural and political moment. In his reflections on Lowell's influence in his contribution to this volume, Gerald Dawe acknowledges that his 'debt to Lowell goes very much deeper than [he had] previously thought.' The various contributions to this volume attest to the breadth and depth of Lowell's

---

8   Paulin, 'The voice of America'.

presence in the Irish poetic landscape, prompting further study of several individual poets and, at the same time, demanding a reassessment of a major American poet's continuing importance and influence outside of the United States, in Ireland and elsewhere.⁹

---

9   For further considerations of Lowell's engagements with Europe and European poets, in particular, see Thomas Austenfeld, ed., *Robert Lowell in a New Century: European and American Perspectives* (Rochester, NY: Camden House, 2019).

ANNA CHAHOUD

The Orator and the Poet: J.V. Luce on Robert Lowell

On 31 May 1976 the University of Dublin held Extraordinary Commencements to mark the bicentenary of the birth of the United States of America. On that day, Robert Lowell, fully robed in scarlet academic dress, processed into the Public Theatre along with fellow writer Saul Bellow, pianist Charles Rosen, astronaut Neil Armstrong, Yale President Kingman Brewster, and American Ambassador Walter Curley. Honorary Doctorates would soon be conferred upon the six distinguished men in recognition of their 'outstanding contribution to scholarship, society, culture and civil society'. The candidates walked down the aisle with the Caput Senatus – Chancellor, Provost and Senior Master Non-Regent – to the podium, where they were welcomed by the Registrar, historian Aidan Clarke, the Senior Proctor, Professor of English William Fitzroy Pyle, and the Public Orator, Erasmus Smith's Professor of Oratory John Victor Luce, who would soon introduce each candidate with an eloquent Latin oration. The Provost at the time was the Irish historian Francis Steward Leland Lyons; the Chancellor of the University of Dublin was Frederick Henry Boland, distinguished diplomat and father of the poet Eavan Boland, who would herself receive an honorary degree on 9 July 2004 on the occasion of the centenary of women accepted for degrees in Trinity College. After the Senate minutes, written in Latin, were read out by the Registrar and approved by the assembled Doctors and Masters, the ceremony began, the Senior Proctor announcing the name of each candidate and summoning him to stand and proceed to the centre of the podium, in order to be presented to the Chancellor and to the Senate by the Public Orator. As the Statutes of Trinity College and of the University of Dublin prescribe that the order of presentation of Degrees be the reverse of the order in which the Degrees were instituted, Robert Trail Spence

Lowell – the full name is traditionally used – was the fourth candidate to be admitted, after Doctors in Music and Science, and before Doctors in Laws. The Chancellor's valedictory formula and the sound of the seventeenth-century organ signalled the completion of proceedings, and the new graduates processed behind the Caput Senatus out of the Public Theatre into Front Square, as is still the practice to this day.

Commencements and the Public Orator

The graduation ceremony preserves all the features of its late medieval origins, and that is one of the reasons why it leaves a long-lasting memory in those who participate in it. Proceedings are as formal as is required by a formal assembly of the University Senate ('Comitia'), and all the more when the Senate meets for the public conferring of degrees ('Commencements', originally so named because candidates do not 'commence' as teachers or Doctors in their Faculty until they obtain their degree).[1] The opening procession is symbolically led by the Porter carrying the Proctors' Book, which contains the signatures of the officers responsible for supplications since 1625, followed by the candidates in ascending order of their Degree, the Mace Bearer with the silver University Mace, the Senior Master Non-Regent, the Provost and the Chancellor.

Every ceremony is memorable in its own right, and especially so on special occasions such as centenary celebrations, anniversaries, and conferring of honorary degrees. One aspect is worth mentioning, in the words of John Luce on the College tercentenary in 1992: 'the ceremonies […] achieved dignity, and indeed splendour, without becoming over-ostentatious.'[2] The comment indeed applies to every ceremony, as anyone who has attended Commencements at least once can testify.

1   Cf. C. Maxwell, *A History of Trinity College Dublin 1592–1892* (Dublin: University Press, 1946), 52 n. 37.
2   J.V. Luce, *Trinity College: The First 400 Years* (Dublin: Trinity College Dublin Press, 1992), 110.

The early history of Honorary Degrees – and in fact any Degrees – in Trinity College is clouded in mystery. The ceremonial was probably modelled on a Cambridge usage,[3] as many other statutory features of the College since its foundation by Queen Elizabeth in 1592. The first conferring of which we have any record is that of James Ussher, on Shrove Tuesday 1601, but one has to wait until the Provostship of Sir William Temple (1609–27) for evidence of Latin orations delivered for prospective Doctors by the Lord Primate at the 'great Commencement' held in St Patrick's Cathedral on 18 August 1614.[4] Over 250 years intervened between that momentous day and the appointment of the first Public Orator in 1869, twelve years after Trinity College was finally granted the Seal as 'The University of Dublin'. The Public Orator is an officer of the University, not of the College.

The *Orator Publicus* is 'the one who pleads in public before the Senate', a title with 'a quasi-juristic implication' reminiscent of the ancient law courts in classical Athens and Rome.[5] Only Cambridge and Oxford have an equivalent position, probably derived from a practice of the medieval University of Paris, and officially recognized for each University by the times of Henry VIII (1521) and Queen Elizabeth (1564) respectively. The Public Orator is the person who traditionally writes and delivers individual orations for each recipient of an Honorary Degree, and the only officer to discharge that function in the University of Dublin. He also writes official letters to institutions on behalf of the University, in Latin if the correspondence is initiated by the University of Dublin, in vernacular if in response to a vernacular letter received by the University of Dublin, as first occurred in 1898.[6]

Why should any of this matter in our times? Robert Lowell, and the other distinguished pioneers of twentieth-century arts and science who joined him on that day, were proclaimed Doctors in 1976, long after the world had taken a radical turn towards a break from the past. And yet, there

3 J.W. Stubbs, *A History of the University of Dublin, from the foundation to the end of the eighteenth century* (London: Longmans, Green and Company, 1889), 34.
4 Dublin University Calendar 1833, 55, 56.
5 C.B. Phipps, Introduction to *Orationes et Epistolae Dublinienses (1914–40)* (Dublin: Trinity College Dublin Press, 1941), vii–viii.
6 Ibid. xviii.

is a symbolic significance in the use of Latin, once the universal language for scholarly and scientific communication, in the admitting of extraordinary individuals who have made a difference to their world into an academic institution which pays tribute to innovation without forgetting tradition. In this sense the old definition of the Public Orator's function retains its full value:

> The office of Public Orator is a natural development of the circumstances of academic life. No University wishes to, or indeed can, live in a state of isolation. Outside her gates events of world-wide importance take place continually of which academic cognisance must be taken – scientific discovery, political, literary and musical achievement, [...] the festive anniversaries and the sorrows of sister Universities. In matters of outstanding importance, such as these, the peculiar practice of the Universities of Oxford, Cambridge and Dublin is to emphasise the dignity of the occasion by entrusting to the Public Orator the duty of penning an official Letter, or introducing in a Latin Oration to the Chancellor distinguished persons whom it is proposed by his hands to admit to Honorary Degrees. Thus the Public Orator primarily is the 'Pen' and the 'Voice' of his University.

John Victor Luce was the eighth Public Orator of the University of Dublin, after W. Bedell Stanford (1970–1), Donald Wormell (1952–70), Sir Robert William Tate (1914–52), Louis Claude Purser (1904–14), Robert Yelverton Tyrrell (1897–1904), Arthur Palmer (1888–97), and Thomas E. Webb (1869–88). His tenure of the office (1971–2005) was the longest after Tate's, although the number of his orations greatly exceeds those composed by Tate.[7] By his retirement in July 2005, John Luce had written 346 public orations, as well as numerous official letters to Universities,

---

7   All published, along with select official letters, in R.W. Tate, *Orationes et Epistolae Dublinienses (1914–40)*, Dublin 1941. The collection includes a substantial Introduction, in which Tate's friend C.B. Phipps gives a detailed account of the history of the office of Public Orator in Dublin, Oxford and Cambridge (vii–xix). Orations of Tate's predecessors, from 1888 to 1908, were published by Robert Y. Tyrrell in *Trinity College, Dublin: Speeches of Public Orators delivered at the Comitia held for conferring Honorary Degrees*, Dublin 1909; no records apparently survive of Webb's orations (cf. Tyrrell, *Praef.* vi).

and the eloquent introductory 'Exordium' to the Quatercentenary celebrations on 'Charter Day', 13 March 1992.[8]

'The Orator is the "Pen" and the "Voice" of his University': a deep awareness of this responsibility guided John Luce throughout the thirty-four years of his tenure, and he often recalled it as an encouragement (and a benevolent warning) to his successors.

The Oration

Unlike most of his predecessors, who wrote only in Latin for an audience inevitably educated in the ancient idiom, John Luce had to rise to the challenge of capturing the essence of his honorands in both Latin and English. From the mid-twentieth century orations for the conferring of Honorary Degrees were required not only to be composed and delivered in elegant Latin style, but also to offer an equally effective written English version. A literal translation would not do, because the two languages work differently, and stylistic features that are desirable in one language may make the other sound pompous or inane. Nevertheless, there can be only one oration, and the English text must reflect faithfully the sentiments of the Latin original. The oration written for Robert Lowell is a splendid example of John Luce's excellence in this arduous task.

The 'careful control' (*numeris sedulo moderatis*) that Luce praises in Lowell's poetry is also a characteristic of the orator's laudatory prose. It is no surprise that the Lowell oration is singled out for special praise in John Dillon's introduction to the first collection of Luce's speeches: 'it might equally well be said of our orator that he manages again and again to illuminate the praise of his honorands, which could so easily become a

---

8   A first selection of J.V. Luce's orations may be found in *Orationes Dublinienses Selectae (1971–1990)*, published in 1991 as No. 5 in the 'Trinity College Dublin Quatercentenary Series', with an Introduction by John Dillon, Regius Professor of Greek. A second volume *Orationes Dublinienses Selectae II 1991–2002*, appeared in 2004, with an Introduction by T.N. Mitchell, Provost 1991–2001.

pedestrian catalogue of honours and distinction, *fulguribus ingenii*'.⁹ The metaphor created for Lowell's 'lightning-flashes' capable of 'illuminat[ing] the "darkling plain" of our world' (*planitiem tenebris obductam*) is indeed impressive, as it combines a biblical allusion – the last hour of Christ's passion, *caelum tenebris obductum*¹⁰ – with a poetic one – the last stanza of Matthew Arnold's 'Dover Beach', 'And we are here as on a darkling plain, / swept with confused alarms of struggle and strife'.¹¹

In his Introduction to the second collection of Luce's orations, Provost Mitchell wrote:

> His style is markedly Ciceronian in its learned allusions, epigrammatic wit, the balance of rhythm of its sentence structure, and the eloquence of the phrasing, even when the esoteric mysteries of molecular biology or computer hardware have to be expounded in Latin dress. And their impact was always enhanced on the day by a resonant voice and faultless delivery.¹²

The truth of this appreciation is not open to question. John Luce excelled in all four of the five requirements of classical oratory – the finding of cogent arguments, the skilful construction of the speech and of its individual elements, the adoption of a style appropriate to the subject, and powerful and persuasive delivery; unlike Cicero and his contemporaries, modern-day University Orators are not expected to memorize their Latin speeches.

The Lowell oration is neatly framed by the eulogy of the candidate's chief quality: the power and originality of his poetry. The opening and closing sentences mirror each other (*carminum … ubertatem atque vehementiam ~ poemata et robusta et inusitata*) and are both characterized by appropriate *gravitas*: the emphatic coordinator *atque* (Latin had three words for 'and'!) joins the pair of near synonyms 'richness and power', as per an ancient usage which Cicero inherited from the Elder Cato. The central sentence intertwines alliteration and rhyme to bind together the targets

---

9   See *Orationes Dublinienses Selectae (1971–90)*, xiii.
10 Cf. St Ambrose on Luke 23:44.
11 See Matthew Arnold, 'Dover Beach', available online at: <https://www.poetryfoundation.org/poems/43588/dover-beach>. Accessed 23 April 2019.
12 T.N. Mitchell, *Orationes Dublinienses Selectae* II (2004), xvi.

of Lowell's 'savage onslaught', *crudeli__tatem__ __a__varitiam, Martis __a__trocitatem* – 'cruelty, greeds and the barbarities of war.' The turn of phrase is an apt illustration of the importance that Cicero attached to the choice of words with inherent symmetry (*concinnitas*) in the production of naturally rhythmic clauses.[13] The expression *consentaneum est* [it is appropriate] is almost a cipher of Ciceronian prose, which exhibits it some twenty times, while a mere handful of examples are found in all other classical Latin authors taken together. The oration uses the phrase to introduce the daring connection between the 'lightning flashes' of Lowell's poetry and the name of the poet's birth place, Beacon Hill, thus mitigating the strangeness of an archaic mode of thinking by analogy. As the oration approaches its conclusion, a characteristically Ciceronian rhetorical question (*quid dicam de* ...)[14] announces the tricolon which identifies Lowell's characteristic virtues – diction, imagery, and integrity; assonance (*d__i__ctione ... artificio cali__di__ssimo ... candore prope d__i__vino*) and the classical effect of crescendo in the arrangement of words across the three sense units[15] further highlight and bind them together.

John Luce's ability to vary the formulaic request for approval and applause at the end of the speech was one of the most celebrated features of his style, and this oration is no exception. Where the English version produces an exact balance between the poet and his work ('You, however, should welcome with unrestrained acclamation a poet of great skill and enterprise, who has written so much that is both forceful and original'), the Latin text sustains anaphora and alliteration: *vos __au__tem __au__ctorem tam doctum, tam audacem, qui tot __p__oemata et robusta et inusitata __p__epigit, __p__lausibus effusissimis __p__rosequi debetis*. One might have expected, at least and at last here, a rhythmic clausula in the style of Cicero; this is not the

---

13   Cf., for example, Cicero, *Orator*, 164 and 220.
14   Cicero uses it ten times in his writings; with the exception of two occurrences in his contemporary Varro, the usage is unique in the classical period.
15   Cf. Cicero, *De Oratore* 3.186 *quare aut paria esse debent posteriora superioribus, extrema primis, aut, quod etiam est melius et iucundius, longiora*: 'the later clauses must either be equal to the preceding ones, and the last ones to the first, or they must be longer, which is even better and more pleasing' (trans. H. Rackam, Cambridge, MA: Loeb Classical Library, 1942).

case. Luce does give a cretic base (*prosequi*), but not its normal trochaic sequence to close the sentence, and the oration. Avoidance of Ciceronian *clausulae* is in fact a welcome trait of Luce's Latin style:

> Dr Luce's Latin is easy, fluent and unaffected, and – I cannot be the first to say so – lucid: *nomen omen*. It does not seem to me as 'markedly Ciceronian' as Professor Mitchell characterizes it in his Introduction. The preferred Ciceronian clausulae are not much in evidence, and sentence structure is generally simpler than that remark suggests. To me that is all to the good.[16]

There *can* be too much Cicero, and John Luce knew where to stop.

Finally, the poetry. The main body of the oration is structured around two verse quotations, as befits the encomium of a poet; here the orator unleashes his creativity and wit. The rhetorical expression of rage in Juvenal's line that punctuates the first half of the oration, *quid referam quanta siccum iecur ardeat ira* [How can I tell you of the burning anger in my parched heart?] (Juvenal, *Satires* 1.45), finds an equal match in the second half, where a faultless hexameter renders Lowell's line from the poem 'Hedgehog': 'No fool can pick me up and comb my quills':[17] *Spinas, stulte, meas, deducere pectine noli*. The alliterative sequence of sibilant and plosive in the two initial words, and the interjection of the direct address *stulte* [fool], turn the American poet's scorn into a taunt, in the best tradition of Latin verse satire.

The oration references Lowell's masterpiece *Life Studies* with allusions to the ancient notion that poets are comparable to painters (*velut pictor sollertissimus*). Another collection deserves perhaps a mention here. In *Imitations* Lowell made the words of timeless classics – Homer, Juvenal, Dante, Shakespeare, Rimbaud – his own creatures. Without any undue comparison between oratory and poetry, it is fair to say that John Luce's sketch of Robert Lowell achieved just as successful a combination of distinctive personal style and profound respect for the uniqueness of the

---

16   E.J. Kenney, *Hermathena* 180 (2006), 149–150. Similarly, James Diggle wrote in his review of the first collection: 'Professor Luce has worn the mantle of his office with distinction [...]. His Latin is elegant and exact. His tributes are warm and witty' (*Classical Review* N.S. 42 [1992]: 487).

17   See Robert Lowell, 'Hedgehog' in Frank Bidart and David Gewanter, eds *Collected Poems* (New York: Farrar, Straus and Giroux, 2003), 588.

subject. He accomplished it consistently, hundreds of times, for each and every one of his honorands. An Honorary Degree is the celebration of an extraordinary life; it is the duty – and the reward – of the Public Orator to do it justice, in the space of a few hundred words written in an ancient language.

JOHN VICTOR LUCE

Oration on the Conferral of an Honorary DLitt Degree on Robert Lowell by the University of Dublin, Trinity College, 31 May 1976

LITT.D.
ROBERTUS TRAIL SPENCE LOWELL

Duco ad vos scriptorem laurea nostra prae ceteris dignum, ROBERTUM TRAIL SPENCE LOWELL, qui carminum propter ubertatem atque vehementiam primarium inter poetas locum obtinet, non solum in Republica Americana sed ubicumque terrarum Musae coluntur. Simplicitatem vere Americanam exhibet de rebus penitus ad se ipsum pertinentibus libere scribens, sed scribit plerumque numeris sedulo moderatis et secundum leges exemplaque vatum curiosiorum. Minime mirum si ipse litteris humanioribus excultus Iuvenalem aliquando scite imitatus est, nam licet illi, sicut poetae antiquiori, indignatione sincera exclamare:

Quid referam quanta siccum iecur ardeat ira?[1]

Saepenumero carminibus prioribus crudelitatem, avaritiam, Martis atrocitatem saevo impetu castigavit. Media aetate, inter alia scripta insignissima et valde nova, opus Vitae Figuras *nominatum excussit, in quo, velut pictor sollertissimus, parentum et familiarium imagines, nec non ipsius simulacrum, accuratissime depinxit. Consentaneum est, ut opinor, virum in Colle Lampadis nutritum aetatem nostram, velut planitiem tenebris obductam, fulguribus ut ita dicam, ingenii illustravisse. Quid dicam de dictione stricta et nervosa, de iuncturis similitudinum artificio calidissimo fabricatis, de auctoris ipsius candore prope divino? Sed vereor ne me fusius opera laudantem sic versu proprio obiurget:*

[1] See Juvenal, *Satire* I.

Spinas, stulte, meas, deducere pectine noli.[2]

Itaque ad finem propero. Vos autem auctorem tam doctum, tam audacem, qui tot poemata et robusta et inusitata pepigit, plausibus effusissimis prosequi debetis.

LITT.D.
ROBERT TRAIL SPENCE LOWELL

I present to you a writer most worthy of our laurels, ROBERT TRAIL SPENCE LOWELL, who, by the richness and power of his works, has won a place among the front rank of poets, not only in America, but wherever fine literature is honoured throughout the world. He shows a true American forthrightness in writing freely about his deepest concerns, but yet he composes for the most part in carefully controlled rhythms and following the principles and example of poets distinguished for their careful craftmanship. It is hardly surprising that one who was educated in the classics should have given us some elegant adaptations of Juvenal, for, like that ancient poet, he can exclaim with unfeigned indignation:

How can I tell you of the burning anger in my parched heart?[3]

In his earlier poems he made many savage onslaughts on cruelty, on greed, and on the barbarities of war. In the works of his later period, among many distinguished and highly novel pieces, he composed *Life Studies*, in which, like a skilled painter, he executed minutely detailed portraits of members of his family, of his friends, and even of himself. It is appropriate, I think, that one who was reared on Beacon Hill should have illuminated the 'darkling plain' of our world with what I make bold to call the lightning-flashes of his genius. How can I describe to you the compression and energy of his diction, the complex and subtle interplay of his imagery, the inspired integrity of the writer himself? But I fear that if I praise his works without due restraint he may rightly scold me with one of his own lines:

---

2   J.V. Luce's translation of Lowell's line.
3   J.V. Luce's translation of Juvenal's text.

No fool can pick me up and comb my quills.[4]

And so I hasten to conclude. You, however, should welcome with unrestrained acclamation a poet of great skill and enterprise, who has written so much that is both forceful and original.

---

4 See Robert Lowell, 'Hedgehog' in Frank Bidart and David Gewanter, eds, *Collected Poems* (New York: Farrar, Straus and Giroux, 2003), 588.

PAUL MULDOON

Robert Lowell at Castletown House[1]

1

This afternoon the chimney made a clean breast
of the matter as Caroline and he took turns
to argue for her hightailing it to London. Tomorrow he'll fly west
to Lizzie, her own recalcitrance

the recalcitrance of a mare that will kick out
because she's too often been confined to the stable
'for her own good'.
As it is, he's managed to at once disable

the burglar alarm and lock
himself in. He picks up the phone to hear his father mutter
something about Lafcadio Hearn

in a closet. The night is coming at a lick
across the stubble-fields even as the downpipe from a gutter
is mouthing the word 'rain'.

2

Everything that went against the grain.
Everything that had rattled its chain.
Everything that had gone down the drain
because of the lack of a little salt in the brain.

3

The spot where the Vartry river meets the sea should be a marsh
yet the going yesterday had been firm

---

[1] This poem was first published in the *Times Literary Supplement* in September 2017 and subsequently published in *Frolic and Detour* (2019). It is reproduced here with the permission of the author.

enough till he somehow crossed Caroline, his penalty so harsh
it was handed down in cruciform

by Ur-Nammu. He hangs on the cusp
between a wood nymph from The Age of Fable
and a self-styled 'gossip'
from Kentucky. The Transatlantic Telegraphic Cable

turns out to have been spun from straw.
Even it's slightly unhinged, the shutter.
When one's weighing wives one must sometimes set a thumb

on the scale. Though it had been all washed up in the estuary,
leaving high and dry both cabin cruiser and cutter,
the ocean was back to throwing dirt on him.

4
Partly because the chances were slim
her light would ever but briefly dim
it had seemed, after vodkas and Pimm's,
the moon might still love nothing more than a midnight swim.

5
The amount of molasses one might add to her warm bran mash
would generally takes its tone
from how a mare has handled the 100-yard dash
towards the ha-ha. What is the Palladian

golden ratio might apply to gin and vermouth? The empty grate
is a cast-off and the card table
itself a discard.
Now there's a smoke stain on the gable

and it looks as if night has already fallen at the first fence.
In the long gallery a candle splutters
like yet another sylph.

That glass chandelier, meanwhile, was shipped from Venice
in a cask of butter
so as to save it from itself.

STEVEN GOULD AXELROD

Robert Lowell in Dark Times

Dark Times

Robert Lowell (1917–77) was a poet of dark times – to some degree *our* dark time as well as his own.[1] The American psychiatrist Allen Frances has termed the present era 'a dystopic Trumpean dark age' composed of 'ignorance, incompetence, impulsivity and pursuit of dictatorial powers'.[2] I would add that this 'dark age' has not arisen from the executive branch alone but also from other governmental branches, social institutions, and material and cultural conditions. It should not have been a surprise; Jane Jacobs predicted it in her prophetic last book *Dark Age Ahead* (2004).[3] Granted, Lowell's dark time was rhetorically and conceptually different from our own. Whereas the Cold War featured a relatively straightforward opposition between capitalism and communism, our own era features (in Timothy Snyder's words) 'actual fascists calling their opponents "fascists"', while authoritarian cohorts 'turn away from democracy and the rule of law'.[4]

---

1 This essay is based on the 2017 H.O. White Memorial Lecture which was delivered in Trinity College Dublin on 3 March 2017. Thanks to Eve Cobain, Philip Coleman, Michael Hinds and Stephen Matterson who invited and welcomed me to the *Robert Lowell and Ireland* centenary symposium at Trinity College Dublin in 2017; to Grzegorz Kość, my co-editor of Lowell; and to Rise B. Axelrod, my writing partner and life partner.
2 Letter to the Editor, *New York Times*, 15 February 2017, A26.
3 Jane Jacobs, *Dark Age Ahead* (New York: Random House, 2004).
4 Timothy Snyder, *The Road to Unfreedom: Russia, Europe, America* (New York: Penguin Random House, 2018), 145, 274.

In writing of Lowell's defensive reaction to dark times, I refer to two distinct but interrelated contexts: the political and the psychological. First, alluding to *Men in Dark Times,* published by Lowell's close friend Hannah Arendt in 1968,[5] I mean dark times in the public realm – times of political destabilization, de-democratization, and the haunting threat of monstrosity. Arendt, a Jewish refugee from Nazi Germany, rejected the appealing option of withdrawing into private thought in such times, writing that with each retreat 'an almost demonstrable loss to the world takes place; what is lost is the specific and usually irreplaceable in-between which should have formed between this individual and his fellow men'.[6] For Arendt, it is one's duty to enter into the fraught public world, 'which can form only in the interspaces between men in all their variety'.[7] To speak of and to that public world is ultimately the only source of 'light and illumination'.[8] In just that spirit, Lowell functioned in the mid-twentieth century as a public poet and (in Richard Poirier's phrase) 'our truest historian'.[9] Such poems as 'For the Union Dead', 'Waking Early Sunday Morning', and 'For Robert Kennedy 1925–68' spoke to the omnipresent dangers and iniquities of the Cold War era.

Reflecting on the Nazi death camps, Lowell said, 'Genocide has stunned us. We have a curious dread it will be repeated'.[10] Later, as the Vietnam War began to escalate, he warned, 'This has been an age of barbarous manslaughter [...] Every man belongs to his own nation and to the world. He can only, as things are, belong to the world by belonging to his own nation. Yet the sovereign nations, despite their feverish last-minute existence, are really obsolete. They imperil the lives they were created to protect'.[11] Six years later, after the mass murder of 400 unarmed Vietnamese

---

5   Hannah Arendt, *Men in Dark Times* (New York: Harcourt Brace, 1968).
6   Ibid. 4–5.
7   Ibid. 31.
8   Ibid. 30.
9   Richard Poirier, 'Our Truest Historian', *New York Herald Tribune Book Week* (11 October 1964): 1, 16.
10 'In Bounds', *Newsweek* (4 October 1964), rpt Jeffrey Meyers, ed., *Interviews and Memoirs* (Ann Arbor: University of Michigan Press, 1988), 93.
11 Jane Howard, 'Applause for a Prize Poet', *Life* (19 February 1965), rpt Meyers 95.

farmworkers by American soldiers at My Lai, Lowell lamented, 'No stumbling on the downward plunge from Hiroshima [...] In a century perhaps no one will widen an eye at massacre, and only scattered corpses express a last histrionic concern for death.'[12]

Lowell's sense of darkness was conditioned by the poetry and prose of William Butler Yeats. He turned to Yeats despite their obvious political differences and perhaps because of a similar contradiction – their mutual horror of violence combined with a countervailing fascination with authoritarianism.[13] Most compellingly, Yeats had constructed a modernist rhetoric filtered through an artist-observer often depicted 'raging in the dark'.[14] Lowell revised Yeats's language of shock into surreal evocations of both a broken *oikia* and *polis*: 'how will you hear my answer in the dark?' and 'peace to our children when they fall / in small war on the heels of small / war – until the end of time'.[15] Whereas Yeats registers political horror with 'the night can sweat with terror', Lowell confesses existential angst with 'my life's fever is soaking in night sweat'.[16]

As an apprentice poet in his twenties, Lowell copied Yeats's 'All Souls' Night' and 'The Second Coming' into his notebooks for inspiration.[17] Later, he rarely mentioned Yeats, and then often in terms of their 'technical' differences.[18] He praised Yeats in conventional terms to Santayana

12 'Judgment Deferred on Lieutenant Calley', *New York Review of Books* (6 May 1971): 37.
13 See 'Philosophy and a little passion: Roy Foster on WB Yeats and politics', *The Irish Times* (10 June 2015), <http://www.irishtimes.com>, n.p. See also Ian Hamilton, *Robert Lowell: A Biography* (New York: Random House, 1982), 84–85, 209–212, 315, 355–356, 449, 465.
14 Yeats, 'The Choice', *Poems*, ed. A. Norman Jeffares (London: Macmillan, 1989), 362.
15 Lowell, 'The Flaw' and 'Waking Early Sunday Morning', *Collected Poems* (New York: Farrar, Straus and Giroux, 2003), 374, 386. Hereafter *Collected Poems*.
16 Yeats, 'Nineteen Hundred and Nineteen', *Poems* 315; Lowell, 'Night Sweat', *Collected Poems* 375. Lowell came closer to Yeats's sense of political terror in his poem about nuclear crisis, 'Fall 1961': 'the moon lifts, / radiant with terror' (*Poems* 329).
17 Lowell Papers, Harvard; noted in Steven Gould Axelrod, *Robert Lowell: Life and Art* (Princeton, NJ: Princeton University Press, 1978), 246.
18 Meyers 59, 89. Thomas Travisano (with Saskia Hamilton), ed., *Words in Air: The Complete Correspondence between Elizabeth Bishop and Robert Lowell* (New York: Farrar, Straus and Giroux, 2008), 160–162.

who apparently remained sceptical.[19] Then in 1965 Yeats suddenly mattered more. The Vietnam War era, with its protests and violence, must have reminded Lowell of Yeats's poems of civil war. In addition, 1965 was the centennial of Yeats's birth, which generated from Columbia University an invitation to give a lecture. After an introduction by an unidentified professor who asserted that 'what [Yeats and Lowell] share [...] is a sense of greatness', Lowell began to speak, and he seemed to want to clarify what the professor might have meant.[20] Dismissing Yeats's early poetry was 'rather innocent, I'd say inconsequential', Lowell identified Yeats's greatness with the political engagement of his later work:

> He was very lucky I think – it was certainly very important – that he was born in Ireland, a small country where one knew everyone else more or less in Dublin, in a small country that was on the verge of revolution and independence, so that politics became something that one felt in one's blood. And the other thing I think was perhaps most important for Yeats was his long love affair with Maud Gonne, the beautiful woman who was interested in Irish politics. Yeats tried in vain to move away from politics, and it involved him in them.[21]

In that same year Lowell wrote to Elizabeth Bishop that his head 'rang' with Yeatsian resonances as he was writing 'Waking Early Sunday Morning'.[22] In Yeats's reluctant involvement in the politics of his time, Lowell saw something like his own.

But he saw even more in Yeats. He described Yeats as split between a solitary person and a gregarious one. The latter self 'mixed in affairs [...] not only in Irish politics, but writing plays and managing the theater, engaging in polemical controversies'; the other side 'made him bruisable'.[23] Here we have an interpretation not only of Yeats but also of Lowell himself: politically engaged but also vulnerable to psychic wounding. His portrait of

---

19 Robert Lowell, *Letters*, ed. Saskia Hamilton (New York: Farrar, Straus and Giroux, 2005), 100, 110, 125.
20 Lowell, 'Yeats Memorial Lecture', Low Library Rotunda, Columbia University, 1965 (unpublished); archived as 'A Talk on the Poetry of William Butler Yeats', Low Library, Columbia University.
21 Ibid. 3.
22 *Letters*, 467.
23 Lowell, 'Yeats Memorial Lecture', 3–4.

Yeats prefigures the portrait of Lowell I am presenting here: 'battered' and yet 'able to stand that battering and survive'.[24]

Another resonance of Lowell's 'dark times' came from his friend – barely a friend, more a rival – Theodore Roethke. In 1964, four years before Arendt published *Men in Dark Times* and a year before Lowell composed 'Waking Early', Roethke published his great lyric, 'In a Dark Time', which begins: 'In a dark time, the eye begins to see / I meet my shadow in the deepening shade'.[25] Roethke's poem explored the psychic and spiritual uses of depression. Lowell, who suffered from a severe bipolar mood disorder throughout his life,[26] knew what Roethke was talking about. His poem 'Skunk Hour', composed in 1957 and published in *Life Studies* (1959), had similarly employed the metaphor of a dark night, derived from St John of the Cross as well as from the existentialists Jean-Paul Sartre and Albert Camus:

> One dark night,
> my Tudor Ford climbed the hill's skull;
> I watched for love-cars. Lights turned down,
> they lay together, hull to hull,
> where the graveyard shelves on the town ...
> My mind's not right.[27]

As a result of such poems, Lowell instantly became famous or notorious as a pioneer of 'poetry as confession'.[28] Whereas 'Skunk Hour' suggested

---

24 Ibid. 4.
25 Theodore Roethke, *Collected Poems* (New York: Doubleday, 1966), 239.
26 The most informed study of Lowell's manic-depressive illness is Kay Redfield Jamison, *Robert Lowell: Setting the River on Fire* (New York: Alfred A. Knopf, 2017). Another valuable interpretation of Lowell's struggle to make sense of his fragmented selfhood is Nikki Skillman, 'Robert Lowell and the Chemistry of Character', *The Lyric in the Age of the Brain* (Cambridge, MA: Harvard University Press, 2016), 47–86.
27 Robert Lowell, *Life Studies* (New York: Farrar, Straus and Giroux, 1959), rpt *Collected Poems*, 191.
28 M.L. Rosenthal, 'Poetry as Confession', *Nation* (19 September 1959), rpt Steven Gould Axelrod, ed., *The Critical Response to Robert Lowell* (Westport, CT: Greenwood Press, 1999), 64.

the 'dark night' of the soul, 'Waking in the Blue' suggested that 'azure day' only made his agony 'bleaker',[29] while later poems returned to the trope of seeing 'darkly'.[30] Although Lowell came to accept that his best work derived from his 'manic depressive breakdowns',[31] he also insisted that for poems to emerge, 'a huge amount of health has to go into the misery'.[32] Perhaps there is also some connection here to Randall Jarrell, who was similarly disabled. Jarrell had written in '90 North': 'Pain comes from the darkness / And we call it wisdom. It is pain'.[33] As if in response, Lowell wrote to him a partial dissent a decade later: 'Darkness honestly lived through is a place of wonder and life. So much comes from there'.[34]

Lowell's exploration of psychic suffering differed from Roethke's and resembled Yeats's and Jarrell's in connecting it to the public arena. Lowell problematized the binary between public and private realms by presenting them as interrelated. After his first hospitalization, he described to Santayana his 'fascinated spirit watching the holocaust of irrationality',[35] much as Sylvia Plath was later to write about 'this holocaust I walk in'.[36] Lowell's texts of inwardness frequently evoked the politics of the domestic or public sphere. Whereas in *The Human Condition*, Arendt had noted the gap between *polis* and *oikia* in ancient Greece, between the 'space of exposure' and the 'shelter' of the household, and whereas Foucault problematized binary spaces such as public and private by positing an 'other space' of 'heterotopia',[37] Lowell evoked a variegated space with communal,

---

29 Lowell, *Collected Poems*, 183.
30 Ibid. 334, 345, 385.
31 *Letters*, 354.
32 Stanley Kunitz, 'Talk with Robert Lowell', *New York Times Book Review* (1964), rpt Meyers 89.
33 Jarrell, '90 North' (1955), rpt *The Complete Poems* (New York: Farrar, Straus and Giroux), 114.
34 *Letters*, 298.
35 Ibid. 151.
36 'Mary's Song' (1966), rpt *Collected Poems of Sylvia Plath* (New York: Harper, 1981), 257.
37 Arendt, *The Human Condition* (1958), rpt (Chicago: University Chicago Press, 1989), 22–78; Foucault, '*Des espaces autres*' (1967), rpt as 'Of Other Spaces', *Diacritics* 16 (Spring 1986): 22–27.

domestic, *and* personal features, thereby reconfiguring our geography of being-in-the-world. If the 'terror' of Yeats's 'night' was civic, in Lowell's metalepsis it becomes both personal and communal. '*My* life's fever is soaking in night sweat', but 'the downward glide / and bias of existing wrings *us* dry'. The very next poem in the sequence, 'For the Union Dead', underlines the communal aspect of the anguish being evoked. Lowell finds pain wherever he looks, whether in the 'night sweats of the spirit' or in the 'fear, glory chaos, rout' of political protest.[38]

Lowell once wrote, rather disingenuously I think: 'In truth I seem to have felt mostly the joys of living; in remembering, in recording, thanks to the gift of the Muse, it is the pain'.[39] But the poet, reflecting Freud's great essay 'Negation', admitted a few years later, in a letter to me: 'How we mean the opposite of what we first say or habitually say'.[40] Jamison's *Robert Lowell: Setting the River on Fire* makes clear the suffering that was a constant of his daily existence. As Patrick Cosgrave wrote long ago, 'Even in his lightest moments he was forever in turmoil'.[41] I think it was just the reverse of what Lowell initially wrote: he experienced the pain of living and the joy of artistic creation. 'One life, one writing!':[42] it was the latter that consoled for the former.

Lowell was briefly institutionalized in January 1976, the last in a series of sixteen hospitalizations. In his poem, 'Home', composed that same month, an unidentified voice describes him as a King Lear figure: '*seeing too much and feeling it / with one skin-layer missing*'.[43] In March 1976, he wrote to Elizabeth Bishop: 'One needs to hold a shield before one's feelings and the reader'.[44] He conceived of poetic device as one such shield, and his wonderful sense of humour was another. He was willing to lie

---

38   Lowell, *Collected Poems*, 375, 545.
39   *Notebook 1967–68* (New York: Farrar, Straus and Giroux, 1969), 160.
40   Lowell to Axelrod (10 February 1974), rpt Axelrod, *Robert Lowell: Life and Art*, 169 and Lowell, *Letters* 624.
41   Patrick Cosgrave, 'Robert Lowell', *Spectator* (24 September 1977), rpt Meyers 222.
42   Lowell, *Collected Poems*, 375.
43   Ibid. 825. Cf. *King Lear* 5.3: 'We that are young / Shall never see so much, nor live so long'.
44   Travisano, *Words in Air*, 785.

down among 'the sweepings of the street', in the 'foul rag-and-bone shop of the heart',[45] but he needed a shield and 'health' to make the poems possible.[46]

In early June 1976, about three months before his death, Lowell felt well enough to receive an honorary doctorate in literature from Trinity College, Dublin. At the ceremony John V. Luce, a professor of classics and for many years the College's Public Orator, celebrated the power of Lowell's public poetry in words that must have made him happy. Professor Luce said that Lowell made 'many savage onslaughts on cruelty, on greed, and on the barbarities of war', adding that the poet 'illuminated the 'darkling plain' of our world with what I make bold to call the lightning flashes of his genius'.[47] These were justified compliments. I think it's fair to say that Lowell excelled in portraying both the psyche and the polis in turmoil, and in intimating such survival strategies as humour, meditation, courageous speech, and active resistance.

The Disabled Psyche

Let's start with Lowell's personal pain, and situate ourselves at the beginning of that, in his childhood, when he lived amid the ever-present tensions of his dysfunctional upper-class family on Beacon Hill in Boston. The family consisted of his mother, Charlotte Winslow Lowell, controlling, exhausting, brilliant, and probably bipolar herself; his father, Robert Lowell III, remote, depressed, and haunted by his failures; and young Lowell himself, Robert Lowell IV, an only child, difficult and unhappy even then. Here they are in 1930, at the breakfast table. As we look in, young Lowell is 13 and being sent away that very day, against his will, to a

---

45 Yeats, *Poems*, 472.
46 Kunitz, 'Talk with Robert Lowell', 89.
47 J.V. Luce, 'Oration on the Conferral of an Honorary DLitt. Degree on Robert Lowell by the University of Dublin, Trinity College, 31 May 1976', reprinted in the present volume.

posh boarding school called St Mark's. The source is Lowell's unpublished childhood memoir, which Grzegorz Kosc and I are preparing for publication in a volume of Lowell's *Memoirs*:[48]

> Mother, down for breakfast to give verve to the occasion of my leaving for prep school, was like the youngish Napoleon writing dispatches on a drumhead before the Battle of Marengo. Her hand moved with decisive, dramatic thrusts, as she checked off items of clothing on a two-foot list. 'What is l'Aiglon, I mean your royal highness, thinking of?' …
>
> Mother talked on with a hard, hopeless bravado. It was maddening to be talking to a stone and stuck with a theme that ruled out humor and all her wonderfully good-natured and detailed exaggerations. Still, she had lived all summer on just this. Now, [what] if the hot bath she had so lovingly drawn should turn out to be a rock pile?
>
> She wasn't so common and nouveau riche as to name or even quite remember the exact figures; still, anyone could see that this gross tuition was something in black and white, a cold demonstrable proof of giving. *Money talks.* She might have said this if she had had more of it, and a less puritan, less genteel conscience. What she so deeply felt was that only spiritual pain is deserving, and that if, despite her feelings, she had had oceans of just this, oh nauseating oceans, and all nearly impossible to exhibit to others … well, she deserved a vacation she could pay for. Ever since her marriage she had been modeling a statue called *I am a mother*. If sending me off to boarding school was buying the pedestal ready-made, surely she had shown genius in her choice.
>
> In all this vibrating torment, it was as though Mother and I were battling down a list of statements and answers.
>
> STATEMENT: your father and I are paying a great deal to give you the advantage of St. Mark's.
> ANSWER: I only thank for what I ask for.
> STATEMENT: $2000.
> ANSWER: my allowance is twenty-five cents a week.
> STATEMENT: the return we expect is improved conduct.
> ANSWER: love and admire what I already am!
> STATEMENT: most boys are unable to go to St. Mark's.
> ANSWER: that means I can't play with [my friend] Ernest Manahan.
> STATEMENT: your great-grandfather was headmaster of St. Mark's.
> ANSWER: I am afraid to mention him [there].

48 Lowell Papers, Houghton Library, Harvard University.

STATEMENT: he was a great man.
ANSWER: probably he was mean and couldn't keep order.
STATEMENT: we are giving you the best education.
ANSWER: you mean blue serge suits seven days a week and music lessons.

And so on; at the end of the list Mother wrote: 'we are breathless, someone else must take over'. I said, 'Eskimos fish every day of the year, except when they are hibernating'. Mother and I loved knocking our heads together until they bled. Worn, jumpy, exhilarated from such bloodletting, we could not live a day without it. My father drained his great cereal bowl of a coffee cup. 'Maxwell House', he said, 'good *except* for the last drop'.

In this battle of wills, the son purposely antagonizes his mother while identifying with her. The self-absorbed mother wants the best for her son, but also desperately wants him gone. The recessive father is out of it, hiding behind a meaningless parody of the advertising slogan for Maxell House coffee. Decades later, Lowell wrote that his mother's name had been misspelled 'Lovel' on her coffin.[49] Not literally true, this comment implies that from his perspective his mother's real name – and perhaps his family's name – was not Lowell but Loveless. Lowell's childhood was shaped by his brutal rebellions against his judgemental, disapproving mother, who told him she had not wanted to give birth and who found nothing in him of which to approve. In a letter to his psychiatrist in the 1950s, Lowell wrote that from the age of 4 'I already felt the stirrings of revolt against my mother's judgment'.[50] His rage, defiance, and verbal facility, clearly on display in his childhood memoir, only increased as he grew to adulthood.

As a young adult he underwent recurrent and increasingly severe cycles of what he called 'enthusiasm' and 'depression'. These bipolar episodes intensified in his thirties, and lasted throughout his life. In a typical cycle, he would start out feeling fine; then he would sense his mind was racing. In full-blown mania, he might commence passionate affairs with newly met women or threaten violence against friends or strangers; he would fall under the grip of fantasies or delusions. For example: "'Do you smell

---

49 Lowell, *Collected Poems*, 180.
50 Jamison, *Robert Lowell: Setting the River on Fire*, 57.

that?" Lowell asked, and when [his friend Peter] Taylor said he couldn't, told him it was the smell of brimstone. Then Lowell began looking around the room, trying to locate the devil'.[51] At another point in the manic episode, he held his frail mentor, the poet Allen Tate, out a second story window of an apartment building while reciting one of his poems.[52] He would inveigh against Communists or, conversely, insist on Alger Hiss's innocence, barricade himself in his room or wander streets all night, foam at the mouth, talk nonstop, and wind up in police custody and then in a hospital room or padded cell. After his first hospitalization in 1949, his manic illness was 'unrelenting'.[53]

Following the death of his ambivalently loved mother in February 1954, Lowell suffered his worst manic attack yet, resulting in electroshock treatment at a Cincinnati hospital and then transference to a locked cell in New York's Payne Whitney Clinic. From that point forward, all of his major manic attacks culminated in stays at a psychiatric institution – generally McLean Hospital just outside of Boston, the setting of 'Waking in the Blue'. Initially he was involuntarily committed but then, as he gained understanding of his condition, he voluntarily admitted himself. In the hospital, he would descend into quietude, remorse, and self-criticism. And then, often quickly, he would recover – for a while.[54]

Following his lengthy 1954 stay at Payne Whitney, psychiatrists encouraged Lowell to write about his experiences there. Taking the advice, he wrote a prose memoir of his illness and recovery called 'The Balanced

---

51   Paul Mariani, *Lost Puritan: A Life of Robert Lowell* (New York: Norton, 1994), 182–183.
52   Mariani, 181–182. For other scenes of mania mentioned in the next sentence, see Mariani 176–188, 214–219; Jamison 102–116, 121–130, 135–147, 150–155; and Ian Hamilton, 154–163, 189–196.
53   Jamison, 113.
54   Lowell was hospitalized in sixteen of the twenty-eight years between 1949 and 1977. In fifteen of those sixteen years, he was not being treated with lithium before the manic attack. He was hospitalized only once in the seven years when he was taking lithium (Jamison 179).

Aquarium'. I will quote a passage here, which conveys a sense of both irony and horror.[55]

> When Mother died, I began to feel tireless, madly sanguine, menaced and menacing. I entered the Payne Whitney Clinic for 'all those afflicted in mind'. One night I sat in the mixed lounge, and enjoyed the new calm which I had been acquiring with much cunning during the few days since my entrance. I remember coining and pondering for several minutes such phrases as 'the Art of Detachment', 'Offhanded Involvement', and 'Urbanity: A Key to the Tactics of Self-Control'. But the old menacing hilarity was growing in me. I saw Anna and her nurse walk into our lounge. Anna, a patient from a floor for more extreme cases, was visiting our floor for the evening. I knew that the evening would soon be over, that the visitor would probably not return to us, and that I had but a short time to make my impression on her. Anna towered over the piano, and thundered snatches of Mozart sonatas, which she half remembered and murdered. Her figure, a Russian ballerina's or Anna Karenina's, was emphasized, and *illuminated*, as it were, by an embroidered, middle-European blouse that fitted her with the creaseless, burnished, curved tightness of a medieval breastplate. I throbbed to the music and the musician. I began to talk aimlessly and loudly to the room at large. I discussed the solution to a problem that had been bothering me about the unmanly smallness of the suits of armor that I had seen 'tilting' at the Metropolitan Museum. 'Don't you see?' I said, and pointed to Anna, 'the armor was made for *Amazons*!' But no one took up my lead ...
> Roger, an Oberlin undergraduate and fellow patient, sat beside Anna on the piano bench. He was small. His dark hair matched his black flannel Brooks Brothers' suit; his blue-black eyes matched his blue-black necktie. He wore a light cashmere sweater that had been knitted for him by his mother, and his yellow woolen socks had been imported from the Shetlands. Roger talked to Anna with a persuasive shyness. Occasionally, he would stand up and play little beginners' pieces for her. He explained that these pieces were taken from an exercise book composed by Béla Bartók in protest against the usual, unintelligibly tasteless examples used by teachers. Anna giggled with incredulous admiration as Roger insisted that the clinic's music instructor could easily teach her to read more skillfully. Suddenly, I felt compelled to make a derisive joke, and I announced cryptically and untruly that Rubinstein had declared the eye was of course the source of all evil for a virtuoso. 'If the eye offends thee, pluck it out'. No one understood my humor. I grew red and confused. The air

[55] Lowell Papers, Houghton Library, Harvard University. This memoir, which will appear in our forthcoming edition of Lowell's *Memoirs*, to be published by Farrar, Straus and Giroux, differs significantly from the version Robert Giroux presented, under the title 'Near the Unbalanced Aquarium in Lowell's *Collected Prose* (New York: Farrar Straus and Giroux, 1987), 346–363.

in the room began to tighten around me. I felt as if I were squatting on the bottom of a huge laboratory bottle and trying to push out the black rubber stopper before I stifled. Roger sat like a rubber stopper in his black suit. Suddenly, I knew I could clear the air by taking hold of Roger's ankles and pulling him off his chair. By some crisscross of logic, I reasoned that my cruel boorishness would be an act of self-sacrifice. I would be bowing out of the picture, and throwing Roger into the arms of Anna. Without warning, but without lowering my eyes from Anna's splendid breastplate blouse, I seized Roger's yellow ankles. I pulled; Roger sat on the floor with tears in his eyes. A sigh of surprised repulsion went round the room. I assumed a hurt, fatherly expression, but all at once I felt eased and sympathetic with everyone [...]

Lowell was immediately transferred to a new floor for more seriously disturbed patients. Deprived of his belt, pyjama cord, and matches, he was heavily sedated with Chlorpromazine and encouraged to watch Liberace and baseball on TV – an interesting pair of gender models. His 'blood became like melted lead'. He 'could hardly swallow' his breakfast. He 'sat gaping through Scrabble games unable to form the simplest word'. Reaching a nadir, he returned to his room and wound the window open to its maximum 6 inches:

Below me, patients circled in twos over the bright gray octagonal paving stones of the courtyard. I let my glasses drop. How freely they glittered through the air for almost a minute! They shattered on the stones. Then everyone in the courtyard came crowding and thrusting their heads forward over my glasses, as though I had been scattering corn for pigeons. I felt my languor lift and then descend again. I already seemed to weigh a thousand pounds because of my drug, and now I blundered about nearly blind from myopia. But my nervous system vibrated joyfully, when I felt the cool air brushing directly on my eyeballs. And I was reborn each time I saw my blurred, now unspectacled, now unprofessorial face in the mirror. Yet all this time I would catch myself asking whining questions. Why don't I die, die? I quizzed my face of suicide in the mirror; but the body's warm, unawed breath befogged the face with a dilatory inertia.

In this set of passages, Lowell has oscillated between slapstick comedy and suicidal cognition. His memories resemble a Jamesian sponge; he squeezes one, and it exudes vivid memories and figures of speech. Writer's block had been a problem – 'five messy poems in five years'[56] – and remembrance was the solution. Lowell wrote three significant autobiographical

---

56 Ian Hamilton, 'A Conversation with Robert Lowell', *The Review* (Summer 1971), rpt Meyers 156.

works in the 1950s: his memoir of psychosis and recovery ('The Balanced Aquarium'); his memoir of childhood ('My Autobiography'); and most famously, his poetic sequence 'Life Studies'. All three evoke his inward suffering, and they all end with tropes of healing. These autobiographical texts balance Roethke's uncanny introspection with Yeats's civic anxiety and Arendt's redemptive vision of a lively world.

In 'The Balanced Aquarium', Anna and Roger are to some extent projected images of Lowell's psychic disturbance, glimpsed in what George Lensing once termed his 'associative mirror';[57] but they are also autonomous others, with issues different from his own. The clinic's patients and staff form a functioning alternative community, one that Lowell ultimately finds more satisfying than either his biological family or the conformist society outside the hospital's walls. In Lowell's personal waste land, the hospital resembles Eliot's public bar 'where fishmen lounge at noon.'[58] It is another space of group identification and healing. As Lowell prepares to leave, his fellow patients asked him how it feels: 'I answered that I was pleased, but that of course it hurt'. There is a distinct line leading from the marginal community achieved at Payne Whitney to Lowell's participation in acts of political resistance in the 1960s; and another line connecting such psychological texts as 'Skunk Hour' and 'The Balanced Aquarium' to such political ones as 'Waking Early Sunday Morning' and 'For Robert Kennedy 1925–68'.

Political Engagement

Now let's turn to Lowell's enactment of citizenship. As a prep school student, Lowell nursed imperialistic and proto-Fascist sentiments that were not necessarily out of place in his milieu.[59] By the 1940s his politics had

---

57 'Memories of West Street and Lepke', *Concerning Poetry* 3 (1970): 23–26.
58 T. S Eliot, *The Waste Land* (1922), rpt *The Complete Poems and Plays 1909–1950* (New York: Harcourt, Brace & World, 1971), 45.
59 See, for example, his essay 'War: A Justification', *The Vindex* 59 (1935), 156–158, excerpted in Axelrod, *Robert Lowell: Life and Art*, 15–16.

evolved into an unsorted mix of sensitivity and callousness, empathy and anger. Jerome Mazzaro refers to this mindset as Lowell's 'early politics of apocalypse', and Randall Jarrell famously called it a 'conflict of opposites'.[60] In mania, his sympathies remained with the right, as indicated by his recurrent fascination with *Mein Kampf* and his successful witch-hunt in 1948 against the director of the Yaddo Writer's Colony, Elizabeth Ames.[61] But in his saner moments he had become by 1952 a thoughtful consensus liberal, a supporter of Adlai Stevenson, as we sense in 'Inauguration Day', and a supporter of the civil rights movement, as we see in 'For the Union Dead' and 'Two Walls'.

In 1965, however, his politics evolved again. In his sane periods, he migrated even further to the left, lending his name and persuasive skills to the anti-Vietnam War movement and other progressive causes. He reentered 'the space of exposure' for the first time since he had gone to jail as a Conscientious Objector in 1943. Rebelling against the narrow ethnocentricity of his upbringing, he turned to three Irish-identified figures to help him make this transition: the Irish poet, William Butler Yeats; the Irish-German-American senator from Minnesota, Eugene McCarthy; and the Irish-American senator from New York, Robert Kennedy.

Lowell once told an interviewer, 'When your private experience converges on the nation's experience, you feel you have to do something.'[62] In spring 1965, Lowell, like many others, became aware of the nation's push toward war in Southeast Asia. When President Lyndon Johnson was inaugurated for his full term in January of that year, the US had only 20,000 'military advisors' in Vietnam, none of them combat soldiers. Responding to deteriorating military conditions, Johnson sent 3,500 Marines to South Vietnam in March. He then authorized additional troops in April, May, June, and July, raising the total to almost 100,000. Scenes of civilian casualties appeared on the evening news, and public protests began. In April

---

60 Mazzaro, 'Robert Lowell's Early Politics of Apocalypse', *Modern American Poetry* (New York: David McKay, 1970), 321–350; Jarrell, 'From the Kingdom of Necessity', *Nation* 1947; rpt Axelrod, *Critical Response*, 30–37.
61 Mariani 22, 262, 308, 329, 455; 177–178.
62 Richard Gilman, 'Life Offers No Neat Conclusions', *New York Times* (1968), rpt Meyers 122.

and June, Senator William J. Fulbright made major statements opposing the war. Lowell described his complicated political position thusly: 'I was never, I think, anti-Communist, but I was and still am anti-Stalinist [...] I suppose, if I had been called up for the Korean draft, I would have been a conscientious objector. A helpless, inconsistent position, but I have never gotten over the horrors of American bombing [in the Second World War]. For me anti-Stalinism led logically – oh, perhaps not so logically – to my being against our suppression of the Vietnamese'.[63]

In the midst of the escalation, in May 1965, Lowell received an invitation to recite his poetry at a White House 'Festival of the Arts'. He had been to the White House once before, invited to dinner by John F. Kennedy, and though he had enjoyed the occasion, he had felt qualms afterward: 'The next morning you read that the Seventh Fleet had been sent somewhere in Asia and you had a funny feeling of how unimportant the artist really was'.[64] Lowell first accepted Johnson's White House invitation, then reconsidered and refused. His refusal was reprinted on the front page of the *New York Times* and became a *cause célèbre*. Laura Bush's failed White House poetry reading in 2003 was but a weak echo of what occurred in 1965. In 1965 the invitations to writers came from the President; in 2003 they came from the First Spouse; and now they do not come at all. Even if they did come, few American poets today have the cultural authority of Robert Lowell, which allowed him access to the front page of the nation's leading newspaper and permitted him to generate a national debate.

Lowell wrote to Johnson that he was following 'our present foreign policy with the greatest dismay and distrust', adding that 'we are in danger of imperceptibly becoming an explosive and suddenly chauvinistic nation.'[65] Hannah Arendt, John Berryman, Stanley Kunitz, Philip Roth, W.D. Snodgrass, and Robert Penn Warren, and many others publicly endorsed Lowell's protest.[66] When President Johnson learned of Lowell's refusal,

---

63 'Liberal Anti-Communism Revisited: A Symposium', *Commentary* 44 (September 1967): 54.
64 A. Alvarez, 'A Talk with Robert Lowell', *Encounter* (February 1965), rpt Meyers 101.
65 Robert Lowell, 'Letter to President Lyndon Johnson', *New York Times* (3 June 1965), rpt Lowell, *Collected Prose* 371.
66 Axelrod, *Life and Art* 181.

according to one person who was there, 'the roar in the Oval Office could be heard all the way into the East Wing'.[67] Johnson became convinced that poets and intellectuals 'were not only "sonsofbitches" but they were "fools", and they were close to traitors'.[68] Poets played the role then that the media are playing today: enemies of the people, in the president's eyes.

Lowell wrote 'Waking Early Sunday Morning' in direct response to the incident, including President Johnson and his staff as characters. In addition, Yeats played a role as a kind of type to Lowell's antitype. In his Yeats lecture in that same year, Lowell said, 'If you ask people what Yeats stands for, I don't know what it would be exactly, perhaps it would be for grandeur of thought getting into verse'.[69] Here is Lowell's haunting attempt to achieve a darkened and prophetic grandeur of his own:

> Pity the planet, all joy gone
> from this sweet volcanic cone;
> peace to our children when they fall
> in small war on the heels of small
> war – until the end of time
> to police the earth, a ghost
> orbiting forever lost
> in our monotonous sublime.[70]

In these lines we hear faint echoes of contrasting discourses: the journalistic discourse of 'small wars' and 'police the earth'; and Yeatsian images of 'widening gyre', 'anarchy [...] loosed upon the world', and a 'ghost' stricken by 'the injustice of the skies'.[71]

Between 1965 and 1968 Lowell threw himself into political controversies and activities. He participated in anti-war readings, published public letters and statements, signed petitions, and contributed to political symposia.

67 Eric Goldman, *The Tragedy of Lyndon Johnson* (New York: Knopf, 1969), 429.
68 Ibid. 447.
69 Lowell, 'Yeats Memorial Lecture', 6.
70 Lowell, *Collected Poems*, 385–386.
71 Walter Lippmann, 'The All-Purpose Myth', *Newsweek* 65 (24 May 1965): 23; Irving Howe 'I'd Rather Be Wrong', *New York Review of Books* 4 (17 June 1965): 3–4; Yeats, 'The Second Coming' and 'The Cold Heaven', *Poems* 227, 294. Lowell spoke feelingly about both poems in his Yeats lecture (16, 23–24).

At a reading he introduced the Russian poet Andrei Voznesensky by saying, 'This is indiscreet, both our countries, I think, have really terrible governments'.[72] In a published statement, he proposed a national 'day of mourning' for 'our own soldiers, for the pro-American Vietnamese, and for the anti-American Vietnamese'.[73]

In 1967 Lowell participated in the March on the Pentagon, along with Norman Mailer, Denise Levertov, and 100,000 other protestors. He famously fled before an advancing phalanx of police, whereas Mailer stood his ground and was arrested. Lowell then became a main character in Mailer's account of the event, *The Armies of the Night*,[74] just as Mailer became the title character of Lowell's sonnet, 'Norman Mailer'.[75] In his book, Mailer evokes Lowell as the anguished poet of conscience, reading 'Waking Early Sunday Morning' at a fund-raiser in a 'fine stammering voice which gave the impression that life rushed at him in a series of hurdles and some he succeeded in jumping and some he did not'.[76] Lowell is also a man of fascinating contradictions, a celebrity, or as Mailer would say, a 'notable', not quite on the fantasy level of Marilyn Monroe, but worth contemplating as a different American archetype, the poet as Puritan. Mailer observes that Lowell 'had something untouchable, all insane in its force; one felt immediately there were any number of causes for which the man would be ready to die, and some he would fight'.[77] Complementing the mania is a quality of holy introspection: 'Lowell gave off at times the unwilling haunted saintliness of a man who was repaying the moral debts of ten generations of ancestors'.[78] It was precisely this kind of mythic persona that made Lowell a powerful cultural figure. Mailer found himself jealous, not of Lowell's poetry but of 'the languid grandeur of [his] slouch'.[79]

72 'Lowell, at Voznesensky Recital Criticizes Both U.S. and Soviet', *New York Times* (18 May 1967): 43.
73 Lowell, 'Day of Mourning', *New York Review of Books* 10 (29 February 1968): 32.
74 Norman Mailer, *The Armies of the Night* (New York: New American Library, 1968), 18–22, 40–46, 63–68, 73–74, 82–84, 124–129.
75 *Collected Poems*, 543.
76 Mailer, 43.
77 Ibid. 40.
78 Ibid. 83.
79 Ibid. 44.

Lowell went on to publish two sonnets in *Notebook 1967–68* concerning the march,[80] which Frank J. Kearful interprets as affirming 'a personal politics of reconciliation' that undermines any notion of irremediable civil conflict.[81] The poems join Mailer's account as one of the sources of contemporary memory of this event, along with Ginsberg's poem 'Pentagon Exorcism', which was recited at the march while Ginsberg himself was in Italy visiting Ezra Pound. Lowell wrote additional sonnets on such public topics as Che Guevara, South American politics, student protests, Dr Spock's trial, the assassinations of Martin Luther King and Robert F. Kennedy, and the presidential election of 1968.[82] His poems on Eugene McCarthy and Robert Kennedy, in particular, exemplify his political poetics.

Lowell originally met McCarthy when he accompanied Elizabeth Hardwick on an interview for an article she was writing about anti-war senators. The two men immediately felt what Lowell called a 'temperamental affinity'.[83] They 'talked and told stories'.[84] Lowell's first meeting with Robert Kennedy was edgier. Jacqueline Kennedy introduced them, and each seems immediately to have gotten on the other's nerves.[85] Lowell tried to read passages from *The Education of Henry Adams* to Kennedy. According to one observer, 'Bobby suddenly got up and excused himself. Lowell followed him right to the door of the bathroom, still reading. Bobby shut the door and said, "If you don't mind." Lowell said, "If you were Louis XIV, you wouldn't mind"'.[86] What a strange comment – like something out of 'The Balanced Aquarium'. Did Lowell think of Robert Kennedy as the Sun King?

---

80 Lowell, *Collected Poems*, 545–546.
81 Frank J. Kearful, 'Poetics and Politics in Robert Lowell's "The March 1" and "The March 2"', *Connotations* 22.1 (2012/2013): 106.
82 Lowell, *Collected Poems*, 540–587.
83 Gilman, 'Life Offers No Neat Conclusions', 121.
84 Ian Hamilton, 'Conversation', 164.
85 Jean Stein and George Plimpton, *American Journey: The Times of Robert Kennedy* (New York: Harcourt Brace Jovanovich, 1970), 192–193.
86 Ibid. 193.

During the 1968 presidential campaign, Lowell took to *The New Republic* to endorse Eugene McCarthy. He was enough of a political figure for his boxed endorsement to matter – not simply to poetry readers but to the entire left. Seeking to guide the undecided, Lowell began: 'Of the announced or seriously offered Democratic or Republican candidates, only Senators Kennedy and McCarthy seem morally or intellectually allowable'.[87] This assertion ruled out Nixon, of course, and it also eliminated Hubert Humphrey, the eventual nominee. Lowell continued: 'Of these McCarthy is preferable, first for his negative qualities: lack of excessive charisma, driving ambition, machinelike drive, and the too great wish to be President'. These were implicit critiques of Kennedy – quite odd, I think. Lowell accuses Kennedy of charisma, drive, and ambition. These are Lowell's own qualities. Moreover, they are qualities essential for electoral success and effective governance. In effect, Lowell sides against Kennedy because he had the better chance of winning and of governing successfully. Lowell concludes by heaping praise on McCarthy: 'But I am for him most for what he possesses, his variable, tolerant and courageous mind, lungs that breathe the air. When the race against President Johnson was hopeless and intractable, he alone hoped, entered and won'.[88] Basically, Lowell is saying that if he read *The Education of Henry Adams* to McCarthy, he would listen. In a way, he's not endorsing McCarthy for the Presidency but for the Academy of American Poets. He's pushing the left away from power and toward moral gesture. As he later admitted, 'It didn't strike me that McCarthy would be President'.[89]

Lowell became McCarthy's travelling companion during the Democratic primaries. Before actively campaigning, Lowell had been divided in his judgement, saying of Kennedy: 'I know him fairly well, and he's a lot better than he seems to a lot of people'.[90] But campaigning with McCarthy in Oregon, he employed what he called 'invective'.[91] In one fantastical speech to a crowd, he claimed that underneath Kennedy's 'charisma

87 'Why I'm for McCarthy', *New Republic* 158 (13 April 1968), 22.
88 Ibid.
89 Ian Hamilton, 'Conversation', 166.
90 Gilman, 122.
91 Stein, 270.

suit' was 'an anti-charisma Bobby-Suit', made of 'steel wool' that 'leaves metal threads in the rash admirer for months'.[92] He added that Kennedy had started a fire that consumed a Portland tire factory that day – a joking comment that was hard to distinguish as a joke. The speech seemed to do McCarthy no harm, and he won Oregon by six points.

Nevertheless, in the decisive California primary a week later, Lowell did injure McCarthy's chances. Arguably he lost the state for the senator. According to Lowell, 'McCarthy wanted to get away from the hail and brimstone of the campaign and talk and relax and talk seriously'.[93] So he conversed with Lowell instead of his political staff. The staff called Lowell one of the 'astrologers' whom they had to circumvent in order to get to their candidate.[94] On the day of the only televised debate, Lowell took it upon himself to visit Kennedy in his hotel room. He wanted to 'harmonize' the two anti-war campaigns after the primary season concluded.[95] Kennedy told Lowell that McCarthy should simply withdraw. Lowell: 'You mustn't talk to me this way'. Kennedy: 'Well, I guess we have nothing more to say'. Lowell: 'I wish I could think up some joke that would cheer you, but it won't do any good'.[96]

After that diplomatic foray, Lowell made his way back to McCarthy. A McCarthy staffer, Andreas Teuber, recalled, 'We tried to keep Robert Lowell from McCarthy at very crucial times because we thought he always took the edge off. Every time Lowell and McCarthy would get together, Lowell, or so we thought, would convince McCarthy that really, he was above all this'.[97] So his advisors hid McCarthy in an unregistered room, attempting to brief him on likely debate questions. But Lowell found him, and the two men started to drink. They got into the limousine together to go to the television studio. First they demanded a detour to see Alcatraz; then they composed 'a 20th century version of "Ode to St. Cecilia's Day" in the back seat'.[98] By the time they arrived at the studio, McCarthy was – as

---

92 Stein, 269.
93 Ibid. 192.
94 Ibid. 302.
95 Ibid. 309.
96 Ibid. 309.
97 Ibid. 311.
98 Ibid. 312.

his staff had feared – 'Shakespearean, distant', like Henry V at Agincourt.[99] A distracted McCarthy lost the debate, and in the aftermath lost California by four percentage points. Kennedy was assassinated at his victory celebration that night.

Lowell pretty clearly revised his complicated feelings toward both men by the time he composed his sonnets to them. The sonnet to McCarthy begins:

> I love you so ... Gone? Who will swear you wouldn't
> have done good to the country, that fulfillment wouldn't
> have done good to you – the father, as Freud says:
> you?[100]

This is pretty equivocal, especially with two line endings of 'wouldn't'. The lines imply that you can't prove McCarthy would have been a bad president, but you can certainly suspect it. They suggest that McCarthy functioned as a father-figure for Lowell – the good father in contrast to Lyndon Johnson's bad father. The sonnet then portrays McCarthy's effort as a worthy but ultimately 'hollow' exercise in aestheticism: 'Picking a quarrel / with you is like picking the petals of the daisy'. At the end, abandoning his flower analogy, Lowell describes the candidate as 'coldly willing / to smash the ball past those who bought the park'. The McCarthy of this conclusion is not as 'tolerant' as the one portrayed in *The New Republic* endorsement. In fact, he seems to possess something very much like the 'machine-like drive' that Lowell previously criticized in Kennedy. In this retrospective sonnet, Lowell seems to be juggling gender stereotypes in order to expose McCarthy's enigmas: he is the good father but also the bad mother, a daisy but also a chilly aggressor.

In contrast, the sonnets for Robert Kennedy frame him as a tragic hero whose death has given rise to a terrible beauty. This Robert Kennedy is very different from the one depicted in Lowell's campaign 'invective'. In the first and best sonnet, initially called 'R.F.K.' and then 'For Robert

---

99   Ibid. 311.
100 Lowell, *Collected Poems*, 572.

Kennedy 1925–68',[101] the poet begins in a mood of mourning: 'Here in my workroom, in its listlessness / of Vacancy […] // […] is loneliness'.[102] The sonnet then turns from the speaker's grief to Kennedy himself, a loyal member of his Irish-American family, a national figure both blessed and cursed. Perhaps Lowell was registering Daniel Patrick Moynihan's comment after the death of John F. Kennedy: 'I don't think there's any point in being Irish if you don't know that the world is going to break your heart eventually'.[103] Lowell portrays Robert Kennedy as a liminal figure poised between being and nothingness. Like the Shakespearean actors evoked in Yeats's 'Lapis Lazuli', Kennedy does not break up his lines to weep:

> Doom was woven in your nerves, your shirt,
> Woven in the great clan; they too were loyal,
> And you too were loyal to them, to death.
> For them like a prince, you daily left your tower
> To walk though dirt in your best cloth.

If McCarthy was the ordinary good man, Kennedy was something more: a complicated Shakespearean or Yeatsian hero who sacrificed himself on behalf of the people.

The poem's conclusion merges Lowell's historical and personal perspectives on Kennedy:

>   I miss
> you, you out of Plutarch, made by hand –
> forever approaching your maturity.[104]

---

101   The poem was called 'R.F.K.' in *The New Republic* (1968), *Notebook 1967–68* (1969), and *Notebook* (1970), but then 'For Robert Kennedy 1925–68' in *History* (1973), *Collected Poems* (2003) and all subsequent publications. The second and third poems of the Kennedy trilogy appeared as 'Another Circle' and 'Another June' in *Notebook 1967–68* and *Notebook*, but in *History* they were merged as 'For Robert Kennedy 2', and they remained in that form subsequently.
102   *Collected Poems*, 571.
103   Daniel Patrick Moynihan, speaking on WTOP radio, 5 December 1963.
104   Lowell, *Collected Poems*, 571.

The line breaks at 'miss', to emphasize that word, which evokes the poet's enduring grief and also the fading of memory and the imprecision of language – his painful inability to recapture Kennedy's presence. The next line begins 'you, you' as if to stutter in bewilderment or to keen for the lost beloved: 'I *miss / you, you* out of Plutarch, made by hand'. Kennedy is not 'machine-like' now but the opposite, a character composed of words, or a manually produced artwork, with a Benjaminian 'aura' of unreproducibility.[105]

Forever approaching his maturity, Kennedy is an object of admiration and desire, eternally young, frozen in time like the figures on Keats's Grecian urn. Perhaps he is also an object of identification: a portrait of the artist as a young man. That identification was clearer in the first four publications of the poem (in *The New Republic*, *Notebook 1967–68*, *Notebook*, and *History*). There, the last line read 'forever approaching *our* maturity'. That pronoun posited Kennedy as a metonym of Americans or of global modernity itself. Additionally, the pronoun reflected the speaker's union with the subject of his elegy. In Kennedy's stilled progress toward maturity, Lowell saw his own similar aspirations dashed. The substitution of 'your' for 'our' appears in the last publication Lowell supervised, in the original *Selected Poems* of 1976. This is the version the definitive *Collected Poems* uses, though it does reproduce the earlier version with 'our' in its Notes, thus preserving a sense that the poem will never truly achieve closure. It oscillates perpetually between an image of Kennedy as our collective alter ego and Kennedy as a unique historical figure.

Lowell's adventures in the public sphere suggest the vitality of political engagement in mid-century poetry. Lowell's summary comment about Yeats seems true of himself: if there hadn't been a political stirring in the air, somehow he 'wouldn't have been the poet he was at all, he would have been a much smaller poet'.[106] Poems such as 'Waking Early Sunday Morning' and 'For Robert Kennedy 1925–68' moved readers in their time and in ours. They made things happen. They resonated and endured. Circulating

---

105 Walter Benjamin, 'The Work of Art in the Age of Mechanical Reproduction' (1936), rpt *Illuminations: Essays and Reflections*, ed. Hannah Arendt, trans. Harry Zohn (New York: Schocken, 1969), 217.
106 'Yeats Memorial Lecture', 20.

through world culture, they helped shape awareness of the social basis of poetry, and they demonstrated the ability of poetry to clarify, to unsettle, and to impel change – even or especially in dark times.

Lowell's Value

Reading Sylvia Plath in the mid-1960s led Lowell to doubt the value of his own writing: 'Sometimes after reading these poems, I have wanted to give up writing. The terrible audacity, rightness and ease of their inspiration make most other poems sound like birthday odes to George the First'.[107] But a dozen years later, in 'After Enjoying Six or Seven Essays on Me',[108] published mere months before his death, Lowell revealed that he had come to terms with the limitations and accomplishments of his very political, very personal life's work.

He began with the political: 'Politics? We live in the sunset of Capitalism. We have thundered nobly against its bad record all our years, yet we cling to its vestiges, not just out of greed and nostalgia, but for our intelligible survival. Is this what makes our art so contradictory, muddled and troubled?'[109] He saw that his ambivalences regarding tradition and change had entered into his public discourse. He had refashioned political poetry by making it both a quarrel with his age and what Yeats called 'a quarrel with oneself'.[110] His entry into the polis, especially in the 1960s, had indeed been a process of 'exposure', as Arendt had said it must be. He retreated in the 1970s, though he produced one additional public poem, 'George III', which was equally about Richard Nixon.[111] Perforating the border between public and private feeling, his poems were acts of self-disclosure as well as

---

107 'Sylvia Plath' (Houghton Library, Harvard University), forthcoming in Lowell's *Memoirs*.
108 *Salmagundi* (Spring 1977), rpt Lowell, *Poems*, 989–993.
109 Lowell, *Collected Poems*, 991.
110 Yeats, *Mythologies* (London: Macmillan, 1959), 331.
111 *Collected Poems*, 843–845.

meditations on the political, economic, and ethical issues that shaped, and continue to shape, our communal existence.

Lowell then turned to the personal: 'Looking over my *Selected Poems*, about thirty years of writing, my impression is that the thread that strings it together is my autobiography [...] My journey is always stumbling on the unforeseen and even unforeseeable.'[112] Living with a severe psychic disorder, which left him awash in moods and emotions he could not always fathom or control, Lowell used his disability to make a powerful kind of poetry, exploring the pain of the interior life. His stumbling journey became a centrepiece of his poetics, and another enduring intervention in the history of poetry.

Lowell concluded his essay thusly: 'I pray that my progress has been more than recoiling with satiation and disgust from one style to another, a series of rebuffs. I hope there has been increase of beauty, wisdom, tragedy and all the blessings of this consuming chance.'[113] The poet who excelled at evoking darkness ends with a prayer that his writing has blessed the world. I think it has.

---

112 Ibid. 992.
113 Ibid. 993.

FRANK J. KEARFUL

Names and Naming: Robert Lowell and the Boston Irish

'Irish need not apply' no longer appears in classified ads of Boston newspapers nor on signs in Boston shop windows, but numerous examples from the 1880s and 1890s can be viewed on YouTube accompanied by the proud, defiant Irish song 'No Irish Need Apply'.[1] The sentence is now part of Boston lore, along with the city's trademark verses frequently anthologized as 'A Boston Toast':

> And this is good old Boston,
> The home of the bean and the cod,
> Where the Lowells talk only to the Cabots,
> And the Cabots talk only to God.

The verses date back to 1910 and a Holy Cross College Alumni dinner where John Collins Bossidy gave a toast to Boston, familiarly nicknamed 'Beantown.' Baked beans and cod were standard fare since the early settlers, who survived on both as did Native Americans before them and Irish immigrants after them, for whom cod was a Friday staple. A golden cod made of pine nearly 6 feet long now hangs over the entrance to the visitors' gallery of the Massachusetts State House on Beacon Hill. Beacon Hill itself was the domain of Boston's inbred traditional aristocracy, known as the Boston Brahmins ever since Oliver Wendell Holmes, Sr called them 'The Brahmin Caste of New England' in Chapter 1 of his

---

[1] See 'No Irish Need Apply: The Signs and Ads that Vilified our Irish Ancestors', available online at: <https://www.youtube.com/watch?v=VJZjEKJllOk>. Accessed 3 June 2018. The samples feature in a documentary video by Bill Fitzpatrick. The iambic trimeter rhythmic variant 'No Irish Need Apply' of 'Irish Need Not Apply' works wonderfully for singing.

novel *Elsie Venner* (1861).² Bossidy needed only to drop the names Cabot and Lowell.

But who was John Collins Bossidy?³ As an Irishman he need not have applied at Harvard in the 1870s, but could at Holy Cross, a Jesuit college in Worcester, Massachusetts, founded in 1843 by the Bishop of Boston as a place where male Boston Irish Catholics and the faithful from throughout his New England archdiocese could receive a college education. Bossidy graduated in 1881 and went on to earn a medical degree at another Jesuit institution, Georgetown University in Washington, DC, and later became a respected ophthalmologist in Boston. His 'Boston Toast' makes fun of the Brahmin elite, from which he himself would forever remain excluded. Let it be said that in some versions of his toast published over the decades it is the Lowells rather than the Cabots who 'talk only to God.' Note: not 'with' but 'to'. In either case, the 'No Irish Need Apply' song, dating from the late nineteenth century, and the mock-toast from 1910, are complementary from a Boston Irish perspective.

Nineteenth-century Harvard-trained historians fostered a myth that Boston's glorious heritage had remained unsullied by immigrants until the 1830s.⁴ John Gorham Palfrey's *History of the Revolution* (1865), for example, maintained that no county in England had 'purer English blood' than that which flowed in New Englanders at the time of the Revolution. In fact, Irish Catholic immigrants began arriving as indentured servants in the early 1600s. According to historian Thomas H. O'Connor, 'Boston had never really accepted Irish immigrants, but at least those who had come over during the 1820s had been physically robust and sturdy – strong enough to swing the picks and shovels on construction jobs and lug heavy cargo on the docks.'⁵ The 'Famine Irish' who arrived in catastrophic numbers after

---

2   Holmes, *Elsie Venner* (Boston, MA: Ticknor and Fields, 1861), 17.
3   See A.M. Juster, 'Cabots, Lowells, and a Quatrain You Don't Really Know', in *Light: A Journal of Light Verse since 1992* (Winter–Spring 2015), available online at: <https://lightpoetrymagazine.com/historical-and-hysterical-winterspring>. Accessed 22 September 2018.
4   See Thomas H. O'Connor, *The Hub: Boston Past and Present* (Boston, MA: Northeastern University Press, 2001), 144–157.
5   Ibid. 152.

the onslaught of the potato blight (1845–9) were emaciated, disease-ridden, and often possessed no skills other than rudimentary farming. On the bright side, by 1851 Boston had its first Irish cop, Barney McGinniskin, a 40-year-old immigrant and Boston resident for twenty-two years. When he arrived for the first time at work he announced himself as 'Barney McGinniskin, fresh from the bogs of Ireland.' The City Marshal objected to his 'outrageously Irish' behaviour.[6]

Bossidy targets the Lowells and the Cabots in his toast, and Robert Lowell returns the favour by giving James Michael Curley (1874–1958) a solo role in the opening paragraph of his 'Antebellum Boston' memoir, written probably in 1957:

> I, too, was born under the shadow of the Boston State House, and under Pisces, the Fish, on the first of March 1917. America was entering the First World War and was about to play her part in the downfall of four empires. At this moment, the sons of most of the old, aristocratic Republican Boston families were waiting on their doorsteps like spent hounds. They were, these families and sons, waiting and hoping for a second wind. James Michael Curley was out of jail and waiting for a mandate from the people to begin the first of his many terms as Mayor of Boston. Nothing from now on was to go quite as expected – even downhill.[7]

Curley had dominated Boston's politics for fifty years and was recently fictionalized in Edwin O'Connor's bestselling, critically acclaimed novel *The Last Hurrah* (1956), followed in 1958 by a film adaptation staring Spencer Tracy as the Curley figure. Lowell associates himself, however, with Henry Adams (1838–1918), whose classic autobiography *The Education of Henry Adams*, written in the third person, was privately printed for friends in

---

6   See Stephen Puleo, *A City So Grand: The Rise of an American Metropolis, Boston 1850–1900* (Boston, MA: Beacon Press, 2010), 52–55.

7   Robert Lowell, *Collected Prose*, ed. Robert Giroux (New York: Farrar, Straus, and Giroux, 1988), 291. Ann Walsh examines how 'Lowell's poetic utilization of the American-Irish as antithetical foil to his own élite New England community forms part of the poet's complex account of a rapidly changing society, where the influence of a massive tide of immigration had eroded the old order.' See Walsh, 'Robert Lowell and the "Lace-Curtain Irish": Identification and Identity' in Ruth Connolly et al., eds, *New Voices in Irish Criticism* 5 (Dublin: Four Courts Press, 2005), 263–276.

1907 and published posthumously in 1918. Beginning like Lowell's under the shadow of the Boston State House, Adams' long first clause ascends to his birthplace on the summit of Beacon Hill, near Lowell's birthplace at 18 Chestnut Street.

> Under the shadow of Boston State House, turning its back on the house of John Hancock, the little passage called Hancock Avenue runs, or ran, from Beacon Street, skirting the State House grounds, to Mount Vernon Street, on the summit of Beacon Hill; and there, in the third house below Mount Vernon Place, February 16, 1838, a child was born, and christened later by his uncle, the minister of the First Church after the tenets of Boston Unitarianism, as Henry Brooks Adams.[8]

Adams was no less an ironist than Lowell and would have expected readers to hear an allusion to Isaiah 9:6, 'For unto us a child is born', which resounds in Händel's *Messiah*. Boston's honorific 'a city built on a hill' links Beacon Hill and its denizens with Matthew 5:14 and the Sermon on the Mount, which the Geneva Bible (1576), the Bible of the Puritan settlers, renders: 'Ye are the light of the world. A city that is set on a hill, cannot be hid. ('You are the light of the world. A city built on a hill'). Governor John Winthrop used the 'city on a hill' biblical allusion when addressing the Massachusetts Bay Colony settlers while still onboard the Arabella before it landed in 1630. That Winthrop was referring prophetically to Beacon Hill and its chosen people as 'the light of the world' goes without saying.

In his second paragraph Adams assumes a prophetic role and forecasts his twentieth-century fate as one of the chosen people of a city built on a hill. Exchanging the State House for the Temple of Jerusalem, he adopts the name Israel Cohen:

> Had he been born in Jerusalem under the shadow of the Temple, and circumcised in the Synagogue by his uncle the high priest, under the name of Israel Cohen, he would scarcely have been more distinctly branded, and not much more heavily handicapped in the races of the coming century, in running for such stakes as the century was to offer; but, on the other hand, the ordinary traveller, who does not enter the

---

8   Adams, *Novels, Mont Saint Michel, The Education*, eds Ernest Samuels and John N. Samuels (New York: Library of America, 1983), 723.

field of racing, finds advantage in being, so to speak, ticketed through life, with the safeguards of an old, established traffic.[9]

The horseracing term 'handicapped', for heavier weights assigned some horses to equalize chances of winning for others, points to the added weight of the Adams name that Henry Adams bore, which might prove a handicap in the new century. Lowell converts horseracing to dog racing and hounds already spent. He was also 'ticketed through life' by his name and enjoyed the 'safeguards on an old, established traffic' that obviated having to traffic with the Boston Irish underclass. Henry Adams was yet more 'distinctly branded' as the great grandson of the nation's second president, John Adams, and the grandson of the sixth, John Quincy Adams.

The Boston Irish themselves proved adept politicians, skilled at forging ethnic coalitions and running a political machine that provided essential assistance for impoverished immigrants. The Democratic Party, represented in person by the voting ward machine boss, was a godsend for generations of Irish and other disadvantaged ethnic groups. Each would get a share of the pie, cut however by the Irish. Boston's first Irish-born mayor, Hugh O'Brien from County Cork, served four one-year terms (1885–9), followed by Patrick Collins, also from County Cork (1902–5), who died in office. From 1930 to 1993 Boston's mayors were all of Irish descent, suggesting that only Irish need apply. There have been fourteen, including Martin 'Marty' Walsh, in office since 2014, whose parents emigrated from County Cork in the 1950s.

When Lowell records that 'James Michael Curley was out of jail and waiting for a mandate from the people to begin the first of his many terms as Mayor of Boston' he also covertly alludes to one of his own, Federal Judge Francis Cabot Lowell, whose name incarnated in one person both interlocutors with God in Bossidy's verses. For his part, Curley called the waning Brahmin aristocracy 'clubs of female faddists, old gentlemen with disordered livers, or pessimists croaking over imaginary good old days and ignoring the sunlit present.'[10] One of these 'gentlemen' sentenced Curley

9   Ibid. 723.
10 James Michael Curley, *I'd Do It Again: A Record of All My Uproarious Years* (Englewood Cliffs. NJ: Prentice-Hall, 1957), 114.

and an accomplice to two months in the Charles Street Jail for 'combining, conspiring, confederating, and agreeing together to defraud the United States' by taking a Post Office civil examination for two fine and decent Irish immigrant lads who aspired to become letter carriers but were not gifted writers. Curley told constituents that he 'he did it for a friend,' which proved a winning campaign slogan.[11]

Curley revolutionized the Boston political machine by making himself not simply the boss of ward bosses, instead the only boss. The others were all 'chowderheads'. Nor did he let other Boston Irish politicians stand in his way. John F. 'Honey Fitz' Fitzgerald, the maternal grandfather of President Jack Kennedy, was mayor of Boston 1906–8, 1910–4 and would have run for another term, but Curley threatened to expose his extramarital affair in a public lecture on 'Great Lovers, from Cleopatra to Toodles', the latter with reference to one Toodles Ryan, a cigarette girl of Fitzgerald's acquaintance. Fitzgerald dropped out of the race, making room for Curley.[12] When elected mayor for the fourth time in 1945, he was already indicted on charges of corrupt practice in office, but he got off lightly in June 1947 with six to eight months in the Federal Correctional Center in Danbury, Connecticut. Pardoned by President Truman after five months, when he arrived at a Boston train station 'thousands of friends, supporters and well-wishers greeted him, cheering and ringing cowbells while a brass band played "Hail to the Chief."'[13] After his first day back on the job as mayor he trumpeted: 'I have accomplished more in one day than has been done in the five days of my absence.'[14]

What does all this have to do with Robert Lowell? This time no Lowell had sentenced Curley to jail, but Lowell himself had served time in the Danbury Correctional Center. On 13 October 1943, he was sentenced to serve a year and a day there as a conscious objector after the firebombing of Hamburg in Operation Gomorrah, the mining of German dams, and

---

11   See Thomas H. O'Connor, *The Boston Irish: A Political History*, 181.
12   Ibid. 185.
13   Ibid. 210.
14   Jack Beatty, *The Rascal King: The Life and Times of James Michael Curley (1874–1958)* (Reading, MA: Addison-Wesley Publishing Co., 1992), 482. Beatty cites *The Boston Globe*, 28 November 1947.

Names and Naming: Robert Lowell and the Boston Irish 55

the Allies' insistence on unconditional surrender. Lowell was not a pacifist, and had sought to enlist after Pearl Harbor, but his conversion to Roman Catholicism in 1941 brought with it a commitment to just war doctrine that underpinned his conscientious objection. When Lowell chose Michael Curley as the single twentieth-century Boston luminary he did it for a jailbird friend.

In another memoir, '91 Revere Street', Part Two of *Life Studies*, Lowell recreates his Beacon Hill childhood from ages 8 to 10 during the years 1925–7, 'when the Republican party and what were called 'people of the right sort' were no longer dominant in city elections.'[15] Indeed. Curley had already served his first term as mayor and was working on his second, 1922–6. Beacon Hill nonetheless was still occupied mainly by people of the right sort in 1925, when 'we bought the 91 Revere Street house, looking out on an unbuttoned part of Beacon Hill bounded by the North End slums.' Things could have gotten worse, but '[i]n the decades preceding and following the First World War, old Yankee families had upset expectations by regaining this section of the Hill from the vanguard of the lace-curtain Irish,' also dubbed two-toilet Irish. Nonetheless, all was not well on Revere Street: 'Houses, changing hands, changed their language and nationality. A few doors to our south the householders spoke "Beacon Hill British" or that flat *nay nay* of the Boston Brahmin. The parents of the children spoke mostly in Italian.'

Lowell's mother grimly observed, 'We are barely perched on the outer rim of the hub of decency,'[16] applying Boston's favourite nickname for itself, the 'Hub', short for the 'Hub of the Universe'.[17] By 1925, the situation had alarmingly deteriorated at the bottom of Beacon Hill, where 'the historic Boston Common' was 'a now largely wrong-side-of-the- tracks park.'

---

15   Robert Lowell, *Collected Poems*, eds Frank Bidart and David Gewanter (New York: Farrar, Straus and Giroux, 2003), 124. Subsequent quotations from '91 Revere Street' are from page 137.
16   Ibid.
17   Oliver Wendell Holmes, Sr named the Massachusetts State House the 'Hub of the Solar System' in an 1858 *Atlantic* magazine essay (vol. 1, no. 6) and included it in his essay collection *The Autocrat of the Breakfast-Table* (New York: Macmillan, 1906), 104.

On the other side of Charles Street there was still the Public Garden and its 'polite, landscaped walks', a refuge for Bostonians of the better sort. There Lowell and his fellow pupils strolled in spring, supervised by their teachers. Pressing against an iron gate, he would 'gape longingly' toward the Common, which offered everything that his Revere Street bastion of gentility and Brimmer School did not, notably 'gangs of Irish, Negroes, Latins.' 'Latins' suggests how vague a notion Lowell had of alien children not precisely classifiable like 'Irish' or 'Negroes'. Fortunately, 'keen young policemen, looking for trouble, lolled on the benches. At nightfall a police lieutenant on horseback inspected the Common'. In the Public Garden there was no such need: 'there was only Officer Lever, a single white-haired and mustached dignitary, who had once been the doorman at the Union Club. He now looked more like a member of the club.' The gentlemen's club founded in 1863 for proper Bostonians is located at 8 Park Street on Beacon Hill, adjacent to the State House and overlooking the Common. Irish, Negroes, and miscellaneous 'Latins' did not need to apply. As an adult Lowell didn't bother.

In the 'Henry Adams' portion of his essay 'New England and Further', Lowell recalls a passage on 'bloody snowball fights between the Boston bluebloods and the Irish' in Chapter 3 of *The Education*, where Adams notes they could occur anytime that the snow on the Common was soft enough to make snowballs, some containing rocks. This sounds a lot more exciting than any visual contact Lowell may have had as a child with gangs of Irish et al. Adams describes one battle in which he joined the 'Beacon Street boys' against their Irish counterparts, 'blackguards from the slums, led by a grisly terror called Conky Daniels, with a club and a hideous reputation' (757). When Daniels 'left untouched' the brave Beacon Street boys who 'stood still and waited immolation' by Daniels and his charging horde, the 'obvious moral' for the 12-year-old Adams was that 'the blackguards were not so black as they were painted' (758). This was part of the education of Henry Adams.

One Irish name is conspicuous, or inconspicuous, by its absence in 'The Park Street Cemetery,' which inaugurates Lowell's first book, *Land of Unlikeness* (1944). Boston's Park Street Church was built in 1809 on the site of a grain storage building, or granary; the Old Granary Burying

Ground, which abuts the church, dates back to 1660 and accommodates the remains of leading figures of early American history. Stanza one highlights 'the stern surnames' on the tombstones, recited in a slow march of trochees briefly varied by only one iamb: 'Adams, / Otis, Hancock, Mather, Revere; / Franklin's mother rests in hope.' After 'Revere' and a semicolon, the march resumes. 'Franklin's mother rests,' not as it turns out 'in peace,' but 'in hope.' By contrast, the 'stern' surnames on the tombstones of founders of the American republic express disapproval of the state of the nation and its apparent future direction.[18]

One name sticks out oddly in the roll call of Founding Fathers, 'Mather,' indelibly linked with the seventeenth-century Salem witch trials and both Increase Mather (1639–1723) and his son Cotton Mather (1663–1728). Increase's father, Richard Mather (1596–1669), had nothing to do with witch trials nor anything else of historical note. But what makes 'Mather' stand out all the more is that none of the three Mathers is buried in the Old Granary Burial Ground. Increase and Cotton were laid to rest in Copp's Hill Burial Ground, and Richard in the North Dorchester Burying Ground. Lowell's injection of 'Mather' among the great and the good buried in the Old Granary Burial Ground sabotages Boston's self-naming as 'The Cradle of Liberty,' and 'The Athens of America.'[19]

Cotton Mather it so happens was the chief accuser against Ann Glover, a Gaelic-speaking Catholic born in Ireland and the last person to be hanged as a witch in Boston (1688). When a 13-year-old girl, Martha Godwin, accused Glover's daughter of stealing, Glover replied to her harshly and Martha was 'suddenly visited with strange fits' recorded in Mather's *Memorable Providences, Relating to Witchcraft and Possessions* (1689). Then Martha and her brother suddenly experienced sharp pains and were struck 'Deaf, sometimes Dumb, and sometimes Blind.' They crawled on all fours, barked like dogs, and imaginary knives wrought excruciating pain. Mather describes Glover as 'an ignorant and scandalous old Woman' whose deceased husband had 'complained of her that she was undoubtedly a Witch.' Her

18   Lowell, *Collected Poems*, 861.
19   The Cradle of Liberty refers specifically to Faneuil Hall, where political meetings leading to the Revolution took place; Boston as the 'Athens of America' has competed with Edinburgh as the 'Modern Athens' since the nineteenth century.

Gaelic was clearly the language of the Devil, and her inability to recite the Lord's Prayer in English, only in Latin, was proof positive that her husband was right. Glover ultimately confessed to being a witch.[20] You won't find Cotton Mather's earthly remains in the Old Granary Burial Ground, but if you look hard you may find Ann Glover's unmarked grave. Try to go on 16 November, which the Boston City Council named Goody Ann Glover Day in 1998, 300 years to the day after her hanging at the public gallows on Boston Common.

The second stanza closes dramatically: 'The dead cannot see Easter crowds / On Boston Common, or Beacon Hill / Where the Irish hold the Golden Dome.' Ironically, Ann Glover was among those dead. Especially in his early poetry (e.g. 'The Exile's Return,' 'Mr. Edwards and the Spider'), Lowell employs 'where / when / what' clauses strung together in long sentences for Miltonic rhetorical effect. Here a 'where' clause brings an entire stanza to a close, with 'hold' and 'Golden' rhyming internally and assonantal 'Dome' resounding at the very end. The magnificent Golden Dome, a synecdoche for the Massachusetts State House, was designed by Charles Bulfinch and completed in 1798. It was held by Curley himself as Governor for a single term (1935–7) marked by raffish one-man showmanship, diverse scandals, and malfeasance in office. He never made it to the White House.

In Lowell's poetry the Boston Irish are present occasionally, beginning with 'where the Irish hold the Golden Dome' in 'The Park Street Cemetery.' Lowell slightly alters the line in 'At the Indian Killer's Grave' in *Lord Weary's Castle* (1946) by adding something new to begin the next line: 'Where strangers hold the golden Statehouse dome / For good and always', which is a good instance of Lowell's penchant for playing with and upon idiomatic phrases.[21] In this case he adds to his original text an apparent pleonasm, 'For good and always,' which begins the new line in a markedly different register and solicits two interpretations. First, emphasis: the Irish will hold it forever, there is no chance of our ever getting it back. Second,

20 My condensed account of Glover's ill fortune draws on Robert J. Allison, *A Short History of Boston* (Carlisle, MA: Commonwealth Editions, 2015), 19–21 and 22.
21 Lowell, *Collected Poems*, 56.

subversive: it is in truth good so. Once the subversive meaning occurs to us, it cannot be got rid of any more than the Boston Irish can be got rid of.

'In Memory of Arthur Winslow,' dedicated to Lowell's maternal grandfather, in whose house on Beacon Hill he was born, is the second poem in *Land of Unlikeness,* and was also virtually unchanged in *Lord Weary's Castle.* Each of its four subtitled parts comprises two ten-line 'Scholar Gipsy' stanzas, rhyming *abcbcadeed* while its iambic pentameter contracts to a trimeter in line 6. Lowell's declamatory rendition of Matthew Arnold's patented stanza includes a brief view of the Boston Irish in the opening 'Death by Cancer' section of the elegy: 'Grandfather Winslow, look the swanboats coast / That island in the Public Gardens, where / The bread-stuffed ducks are brooding, where with tub / And strainer the mid-Sunday Irish scare / The sun-struck shallows for the dusky chub / This Easter'.[22] I take it that Lowell isn't in effect saying, dying isn't so bad given how the Irish are infiltrating the Public Garden – still a gated-community in 'Revere Street 91' – and have even occupied the island around which the Swan Boats have made their pedalled way since 1871, transporting well-behaved children and adults.[23] The scene that the poet bids Grandfather Winslow to observe is highly literary. Lowell's 'the dusky chub' adapts the sort of 'finny tribe' poetic diction that Wordsworth rejected in the *Preface to the Lyrical Ballads* but is appropriate here for a piscatory eclogue.[24] The mid-Sunday Irish, presumably having gone to mass earlier, silently perform their

---

22   Ibid. 862.
23   In a book review and in surrealistic unpublished poetic fragments Elizabeth Bishop recreated the traumatic impact on her as a 3-year-old when on a swanboat ride a swan bit a hole through her mother's kid glove and Bishop saw a drop of blood. See Victoria Harrison, *Elizabeth Bishop's Poetics of Intimacy* (Cambridge: Cambridge University Press, 1993), 134–135.
24   'Piscatory eclogue' may sound fishy, but Google supplies over 40,000 results for 'piscatory eclogues' and over 11,000 for 'piscatory eclogue.' Piscatory eclogues feature fishermen instead of shepherds, catching fish instead of tending sheep, and have their own idyllic 'primitive' locale. See James Edmund Congleton, *Theories of Pastoral Poetry in England 1684–1798* (Gainesville: University of Florida Press, 1952), 132–133. John Donne wittily adapts the piscatory eclogue in 'The Bait' in response to Marlowe's 'The Passionate Shepherd to his Love.'

communal 'primitive' fishing rites, while the 'brooding ducks' sit upon eggs about to be hatched this Easter. Life continues.

'Mary Winslow,' an elegy for Arthur's wife in *Lord Weary's Castle*, begins with two perfect iambic pentameters in a cleverly rhymed, basically iambic sonnet: 'Her Irish maids could never spoon out mush / Or orange-juice enough; the body cools'.[25] Lowell suavely employs 'soon mush,' 'juice enough' sequential assonance framed by 'could, cold' alliteration, before attention turns in lines 4–5 to those in the room besides Mary Winslow and her Irish maids A 'hush' rhyme at once decorous and melodramatic on 'mush' is followed by a gripping trochaic substitution, and then the iambic pentameter continues on unperturbed: 'and a hush / Grips at the poised relations sipping sherry.' While they go on sipping sherry, 'Charon, the Lubber, clambers from his wherry,' eager to pick up his passenger. The baroque theatricality of some of Lowell's early poetry with its classical and Christian 'machinery' self-destructs. Everything in the stanza throws into relief how Mary Winslow's Irish maids humanely attend her as caregivers to the very end. But that's what Irish maids are like.

Lowell came into his own as a humourist in *Life Studies*, where graduated humour becomes a distinctive feature of his 'confessional' voice. 'What use is my sense of humor?' he asks himself in 'Waking in the Blue', and as if to answer his question, he delivers humorous character sketches of two fellow mental patients, Stanley and 'Bobbie,' whose name, foregrounded by quotation marks, summons up Lowell's childhood name 'Bobby.'[26] These superannuated Harvard graduates, now a double act, will never fly over the cuckoo's nest but are good for a laugh. 'Bobbie' is the more the upper crust of the two as 'Porcellian '29,' a quondam member of the socially most exclusive Harvard student club, established in 1791. Neither Jack Kennedy nor his father, both ticketed as Catholics and Boston Irish, succeeded in getting elected.[27] Robert Kennedy didn't try, but he and Jack soon had other elections in mind.

---

25   Lowell, *Collected Poems*, 28
26   Ibid. 183–184.
27   See Thomas Maier, *The Kennedys: America's Emerald Kings* (New York: Basic Books, 2003), 84 and 72.

'Waking in the Blue' also begins on a humorous note: 'The night attendant, a B.U. sophomore, / rouses from the mare's-nest of his drowsy head / propped on *The Meaning of Meaning*. He catwalks down our corridor.'[28] Retooled as a verb, 'catwalks' evokes the policeman's 'cat-like tread' in Gilbert and Sullivan's *Pirates of Penzance* and shows consideration for patients not quite awake. The night attendant's being a Boston University sophomore sets him apart from Stanley and 'Bobbie,' who do not seem to be up to reading anything; but more to the ironic point, Lowell had been teaching since 1955 at Boston University, BU for short, where Anne Sexton and Sylvia Plath were among his students. In 1958 a manic attack led to hospitalization at McLean Hospital which Lowell transformed in 'Waking in the Blue.' One goal was humorously to juxtapose young Boston Irishmen and debilitated Boston Brahmins under their care. Vestiges of the old hierarchy remain, even as Irish maids attended the dying Mary Winslow.

Lowell follows up his portrayals of Stanley and 'Bobbie' with a group sketch of the Roman Catholic day attendants which exploits ethnic clichés: 'In between the limits of day, / hours and hours go by under the crew haircuts / and slightly too little nonsensical bachelor twinkle / Of the Roman Catholic attendants. (There are no Mayflower / screwballs in the Catholic Church.).' Don't Irish eyes always 'twinkle as bright can be,' at any rate 'When Irish Eyes Are Smiling'?[29] Lowell humorously juxtaposes without fear or favour youthful Boston Irishmen, none of them screwballs, and atrophied batty Boston Brahmins.

Lowell represents himself as a humorous observer and commentator, but at the end he stands with other patients before metal shaving mirrors and recognizes himself among the handicapped 'thoroughbred mental cases,' echoing the racing metaphor that Adams used and Lowell adapted. Despite his comparative youth he is an 'old timer.' Things looked a bit different when he wrote in a letter from the hospital to Isabel Gardner on 12 February 1958: 'This business at McLean's isn't exactly very serious [....] I have a private room, my typewriter, my FM radio, a door that will

---

28 Lowell, *Collected Poems*, 183.
29 Wikipedia provides the song's full text, history, and a list of its uses in twenty-nine movies and short subjects.

shut and frequent visitors. I've been reading Kant and Joyce's *Ulysses* and have actually finished a poem that has the admiration of I.A. Richards.'[30] It may have been one of the two poems about his friend that he included in *History* (1973), but in any event I like to imagine how Richards chuckled over 'Waking in the Blue' when he found his name and an old book of his in it. *The Meaning of Meaning: A Study of the Influence of Language Upon Thought and the Science of Symbolism* (1923), by Richards and C.K. Ogden, would be a tough and unusual reading assignment for any sophomore class. I suspect that Lowell himself had read instead, as 'everybody' did, Richards's *Practical Criticism* (1929) and perhaps his *Principles of Literary Criticism* (1924). Surely Lowell chose *The Meaning of Meaning* for the sake of its title and anticipated that Richards would read the poem sooner or later. They shared a sense of humour.

Four days after Robert Kennedy's assassination on 6 June 1968 Lowell sent Jacqueline Kennedy a sonnet titled 'R.F.K' which became, slightly modified, the first of three Robert Kennedy sonnets in *Notebook 1967–68* (1969) and *Notebook* (1970). Lowell transmuted them into two sonnets for *History* (1973), 'For Robert Kennedy 1925–68' and 'For Robert Kennedy 2,' which relates Kennedy to his Irishness and pivots on names and naming in lines 1–5:

> How they hated to leave the unpremeditated
> gesture of their life – the Irish in black, three rows
> ranked for the future photograph, the Holy Name,
> fiercely believed in then, then later held to
> perhaps more fiercely in their unbelief ...[31]

The unrhymed sonnet begins rather like Auden's 'Musée des Beaux Arts,' which gives the pronoun 'they' first, then names whom it refers to: 'About suffering they were never wrong, / The old Masters:'. It might be said that the Irish are also old masters about suffering, from Cromwell to the Great Famine to The Troubles.

30   *Letters of Robert Lowell*, ed. Saskia Hamilton (New York: Farrar, Straus and Giroux, 2005), 12.
31   Lowell, *Collected Poems*, 571.

Lowell's naming of 'the Irish in black' as the referent for the pronoun 'their' is followed by an appositive phrase, 'three rows / ranked for the future photograph,' which anticipates the ending of 'Epilogue' in *Day by Day* (1977): 'We are poor passing facts, / warned by that to give / each figure in the photograph / his living name.'[32] The Irish dressed in black I construe as symbolic mourners whose presence in 'the future photograph,' now developed as the poem, affirms Kennedy as one of their own.

Their clothing differs from the clothing imagery of the first sonnet, 'For Robert Kennedy, 1925–68': 'Doom was woven in your nerves, your shirt / woven in the great clan' (lines 7–8), which evokes the three Fates of Greek mythology, Clotho (hence 'clothing') who spins the thread of life; Lachesis who draws it out; and Atropos who cuts it. There is also the poisoned shirt of Nessus, which dooms Hercules when he wears it to a painful death. At the same time, spinning and weaving have their own Irish historical and cultural associations.[33]

In modern terms the 'great clan' evokes the 'Kennedy Clan,' which foregathered at the 'Kennedy Compound' but was doomed by the 'Kennedy Curse.' It had already struck down Robert's two elder brothers, Joseph in the Second World War and John by assassination. The great clan has been traced back, however, to the ancient Kennedy/O'Kennedy Clan, whose Chiefs are recorded as far back as 1152.[34] Perhaps some are given pride of place in 'ranked' rows of Irish mourners Irish dressed in black. The ensuing train ride with Robert Kennedy's casket became, Thomas Maier records, 'a traveling Irish Wake,' thanks to Jack's 'Irish mafia.'[35]

The five-line opening passage of 'For Robert Kennedy 2' is sonically and rhetorically supercharged, beginning with the emphatic alliterative

---

32   Ibid. 838.
33   See the 'History' section of the Irish Guild of Weavers, Spinners, and Dyers website, <https://weavespindye.ie/history/>. Accessed 4 July 2018.
34   See 'Clan Kennedy: Of Presidents and Kings' at the Irish America website <http://irishamerica.com/2014/03/clan-kennedy-of-presidents-and-kings/>. Accessed 4 July 2018. 'Never mind Thomas Maier's caveat: "As any pub crawler knows, hundreds if not thousands of those with Irish blood in their veins trace their roots to Brian Boru and other long-ago chieftains".' 10.
35   Lowell, *Collected Poems*, 516.

pair 'How' / 'hated,' which leads to askew rhyming of 'hated' / 'unpremeditated,' perhaps fleetingly bringing to mind the premeditated murder of Robert Kennedy. The 'leave' of line 1 morphs through paronomasia into 'life' in line 2, then back through polyptoton to 'believed' and 'unbelief' in lines 4 and 5. The 'future' of line 3 weak rhymes with 'gesture,' before proceeding on its alliterative way, 'future ... photograph ... fiercely,' which in turn spawns the ploce 'fiercely ... fiercely.' The 'rows' of line 2 alliterates with 'ranked' in line 3, while anadiplosis links 'then, then' in line 4, establishing degrees of pastness set off against the 'future photograph.' The keyword 'Irish' is celebrated through assonance and a suturing dash as 'life – the Irish.' The echoic vowel of the emblematic dyad 'l*i*fe *I*rish' occurs nowhere else in the passage.

The comma after 'the future photograph' suggests that an appositional phrase will follow, and indeed 'the Holy Name' links photograph and naming, as in 'Epilogue.' It also insists, however, on initiating a new syntactic chain without the old one having been terminated. This syntactic clash makes 'the Holy Name' stand out all the more, along with that other holy name, 'the Irish.' In religious utterance names can in themselves be holy and revered, as in The Lord's Prayer: 'Our Father who art in Heaven, hallowed be thy name.' The power of the Lord's name is authenticated by several biblical passages, such as 'For whosoever calls upon the name of the Lord shall be saved' (Paul, *Romans* 10: 13), and it is invoked in the Litany of the Holy Name of Jesus. Some Catholic religious orders and communities also derive their own names from the holy name of Jesus, notably the Jesuits. For the laity there is still The Holy Name Society, although its numbers have dwindled, as have the number of Jesuits.

Naming God was a vexed issue in the second *Notebook* sonnet on Kennedy, titled 'Another Circle', which names Lowell's daughter Harriet and alludes to a conversation with her in the volume's opening 'Harriet' sonnet.[36] At ten and half and counting, she pondered the problematics of naming God: 'God's a seaslug, God a queen / with forty servants, God ... she gave up – things whirl / in the chainsaw bite of whatever squares / the

---

36 Ibid. 197.

universe by name and number'.³⁷ In 'Another Circle' Lowell replies: 'We can't hunt God. He hunts us, / and his story is sad ....'³⁸

This sad story leads to Lowell's own problems naming God in 'For Robert Kennedy 2' in *History*. We know God, if we can be said to know him at all, by analogy, and Lowell chooses two grim ones. Lines 8–12 begin with a swallow that kills insects and ends with Gloucester's analogy in *King Lear*, 'As flies to wanton boys are we to th' gods' (IV, i),³⁹ which Lowell circuitously applies to us in lines 10–12: 'Will we / swat out the birds as ruthlessly as flies?'

Harriet's naming quandary gives way to the poet's in lines 13–14: 'No Name can judge their killer, / his guiltless liver, kidneys, fingertips and phallus.' The retention of capitalized 'Name,' stripped of its 'Holy' epithet, strips God of his holiness. But what unholy name can replace it? Seaslug? Better were Nimrod, 'that mighty hunter [...] and men, not beasts shall be his game' (Milton, *Paradise Lost*, XII. 33, 30).⁴⁰ But if God hunts us as ruthlessly as Nimrod hunts men or as men kill Kennedys, or as Irishmen kill Irishmen, how then can one make sense, Irish sense, of the paradox posed in lines 4–6 of 'For Robert Kennedy 2': 'fiercely believed in then, then later held to / perhaps more fiercely in their unbelief'?

The lines might simply reflect a 'hating' to die young, which would loosely correlate with the last line of 'For Robert Kennedy 1925–68': 'forever approaching your maturity' but never reaching it, which sounds like something out of Keats's 'Ode on a Grecian Urn.' But then there are the many, the all too many, who died all too young in The Troubles, including 'the boy' finally named in the last word of Lowell's 'Identification in Belfast (I.R.A. Bombing)' as 'Richard'.⁴¹ Since he goes to 'mass,' we are induced to infer that he was the bomber, slaughtered almost beyond recognition in the mass bombing. As for adult committers of 'premediated' murders,

---

37 Ibid. 21.
38 Ibid. 197.
39 Arden edition, ed. Kenneth Muir (London: Methuen), 149.
40 See Richard F. Hardin, 'Milton's Nimrod', *Milton Quarterly* (1988): 38–44, on Milton's view of Nimrod as a 'hunter of men who is self-tempted, self-depraved, and self-deceived,' 43.
41 Lowell, *Collected Poems*, 838.

their 'hatred' whether of Protestants or Catholics derived in the main from a fiercely held religious belief that they were born into and grew up with. The Troubles incited a yet more militant identification with 'their' Christianity, although they renounced any genuine Christian faith by becoming apostates in deed: 'by their works ye shall know them.' While retaining their denominational ID as an identity marker, they were driven by hatred more ethnic and political than religious.

Lowell's Robert Kennedy sonnets are complaints in three related senses: (1) an elegiac complaint on the death of a young person like Milton's Lycidas, 'dead, dead ere his prime, / Young Lycidas and hath not left a peer,' which is how millions felt after Robert Kennedy's assassination;[42] (2) a vituperation of a malevolent God, an almighty Nimrod; (3) a denunciation of the debasement of religious faith into an exculpation of man's homicidal violence.

Christopher Ricks observes that 'violence was Lowell's central subject, terrible in its variety (of time, of place, of motive, of nature) and terrible in not changing.'[43] Saskia Hamilton adds a codicil of her own: 'Lowell's horror of violence included the violence of doctrines.'[44] Her immediate context is political doctrines rather than religious, but the two reinforced each other during The Troubles. The Boston Irish did not carry out the IRA Provisionals' the Provisional IRA's but does that exculpate their financial support?

In 'For Robert Kennedy 1925–68' Lowell mourns for Kennedy using the simple words 'I miss you.' In 'For Robert Kennedy 2' it is the Irish dressed in black who do the mourning, but who also proffer the consolation along with lament that traditional elegy seeks. The Irish are themselves a singular sign of life that Lowell artfully fashions on their behalf, 'life-the Irish'. The Boston Irish Kennedys prove it, as do in their own ways other Boston Irishmen and Irishwomen who enter Lowell's earlier poems.

---

42 'Lycidas' ll. 3–4, in John Milton, *Complete Shorter Poems*, ed. John Carey (Longman: London, 1997).
43 'The War of Words' in Christopher Ricks, *The Force of Poetry* (Oxford: Oxford University Press, 1984), 282.
44 *The Letters of Robert Lowell*, ed. Saskia Hamilton (New York: Farrar, Straus and Giroux, 2005), xix.

ALEX RUNCHMAN

Weaving the Great Clan: Robert Lowell, Robert Kennedy and Martin Luther King

> And now my death
> Changes the mood, for what in me was purchas'd
> Falls upon thee in a more fairer sort;
> So thou the garland wear'st successively.[1]

In a brief reminiscence, first collected in *New York Magazine* in December 1970, two and a half years after Robert Kennedy's mood-changing assassination, Robert Lowell recalled Kennedy reading aloud Henry IV's deathbed speech to Prince Hal and declaring: 'Henry IV, that's my father'. The New York senator's impromptu reading had been in response to Lowell's provocation that he should instead be cast as Falstaff and that comparing himself to Henry V was 'trite' and, in any case, hardly desirable: 'after his terrible invasion of France', noted Lowell, 'he married a French princess. Five years later he was dead of fever in Paris, leaving a son who was murdered by the English and an occupation force of Englishmen which was ousted and destroyed by Jeanne d'Arc'.[2] At the time, Lowell appears to have intended this almost farcically sped-up precis of genealogical decline, informed as it is by the kind of pat fatalism that could only have been imposed retrospectively, as a way of cutting Kennedy down to size – of exposing the incongruity of a twentieth-century Irish-American politician comparing himself to a fifteenth-century English monarch. After Kennedy's death, however, questions of inheritance within one family (the garland worn

---

1 William Shakespeare, 2 *Henry IV*, 4.iv.198–202.
2 Jean Stein, 'RFK Freshly Remembered', *The New York Magazine*, 14 December 1970, 48.

successively) and of how these might be tied up with national fortunes could no longer be dismissed so flippantly.

Given how central historical analogy-making is to Lowell's method throughout his career, and especially in his late sonnets, his initial resistance to Kennedy's comparison is perhaps surprising. With hindsight, however, he came to understand it as anything but trite: as an acceptance of responsibility rather than vainglorious posturing. Kennedy's father as Henry IV had at first seemed to Lowell a *'non-sequitur'*; but following Kennedy's death, he came to see the comparison as 'very profound'. What R.F.K. meant, Lowell recalled, was 'that he had a very difficult career coming from his difficult but very elevated forebear who made it possible'.[3] While Lowell is clearly talking about Joe Kennedy here, it is impossible to overlook the even greater difficulty for R.F.K. in living up to the legacy of his murdered elder brother. Published alongside Lowell's recollection, the NBC news correspondent Charles Quinn – who had reported on R.F.K.'s assassination – recalls talking to white immigrant voters opposed to the civil rights movement who claimed, despite their political differences, that they would have voted for Kennedy, stating 'We like him for what his brother did'.[4] The anecdote exemplifies the hope that many Americans had of R.F.K. as someone who might have been able to reunify a divided country, but the expectation can only have added to the sense of personal burden. Lowell speculates on this further in the second part of his reminiscence. 'You felt that he [R.F.K.] was doomed', he explains

> and you knew that he felt that. The course he took, it was black, and that gave a kind of tragedy to it all [...] The ambition was a burden ... that he had to run for President, that he was doomed with that possibility and duty [...] He knew that, and he had no middle course possible to him.[5]

Across the two short columns of this piece, the word 'doomed' occurs six times.

---

3 Ibid. 48.
4 Ibid. 54.
5 Ibid. 58.

Conscious that his interpretation may seem overdetermined – would this have still been the case if R.F.K. had not been shot? – Lowell insists that the whole point of the Henry V analogy was 'that it was sort of intuitive and things were left <u>undisentangled</u>'.[6] The *New York Magazine* interview nonetheless offers a very broad elucidation of Lowell's less disentangled *History* sonnet 'For Robert Kennedy 1925–68', in which Kennedy's 'doom' is the abiding concern:

> Doom was woven in your nerves, your shirt,
> woven in the great clan; they too were loyal,
> and you too were loyal to them, to death.[7]

'For Robert Kennedy 1925–68' is the title used when it was published in *History* in 1973, but the poem had first appeared, in a slightly different version, in *The New Republic* on 22 June 1968 (within weeks of Kennedy's death), and then in the various editions of *Notebook*. In *Notebook*, the poem (titled simply 'R. F. K.') is accompanied by two others, 'Another Circle' and 'Another June', which are then dismantled and condensed into one ('Robert Kennedy 2') in *History*.[8] 'For Robert Kennedy 1925–68', though it avoids explicit reference to Henry V, presents Kennedy 'like a prince' and, above all, as a fated figure, the owner of a great life 'out of Plutarch'.[9] The poem is characteristic of the genealogical method that Alex Calder (drawing on Foucault) sees as informing the whole of *History* in that it is at once of its moment and unbound by time: only the title enables us to situate its 'here' and 'now'.[10] Despite references in 'For Robert Kennedy 2' to 'the Irish in black' and in 'Another June' to the deceased as 'pure Celt on the eastern seaboard' (*Notebook*), the doomed figure

---

6 Ibid. 48.
7 Robert Lowell, *Collected Poems*, eds Frank Bidart and David Gewanter (London: Faber, 2003), 571.
8 See Robert Lowell, *Notebook*, 3rd edn (New York: Farrar, Straus and Giroux, 1970), 197–198. Lowell had also sent the *New Republic Version* to Jacqueline Kennedy on 10 June 1968. See Saskia Hamilton, ed., *The Letters of Robert Lowell* (London: Faber, 2005), 503.
9 Lowell, *Collected Poems*, 771.
10 Ibid. 1074.

described in the principle elegy might as easily be Hercules – grappling with the poisoned shirt of Nessus, heroically trying to defy a fate that had already been preordained – as the candidate for the Democratic nomination in the USA in June 1968.[11] As Lowell remarked in his note to *Near the Ocean* – the previous year – perhaps a little disingenuously – 'How one jumps from Rome to the Americas of my own poems is something of a mystery to me.'[12]

However, despite their fluidity of identity and vagueness of location, the intricacy of Lowell's elegies to Kennedy – their woven-ness – only really becomes apparent when analysed within their very precise historical, political, and literary contexts. This essay unpicks some of Lowell's stitches by reading 'For Robert Kennedy 1925–68' (with occasional nods to the other Kennedy poems), first of all, with reference to the national self-questioning that occurred immediately after the assassination, and then in relation to a few crucial lines from Kennedy's 'Mindless Menace of Violence' speech delivered in Cleveland on 5 April 1968, the day after the fatal shooting of Martin Luther King. Lowell's allusion to this speech raises the question of how his elegy might be situated in relation to an intersection of Irish and Black American experience. Through their speeches, King and Kennedy each promoted an overtly hybrid or shared vision of identity and culture. Lowell's perspective on the civil rights movement is far from straightforward, and his depictions of other people's experiences (whatever their ethnicity or social status) are almost always filtered through the lens of his own. All the same, the vast allusive scope of his *History* sonnets, which allows the voices of political speechmakers to resound alongside more intimate and elegiac lyric voices, lends its support to King and Kennedy's visions. This is especially apparent in 'For Robert Kennedy 1925–68'.

R.F.K.'s memory will always be linked to his family – 'the great clan' in which his 'doom was woven', and to which he was so loyal.[13] Lowell himself had been loyal to the clan since J.F.K.'s election at the end of 1960. 'I

---

11 Ibid. 571, 198.
12 Ibid. 381.
13 See Ron Eyerman, *The Cultural Sociology of Political Assassination: from MLK and RFK to Fortuyn and Van Gogh* (New York: Palgrave Macmillan, 2011), 57–73, for an account of RFK's assassination in relation to his brother's.

found I care awfully that Kennedy win,' he wrote to Elizabeth Bishop on 16 November [...] At least we'll have a president for a change'.[14] Lowell was invited to attend the inauguration. 'The Kennedy business is very inspiring', he enthused to Bishop on 15 February 1961:

> with a lot of reservations, I feel like a patriot for the first time in my life. I wrote in the Kennedy guest-book, Robert Lowell, happy that at long last the Goths have left the Whitehouse. Bobby Kennedy read it and said, 'I guess we are the Visigoths'.[15]

Bishop's more cautious response undercuts the imperial overtones of this. 'I don't like that Roman Empire grandeur', she complained: 'I wish K weren't so damned RICH'.[16] Lowell was attracted to the glamour, but recognized how it might sit uneasily alongside responsibility. Following a White House dinner for André Malraux with plenty of cocktails, wine, and champagne, he read 'that the President had ordered our 7th fleet to Laos'.[17] A few years later, after J.F.K.'s death, Lowell described a party of Jacqueline Kennedy's (despite his personal admiration for her) as 'the flash of the jet-set, a little lurid and in bad taste in a world of poverty and blood'. It may have been at this party that he became closer to Bobby Kennedy, describing him as 'the most interesting person to talk to' but also noting that 'there is a scary feeling of ambition and power about him, along with frankness'.[18]

John F. Kennedy's death had a personal effect on Lowell, who was hospitalized for a period afterwards. 'Kennedy's murder was a terrible trauma for all of us', he told Bishop 'I guess it had something to do with my crack-up'.[19] All the same, for the sociologist Ron Eyerman, it was Robert Kennedy's death on 5 June 1968, rather than Jack's, that gave rise to genuine cultural trauma in the US.[20] Shocking as the events in Dallas of 22 November 1963

14 Thomas Travisano with Saskia Hamilton, ed., *Words in Air: The Complete Correspondence Between Elizabeth Bishop and Robert Lowell* (New York: Farrar, Straus and Giroux, 2008), 347.
15 Ibid. 350.
16 Ibid. 352.
17 Ibid. 416.
18 Ibid. 605.
19 Ibid. 518.
20 Eyerman, 57–73.

were, and despite the subsequent murder of the assassin Lee Harvey Oswald and the consequent lack of a purifying trial, security was quickly restored through the peaceful and ordered succession of Lyndon Johnson. But, in June 1968, two months after King's assassination, R.F.K. had represented the best hope for many of reconciling black and white America. As Quinn remarked of the unexpected Kennedy supporters he met in Tennessee, 'all of these people felt that Kennedy would really do what he thought was right for the black people but, at the same time, would not tolerate lawlessness and violence'.[21] With Kennedy's death, that hope was forestalled. For this reason, and because it reopened dynastic wounds that had arguably begun to heal, the assassination prompted a period of collective self-interrogation. Alistair Cooke, who witnessed the murder in LA's Ambassador Hotel first-hand, gave the rationalist perspective in that week's *Letter from America*. 'I have no doubt that this experience is a trauma', he explained, 'and because of it' (not in spite of it),

> I still cannot rise to the general lamentations about a sick society. I, for one, do not feel like an accessory to a crime and I reject almost as a frivolous obscenity the sophistry of collective guilt – the idea that I, or the American people, killed John Fitzgerald Kennedy and Martin Luther King and Robert Francis Kennedy [...] With Edmund Burke, I do not know how you can indict a whole nation [...] It sounds wise and deep but is really a way of opting out of the human situation.[22]

For Cooke, discussion of society's sickness is more likely to provoke than to prevent such arbitrary killings. Pleading collectively guilty legitimizes the actions of those who believe they have a reason to attack society. Cooke advises, instead, an interrogation of individual conscience: 'when Martin Luther King is killed the only people who know that you and I are not like the killer are you and I'.[23]

Lowell's elegies also avoid blaming society. While Cooke had suggested that an appropriate response to the tragedy would include compassion for

21 'RFK Freshly Remembered', 54.
22 Alistair Cooke, 'Letter from America: Bobby Kennedy's assassination, 1968', available online at: <http://www.bbc.co.uk/programmes/p00yqjy8>. Accessed 17 May 2018.
23 Ibid.

Kennedy's killer, Sirhan Sirhan, Lowell's 'For Robert Kennedy 2' seems even to relieve him of accountability for the act. Instead, the poem wonders at the inherent brutality of nature, 'the nesting, sexing tree swallow' that dives 'for eye and brain', 'changed to a danger in the twilight'.[24] Christopher Ricks has discussed how, for a poet like Lowell whose essential subject is violence, it is a challenge to avoid collusion in the violence depicted.[25] The words 'non-violence' and 'non-violent', coined by Gandhi three years after Lowell's birth, are not, for Ricks, satisfactory as words that try to imagine 'an opposite of violence and an alternative to it'; they jar and do not banish actual violence.[26] However, Ricks finds a 'benign and uncollusive apprehension of violence' in many of Lowell's poems, characterized by a summoning up of violence only to tranquilize it. Specifically, Ricks refers to Lowell's use of a kind of 'anti-pun' in which one sense of a word is admitted but another is denied admission.[27] In both of *History*'s Kennedy poems, violence is hinted at but kept at a distance. In 'For Robert Kennedy, 1925–68', for example, 'his gang' simply evokes Kennedy's social set rather than a group of disaffected youth or protesting students; likewise, this gang's now far-off 'hornet yatter' has no sting.[28] In 'For Robert Kennedy 2', when Lowell recalls how Kennedy 'wisecracked through the guests', nothing more than a joke is cracked; nonetheless, the reader attuned to the circumstances of Kennedy's death may strain not also to hear the crack of a pistol.[29] In this poem, it is not so much the case that Lowell avoids describing violence but rather that he describes it so broadly as to make the single horrifying instance that gave the poem its occasion disappear in the general nature of things. 'God hunts us', the poem concludes. 'Who has seen him, who will judge this killer, / his guiltless liver, kidneys, fingertips and phallus?'[30] Is

---

24 Lowell, *Collected Poems*, 571.
25 Christopher Ricks, 'Robert Lowell: "The War of Words"' in *The Force of Poetry* (Oxford: Clarendon Press, 1984), 256–273.
26 Ibid. 261–262.
27 Ibid. 262, 265.
28 Ibid.
29 Ibid.
30 Ibid.

the 'he' here God, the generic assassin, or Sirhan Sirhan himself? It hardly matters: reduced to body parts, this killer lacks motive or intentionality.

However, Lowell's rejection of collective guilt, unlike Cooke's, is also an indulgence: in attributing the assassination to fate – 'doom' – he is mythmaking, perpetuating the notion of the fated house of Camelot. Such an approach offers some consolation because it suggests that nobody could have done anything to prevent what happened. But it is not altogether a rallying cry for people to take individual responsibility. And, even so, the 'general lamentations about a sick society', no matter how ill-founded, could not be reasoned away – not least because the victim, Kennedy, had himself propelled that dialogue; and, before him, so had King, who, a few days before his death, had lamented that 'we live in a sick nation'.[31]

Kennedy's Cleveland commemoration of King was a landmark moment in his campaign for the Democratic candidacy. Diagnosing a sickness that he felt to be contagious, he nonetheless gave enough hope of a remedy to prevent the kind of riots that occurred in other cities when the news became known. 'Violence breeds violence', he remarked. 'Repression breeds retaliation, and only a cleansing of our whole society can remove this sickness from our souls'.[32] In order to cleanse, Kennedy, in Lowell's figuration, was prepared to get dirty: 'You daily left your tower', Lowell writes (accruing connotations of both Yeats's tower and Tennyson's 'many-tower'd Camelot') 'to walk through dirt in your best cloth' – the same cloth, or shirt, presumably in which his doom was woven, or a 'garland' worn 'successively', 'made by hand'.[33] The very conceit seems to pick up a thread from Kennedy's own speech. 'Whenever we tear at the fabric of our lives which another man has painfully and clumsily woven for himself and his children', he insisted, 'whenever we do this, then the whole nation is degraded'.[34] And this itself is cognizant of King's famous invocation in his *Letter from Birmingham*

---

31 Cited in Maurice Isserman and Michael Kazin, *America Divided: The Civil War of the 1960s* (Oxford: Oxford University Press, 1999), 215.
32 Robert Kennedy, 'Mindless Menace of Violence', speech delivered 5 April 1968, Cleveland Ohio, <https://www.youtube.com/watch?v=hhANTymDIYk>, 4.25–4.40 minutes. Accessed 17 May 2018.
33 Lowell, *Collected Poems*, 571.
34 Kennedy, 'Mindless Menace of Violence', 2.21–2.37 minutes.

Jail, first published in *The Atlantic Monthly* five years earlier, that 'Injustice anywhere is a threat to justice everywhere'.³⁵

Given how interwoven the fates of Kennedy and King were, it should not be surprising to hear echoes of King's rhetoric, albeit at a couple of removes, in Lowell's elegy to Kennedy. Lowell had written a sonnet, 'Two Walls', in response to King's murder too, a piece that is more abstracted still than the Kennedy poems. Its beginning is almost a parable, and its driving conceit is not weaving but stone.

> Two white walls face each other;
> their color looks much alike, two shadings of white,
> each living in the shadow of the other.
> How fine our distinctions when we cannot choose!³⁶

King himself only features in the poem, if at all, through a flattening of his voice. Lowell's repetitions of 'white' and 'walls' neutralize the emotive energy of King's own characteristic repetitions and, with only 'shadow' to distinguish tone, the poem conspicuously avoids the word 'black'. This suggests an impasse in the struggle for race equality, although the stone conceit does offer the slightest of hopeful nods to the crescendo of King's most celebrated speech: 'With this faith, we will be able to hew out of the mountain of despair a stone of hope'.³⁷

As in 'For Robert Kennedy 1925–68', the focus at the end of 'Two Walls' switches, via deixis, back to the poet's own persona, an 'I', lying 'here', 'heavily breathing, the soul of New York'.³⁸ In the Kennedy poem, Lowell's 'I' is 'alone in [his] Plutarchan bubble' – a word which evokes the soldier in Shakespeare's 'Seven Ages of Man' speech, 'seeking the bubble reputation / Even in the cannon's mouth'³⁹ but also, as Steven Gould Axelrod has

---

35 Martin Luther King, 'Letter from Birmingham Jail' (1964), *Letter from Birmingham Jail* (London: Penguin, 2018), 1–30; 2.
36 Lowell, *Collected Poems*, 566.
37 King, 'I Have A Dream', speech delivered 28 August 1963, Washington, DC, available online at: <http://www.americanrhetoric.com/speeches/mlkihaveadream.htm>. Accessed 17 May 2018.
38 Lowell, *Collected Poems*, 566.
39 Ibid. 571; Shakespeare, *As You Like It*, 2.vii.152–3.

observed, Lowell's earlier poem, 'For The Union Dead': 'Colonel Shaw / is riding on his bubble, / he waits / for the blessed break'.[40] This is the most anthologized of Lowell's poems to engage with civil rights, but the movement is an implicit context throughout *History*. King wrote in *Letter from Birmingham Jail* that 'Lamentably, it is an historical fact that privileged groups seldom give up their privileges voluntarily', and this is exemplified in Lowell's book, whose opening line is 'History has to live with what was here'.[41] King also wrote in *Letter from Birmingham Jail* that 'Before the Pilgrims landed at Plymouth, *we were here*. Before the pen of Jefferson scratched across the pages of history the majestic word of the Declaration of Independence, *we were here*' (my emphasis).[42] Lowell's scope ranges far beyond the immediate politics of the 1960s but the experience of black Americans is very much one of the 'what was heres' that his book lives with.

The return of focus from the public figure to the individual perceiver in these poems characterizes a feature of Lowell's poetry that Randall Jarrell had recognized in some of his earlier poems: a tendency to mediate moments of literary, historical and political importance through his own experience. In a review of *The Mills of the Kavanaughs*, Jarrell had regretted, half-jokingly, that, in the poem 'David and Bathsheba in the Public Garden', it is almost impossible to tell David and Bathsheba apart: 'they both (like the majority of Mr Lowell's characters) talk just like Mr Lowell'.[43] A later review frames what is essentially the same point much more favourably: Lowell's style, says Jarrell, 'manages to make even quotations and historical facts a personal possession'.[44] In their notes to *History*, Frank Bidart and David Gewanter draw attention to Emerson's call to the reader of history not just to possess the past but to become it: 'We, as we read, must become Greeks, Romans, Turks, priest and king, martyr and executioner, must

---

40   Lowell, *Collected Poems*, 378; Steven Gould Axelrod, *Robert Lowell: Life and Art* (Princeton, NJ: Princeton University Press, 1978), 200.
41   Lowell, *Collected Poems*, 421; King, 'Letter from Birmingham Jail', 7.
42   Ibid. 26.
43   Randall Jarrell, 'Three Books' in *Poetry and the Age* (1953) (New York: The Ecco Press, 1980), 250–265; 254.
44   Randall Jarrell, 'Fifty Years of American Poetry' (1963) in *No Other Book: Selected Essays*, ed. Brad Leithauser (New York: Harper Collins, 1999), 252.

fasten these images to some reality in our secret experience or we shall learn nothing rightly'.[45] (In Lowell's case, Jarrell might have argued for the opposite: Greek, Roman, and Turk becoming Lowell himself.) But no matter how *History* collapses boundaries of time and identity, Lowell never 'becomes' Martin Luther King: 'Two Walls' is too abstracted for that, the shift of focus back from the martyr to the poet indicating how he is affected by the death but nonetheless separated from it.

Lowell's distance from King's experience does not diminish his support for the civil rights movement or his fears about what inter-racial violence might do to the USA. On 8 May 1963, he wrote to Bishop, addressing what he saw as an irrational fear behind Southern racism:

> I suppose you've been reading about the fierce and awful race riots in Birmingham. We've sent a telegram and signed a petition. I can imagine the Southerners, but what they are doing is barbarous, and all for a nightmare of the nerves, something that exists there, but not in fact.[46]

However, unlike his contemporary John Berryman, with his controversial use of black dialect in *The Dream Songs*, Lowell rarely attempted to imagine black experience directly. Even in 'For The Union Dead', the focus is the monument as much as the historical figure of Colonel Shaw, and when the speaker crouches to his television set to see 'the drained faces of Negro school-children rise like balloons,'[47] the TV screen mediates, keeping the experience at a distance. Lowell recognized, in one of his letters to Bishop, that, in relation to civil rights, 'there is no tolerance or place for the unconvinced bystander'.[48] Echoing an earlier insight by Delmore Schwarz that 'there is often a feeling that to be an innocent bystander is in itself one form of guilt', Lowell accepts here that each individual has a responsibility to take a stance.[49] All the same, on this issue

---

45 Lowell, *Collected Poems*, 1075.
46 *Selected Letters*, 422.
47 Lowell, *Collected Poems*, 377.
48 Ibid. 451.
49 Delmore Schwartz, 'The Present State of Poetry', *Selected Essays of Delmore Schwartz*, eds. Donald A. Dike and David H. Zucker (Chicago: Chicago University Press, 1970), 30–50; 48.

his conviction cannot prevent him from being an observer rather than a participant.

Lowell's 1964 play *Benito Cereno* his stage adaptation of Herman Melville's 1855 novella, might seem an exception to his not imagining black experience. However, the actions of the play's slave rebels Babu and Ataful had already been provided by Melville and their speech is too stylized to suggest interiority. Lowell's claims to Ian Hamilton that he couldn't 'feel acted plays are literature', and that he thought of his adaptation as prose, imply that inhabiting the characters was not his intent.[50] Instead, Lowell succumbs to wordplay on the words 'black' and 'white' which, in the context of civil rights, seems a laboured plea for relevance. Episodes from Melville are invested with more overtly symbolic significance by Lowell. For example, Melville describes a Spanish sailor tarring a strap on deck while being watched by a circle of black onlookers; a contrast is noted between the sailor's tar-blackened hand and his fine-featured face, but no explicit interpretation is forced on the reader. Lowell melodramatizes this: his sailor dips white dolls in a tar-pot and then cleans them before smearing his face with tar and crying 'My soul is white!'[51] Such overstated chiaroscuro also characterizes some of Lowell's otherwise serious private correspondences about civil rights. 'Civil Rights seems the clearest of black and white issues', he announced to Bishop in June 1964, elsewhere reflecting that, 'As far as honor goes, I think white America is committed to granting equality to the Negro. How much equality actually will be granted is another darker and unanswerable question.'[52] In these uses of 'black', 'white', and 'darker' there is no Ricksian 'anti-pun' with 'only one sense admitted' while another 'is denied admission': the other sense hammers the door down, adding little to the point being made.[53] However, Babu's final declamation of 'I was the King' (which is entirely absent in Melville), arguably summon up Martin Luther King's surname, only to be refused entry given how at odds

---

50 Lowell, *Collected Prose* (New York: Farrar, Straus and Giroux, 1987), 288, 289.
51 Lowell, *Benito Cereno* in *The Old Glory* (New York: Farrar, Straus and Giroux, 1968), 135–214; 176.
52 *Selected Letters*, 451, 478.
53 Ricks, 265.

Babu's violent revolt is with MLK's non-violent ideology.⁵⁴ Even if this is more potentially evocative than the 'black' and 'white' puns, a far more suggestive motif in *Benito Cereno* – and one that is more in line with Lowell's characteristic imagery of fish-nets and weaving – is that of Spanish oakum-pickers aimlessly knotting rope: when Captain Delano asks one of the sailor's what his knot is for, the reply, evoking the Fates picking at their threads, is simply 'For someone to untie.'⁵⁵

Lowell's allusion to Kennedy alluding to King can be read within a much broader context of US writing that addresses Black and Irish experience from different perspectives. While King and the Irish American Kennedy had advocated the integration of black and white Americans, Malcolm X had used the rise of Irish Americans in politics to illustrate what black Americans should aspire to and seek to surpass. In his autobiography, published after his assassination in 1965, Malcolm X remarked how

> Immigrants once made Tammany Hall the most powerful single force in American politics. In 1880, New York City's first Irish Catholic Mayor was elected, and by 1960 America had its first Irish Catholic President. America's black man, voting as a bloc, could wield an even more powerful force.⁵⁶

It is worth remembering that American's first Irish Catholic president had been decidedly ambivalent on civil rights until he responded to the Birmingham campaign in 1963. It is worth remembering, too, that Bobby Kennedy – in 1968 the supposed unifier of black and white – had authorized the tapping of Martin Luther King's telephones in 1963.⁵⁷ If Black and Irish Americans had once experienced similar injustice (for example, through employment laws), by the 1960s their respective statuses had considerably diverged.

There are more overtly literary examples, too, of the yoking together and then separating out of black and Irish experience. In unpublished

---

54 *Benito Cereno* 213.
55 Ibid. 177.
56 Malcolm X and Alex Haley, *The Autobiography of Malcolm X* (1965) (London: Penguin, 2007), Chapter 16.
57 See Derek C. Catsam, 'Civil Rights' in *A Companion to John F. Kennedy*, ed. Marc J. Selverstone, 540–557.

notes towards a study of T.S. Eliot, Delmore Schwartz, noted that if Eliot's poetry sometimes seemed hostile towards Jews it also expressed, in the Sweeney poems, an 'animus against the Irish'.[58] Rachel Blau du Plessis has stated the charge against Eliot more directly. Sweeney conforms to 'a mid-Victorian stereotype of the savage or simian Irishman' but can equally be seen as African. For du Plessis, he is 'a figure who encodes attitudes toward threatening politically active races, classes, and groups who are (in terms ['Sweeney Among the Nightingales'] proposes) beneath Culture in one sense while exhibiting a lurid, complete and tempting culture of pleasure, avariciousness, and sadism'.[59] Such an ambivalent merging of African and Irish identity into one subversive conglomerate could not seem more remote from Malcolm X's sense of the political power that each group, individually, might wield. Nonetheless, in this interpretation of Sweeney there is likewise a sense of what had hitherto been seen as minority cultures challenging social and political orthodoxy.

Meanwhile, in 2016's Booker Prize winning novel, *The Sellout*, Paul Beatty satirizes black intellectuals who, on one hand, rewrite literary classics to make them 'politically respectful', but, on the other, are guilty of the same kinds of cultural appropriation they rail against.[60] A cameo role by one Jon McJones underlines the hypocrisy. A 'black conservative who'd recently added the "Mc" to his slave name', McJones reads from a memoir entitled *Mick, Please: The Black Irish Journey from Ghetto to Gaelic*, managing to cram references to 'The Emerald Isle', 'hurling' and 'shillelaghs' into a single paragraph.[61] In its context, and despite its sensitive subject matter, the episode is raucous and absurdist, but it does, once again, underline an affinity (assumed or actual) between African American and Irish American experience.

These further meetings of black and Irish experience create a notably wider canvas than the one suggested by the particular nexus of Kennedy

---

58   Delmore Schwartz, *Delmore Schwartz Papers, Yale Collection of American Literature, Beinecke Rare Book and Manuscript Library*, Box 6, Folder 359.
59   Rachel Blau du Plessis, *Genders, Races and Religious Cultures in Modern American Poetry, 1908–1934* (Cambridge: Cambridge University Press, 2001), 153.
60   Paul Beatty, *The Sellout* (New York: Farrar, Straus and Giroux, 2015), 96.
61   Ibid. 215.

and King in Lowell's sonnet. And yet, they all underline – whether they do so competitively, shudderingly, sardonically, or (as King did and Kennedy came to) enthusiastically – an overtly hybrid or shared idea of identity and culture. The scope of Lowell's ambition in *History* invites us to broaden the canvas with every contemporary or historical reference, every half-heard allusion; and so it is perhaps characteristic of Lowell's conflation of cultures and heritages as well as of historical periods that a further, more intimate, voice – one which may, at first, seem unrelated to the other threads discussed in this essay – should make itself heard in his Kennedy elegy: that of Thomas Hardy, or rather, of the 'woman much missed' of Hardy's poem, 'The Voice'. Lowell's persona, in his workroom, 'in its list-lessness / of Vacancy' recalls Hardy's speaker, who seems to hear his former beloved calling to him but then doubts himself:

> Or is it only the breeze, in its listlessness
> Travelling across the wet mead to me here,
> You being ever dissolved to wan wistlessness,
> Heard no more again, far or near?[62]

Substituting an internal rhyme, 'loneliness', for Hardy's more whimsical end-rhyme, 'wistlessness', Lowell softens the allusion without silencing it. Other airs of 'The Voice' also infiltrate 'For Robert Kennedy 1925–68'. Lowell's 'thin smoke thread of vital / air' (*CP*, 571), for example, seems to catch Hardy's 'air-blue gown', his 'breeze', and his 'Wind oozing thin through the thorn from norward'.[63] There is a metrical nod too: the line 'air. But what will anyone teach you now?' tries to break into a Hardy-like anapaestic meter, only to be forestalled by the trochaic 'Doom was woven' at the start of the next line. Most starkly, Kennedy, like the woman of 'The Voice', is much missed: 'I miss / you, you out of Plutarch'.[64] Lowell was a poet who was attentive to voice, and to the qualities of particular voices,

---

62 Lowell, *Collected Poems*, 571; Thomas Hardy, 'The Voice' in *The Oxford Book of English Verse*, ed. Christopher Ricks (Oxford: Oxford University Press), 498.
63 Lowell, *Collected Poems*, 571; Hardy, 498.
64 Lowell, Collected Poems, 571.

throughout his career. Take, for example, his description of Elizabeth Hardwick's in 'Man and Wife':

> the shrill verve
> of your invective scorched the traditional South …
> …your old-fashioned tirade –
> loving, rapid, merciless –
> breaks like the Atlantic Ocean on my head[65]

It is clear, in his elegies to Kennedy, that Lowell had his friend's actual voice in mind: a voice that was 'somewhat woodenly, hoarsely dry',[66] whether wisecracking at a party or calling for an end to violence: 'Surely we can begin to work a little harder to bind up the wounds among us and to become in our hearts brothers and countrymen once again.'[67] Through recordings, and in Lowell's elegies, Kennedy's voice *can* still be heard, far and near, calling for brotherhood, calling for an extension of the 'great clan'.

---

65   Ibid. 189
66   Ibid. 571.
67   Kennedy, 'Mindless Menace of Violence', 9.35–9.50 minutes.

ADAM BEARDSWORTH

From Terrible Beauty to Stale and Small: W.B. Yeats's Influence on Robert Lowell's Political Poetry

In a 1961 letter Elizabeth Bishop, concerned for her close-friend Robert Lowell's well-being following his latest hospitalization for manic behaviour, expressed her hope 'that things are going well, and that your life is matching the splendor and success of your work. Surely we don't have to choose between them quite as narrowly as Yeats says.'[1] Bishop is referring to William Butler Yeats's poem 'The Choice', wherein he asserts that 'The intellect of man is forced to choose / Perfection of the life, or of the work'.[2] Lowell's mental illness, and the havoc it wreaked on his personal relationships, meant leading a perfect private life was never an option. However, as his profile both as a poet and a public figure grew in the 1960s, he began to feel the pressure of living up to the moral authority prescribed by both his work and image. While poems such as such as 'Fall 1961', 'Inauguration Day: January 1953', and 'Waking Early Sunday Morning' showcased Lowell's ability to evince the impact of political and ideological decisions on the private American subject, they also invited suspicion and contempt from those who privileged discourses of unbridled American patriotism. Public statements, such as his 1965 rejection of President Johnson's invitation to the White House Festival of Arts, which voiced in prose form his disdain for what he saw as an increasingly callous disregard for the prospect of 'nuclear ruin' in

1   Thomas Travisano, *Midcentury Quartet* (Charlottesville: University Press of Virginia, 1999), 363.
2   William Butler Yeats, *Yeats's Poetry, Prose, and Drama*, ed. James Pethica (New York: W.W. Norton, 2000), 107.

US foreign policy,[3] further exposed the poet to scrutiny from both the public and the state. Lowell's desire to live up to his words found him measuring the personal toll of writing and speaking from a position of political morality in an anxious Cold War era.

The pressure Lowell experienced as a public poet resembled that experienced by Yeats, suggesting that both writers understood 'the choice' proposed by Yeats's poem. Although Yeats is not typically considered one of Lowell's primary influences, traces of his style and vision can be seen in several of Lowell's works, particularly in early poems such as 'The Quaker Graveyard in Nantucket' and 'To Peter Taylor on the Feast of the Epiphany'. These early poems share Yeats's cyclical vision of history, one where birth and death, renewal and apocalypse, are two ends of the same gyre. However, as Lowell's early poems gave way to the confessional voice of *Life Studies* and after, his Yeatsian vision was replaced by a more purgatorial conceptualization of the subject's place in history. Writing from within a Cold War context that emphasized surveillance, consensus, and conformity as virtues of public life, Lowell's poetry shifted from an investment in the politics of fear to an analysis of how fear was used biopolitically to manage affect in the postwar US. As his work takes its inward turn, Lowell becomes less concerned with the eschatology of historical violence than with the systemic violence that administers and manufactures daily life. For Lowell, then, the choice proposed by Yeats is ultimately a fantasy built into postwar neoliberalism: the terrible beauty of his era lies in the fact that there is no choice; rather, fear of an apocalyptic history is both cultivated and implemented to manage the uncertainty of the present.

While Lowell took seriously the Modernist poets whose careers overlapped with his, Yeats does not appear to be amongst those he most admired. Yeats is only mentioned once in Ian Hamilton's biography of Lowell, and references to him in Lowell's letters suggest more of an academic than devotional interest in the great Irish poet. For Lowell, his more immediate American masters offered greater appeal. He maintained correspondence with William Carlos Williams, visited Pound in St Elizabeth's on more than

---

3 Robert Lowell, *Collected Prose*, ed. Robert Giroux (New York: Farrar, Strauss, Giroux, 1987), 370–374.

one occasion, and fashioned his early verse in the style of Fugitive poets such as Allen Tate, John Crowe Ransom, and Robert Penn Warren. While Lowell's friend John Berryman played the role of acolyte to W.B. Yeats by seeking him out in late 1930s London, Lowell played a similar role with Allen Tate, even going so far as pitching a tent on Tate's Tennessee lawn for three hot months in 1937 in order to be close to his mentor. As Hamilton claims, 'Tate and Ransom, in Lowell's mind, connected America with the exhilaratingly convinced narrowness of European modernism. Ransom had studied at Cambridge, was admired by T.S. Eliot. Tate had served his time in Greenwich Village in the mid-twenties, and then in Paris and London from 1928 to 1930'.[4] While this American connection to a cosmopolitan modernist tradition was appealing to Lowell, the rigid formalism of the Fugitives, driven by the New Critical principles that writers such as Ransom, Warren, and Tate helped formulate, offered Lowell a template for constructing his own lyrically and symbolically dense early verse. In his reminiscence of the 1937 visit to the Tennessee, Lowell recalls how Tate's sharp intellect taught him to appreciate the connection between tradition, history, and modernist literature (or to what Eliot elsewhere referred to as history and the link between history and the individual talent):

> All the English classics, and some of the Greeks and Latins, were at Tate's elbow. He maneuvered through them, coolly blasting, rehabilitating, now and then reciting key lines in an austere, vibrant voice. Turning to the moderns, he slaughtered whole Chicago droves of slipshod Untermeyer anthology experimentalists. He felt that all the culture and tradition of the East, the South, and Europe stood behind Eliot, Emily Dickinson, Yeats, and Rimbaud. I found myself despising the rootless appetites of middle-class meliorism.[5]

While Yeats may not have been the poet who influenced him most, Lowell took seriously Tate's belief that Yeats was a poet whose work could help him transcend the 'rootless appetites of middle-class meliorism' he had come to despise during his formative years as a poet in the late 1930s.

Philip Coleman has argued that the influence of Yeats on Berryman exists not just in the latter's adaptation of Yeatsian formal elements, but in

---

4   Ian Hamilton, *Robert Lowell: A Biography* (New York: Random House, 1982), 45.
5   Robert Lowell, *The Collected Prose* (New York: Farrar, Strauss, Giroux. 1987), 59.

his 'rejection of mainstream American authority', which 'may be traced back to his highly self-conscious turn towards Yeats at the start of his career'.[6] Although Lowell's poetry does not, as Berryman's does, bear signs of the influence of Yeats's style, it does share a similar desire to critique American politics and culture. Indeed, just as the young Berryman was attracted in part to Yeats's aristocratic concerns about the anti-intellectual culture of the Irish middle-class, the young Lowell was attracted by the stately, Southern agrarian air of Tate and Ransom. This attraction led Lowell to enrol as a student at Kenyon College in Ohio, where Ransom had recently moved following a break with Vanderbilt University. While at Kenyon, where he briefly shared an apartment with Randall Jarrell on the second-floor of Ransom's home, Lowell began perfecting the tense, New Criticism-inflected poetic style that marks his early volumes *Lord Weary's Castle*, *Land of Unlikeness*, and *The Mills of the Kavanaghs*, and that would eventually announce his presence as a powerful new American poetic voice.

While the style of Lowell's early poems owes much to the New Critical idiom he learned from Tate, Ransom, Warren, and others, its violent, often harsh symbolism breaks from the more restrained aestheticism of the fugitives. Looking back on his apprenticeship with Tate, Lowell implies that he was ultimately unconvinced by Tate's view of the poem as pure artifice, divorced from public concerns, recalling Tate's belief

> that a good poem had nothing to do with exalted feelings or being moved by the spirit. It was simply a piece of craftsmanship, an intelligible or *cognitive* object. As examples of cognitive objects, Tate brought forward [his gardener] Mr. Norman, the hand-printed edition of *The Mediterranean*, and finally a tar-black cabinet with huge earlobe-like handles. It was his own workmanship. I had supposed that crafts were repeatable skills and belonged to the pedestrian boredom of manual-training classes. However, something warped, fissured, strained, and terrific about this cabinet suggested that it would be Tate's last.[7]

In this tongue-in-cheek account, written twenty-two years after Lowell's stay on Tate's lawn, he humorously rejects Tate's vision of poetry as pure

---

6   Philip Coleman, 'The Politics of Praise: John Berryman's Engagement with W.B. Yeats', *Etudes Irlandaises* 28.2 (2003): 12.
7   Lowell, *Collected Prose*, 59.

craftsmanship, suggesting that Tate's own 'warped, fissured, strained, and terrific' cabinet was not merely a 'cognitive object'. Rather it produced, at least for Lowell at the time, the kind of 'exalted feelings' that Tate argued should be removed from the poem.

It is arguably the combination of New Critical craftsmanship and his own uniquely 'warped, fissured, strained, and terrific' style that distinguished Lowell's early poems. While the presence of his Fugitive masters is visible in his form, the thematic concerns with an increasingly violent, even apocalyptic, historical trajectory appear to owe something to Yeats. Henry Hart figures this division between Lowell's New Critical sensibilities and his Yeatsian themes as proof of his repressed desire to express the sublime. According to Hart,

> Lowell was certainly wary of the sublime at the end of his career because he had come to associate it with his manic delusions of power, but he was wary of it at the beginning of his career as well. Just as Yeats wavered painfully when he contemplated the martyrs of the Easter Rebellion, unsure whether to praise them as heroes or mock them as fools, Lowell agonized over those who sacrificed themselves at the altar of sublimity. For Lowell, as for Yeats, the sublime was a 'terrible beauty', a femme fatale that entranced, bewildered, blinded, and killed. It drove Ahab to death, Lucifer to hell, and Lowell to the madhouse.[8]

The 'terrible beauty' Hart refers to is that described by Yeats in 'Easter 1916', his visceral and conflicted response to the Irish Rebellion that saw Republican nationalists seize key sites in Dublin in a siege that lasted for six days. Following their eventual surrender to British forces, fifteen of the uprising's leaders were executed by British forces. In the poem, Yeats elegizes several of those who were executed while still expressing uncertainty about the violent nature of the uprising, asserting that 'Too long a sacrifice / Can make a stone of the heart', while wondering 'if excess of love / Bewildered them till they died.'[9] Regardless of the motives or rationale behind the uprising, Yeats recognizes that in its wake Ireland has been 'Transformed utterly: / A terrible beauty is born.'[10] The oxymoronic

---

8   Henry Hart, *Robert Lowell and the Sublime* (Syracuse, NY: Syracuse University Press, 1995), 55.
9   Yeats, *Yeats's Poetry, Drama, and Prose*, 74.
10 Ibid.

statement 'terrible beauty' indicates Yeats's conflicted position: he is at once drawn to the possibility of dramatic change offered by violence, and afraid of its potential ramifications.

In early poems such as 'The Quaker Graveyard in Nantucket', Lowell also expresses a conflicted desire for dramatic and violent rupture. Like Yeats's 'Easter 1916', Lowell's poem is also ostensibly an elegy – in his case for a cousin lost during a naval exercise. However, in Lowell's poem the personal elegy is quickly conflated with concerns about the fate of the human in the face of unruly forces. Lowell brings what he sees as the opposing forces of human dominion and nature into conflict as the sailors prepare the drowned victim's body for burial at sea:

> We weight the body, close
> Its eyes and heave it seaward whence it came,
> Where the heel-headed dogfish barks its nose
> On Ahab's void and forehead; and the name
> Is blocked in yellow chalk.
> Sailors, who pitch this portent at the sea
> Where dreadnaughts shall confess
> Its hell-bent deity,
> When you are powerless
> To sand-bag this Atlantic bulwark, faced
> By the earth-shaker, green, unwearied, chaste
> In his steel scales: ask for no Orphean lute
> To pluck life back.[11]

Acting as a reminder that the forces of nature, the powerful 'Atlantic bulwark', cannot be sand-bagged no matter how strong the human desire, the poem evokes Melville's Captain Ahab as a reminder of the consequences of rapacious greed, self-interest, and destruction. For Lowell, Ahab symbolizes fundamentally contradictory elements of United States ideology. His rugged self-reliance, insatiable pursuit of capitalist goals, and desire to exercise dominion over nature all typify individualist elements of the American creed. However, each of these elements is simultaneously a source of violence – against nature, against faith and tradition, and

---

11   Lowell, *Collected Poems*, 14.

against social and individual well-being. These contradictions leave the bones in the Quaker graveyard crying 'out in the long night for the hurt beast / Bobbing by Ahab's whaleboats in the East',[12] a line that echoes Yeats's 'The Second Coming', where the poet wonders in the final apocalyptic lines 'What rough beast, its hour come round at last, / Slouches towards Bethlehem to be born.'[13] Like Yeats, Lowell's poem fears that salvation from a modern world of war – both between nations and against nature – will require a powerful, apocalyptic intervention. When the failures of Ahab continue to be repeated, we have reached, for Lowell, 'the end of the whaleroad and the whale / Who spewed Nantucket bones on the thrashed swell / And stirred the troubled waters to whirlpools / To send the Pequod packing off to hell.'[14] Redemption in the poem comes, as with Yeats, in the form of a second-coming enacted by an unforgiving god:

> Unmarried and corroding, spare of flesh
> Mart once of supercilious, wing'd clippers,
> Atlantic, where your bell-trap guts its spoil
> You could cut the brackish winds with a knife
> Here in Nantucket, and cast up the time
> When the Lord God formed man from the sea's slime
> And breathed into his face the breath of life,
> And blue-lung'd combers lumbered to the kill.
> The lord survives the rainbow of His will.[15]

Lowell's 'The Quaker Graveyard in Nantucket', it would seem, shares much in common with poems such as Yeats's 'Easter 1916' and 'The Second Coming'. Just as Yeats memorializes the dead of the Easter Uprising while simultaneously worrying about the consequences of their actions for Ireland at large, Lowell elegiacally laments the death of his navy officer cousin while using him as a stand-in for the violence enacted upon individuals in an America burdened by both war and the greed of capitalism. Like Yeats, Lowell looks to the 'terrible beauty' of a hostile

12   Ibid.
13   Yeats, *Yeats's Poetry, Drama, and Prose*, 76.
14   Lowell, *Collected Poems*, 16.
15   Ibid. 18.

Lord who 'survives the rainbow of his will' as He invites the destruction of the wicked. As with Yeats, Lowell's speaker in 'The Quaker Graveyard in Nantucket' appears torn between his attachment to the industry, history, and tradition evoked by the poem's titular graveyard, as well as its images of naval industry, and the imperious ends to which that industry is being used in his contemporary America.

While the formal rigour of his New Critical antecedents is on display in poems such as 'The Quaker Graveyard in Nantucket', it also seems that Lowell inherited from Yeats a poetics of fear. This poetics transcends the cloistered craftsmanship preached by Tate and others and engages with concerns about a world that Lowell, like Yeats before him, saw as moving inevitably towards an apocalyptic crisis. The young Lowell's uncertainty about how to respond to this inexorable historical movement shares Yeats's tendency towards vacillation in the face of crisis. As James Pethica notes, in Yeats's poems of the 1920s, 'vacillation becomes a dominant mode, with neither the choice of withdrawal from the world in favor of spiritual discipline, nor the choice of engagement with the realm of the physical, providing satisfaction for long.'[16] Yeats lays these choices bare in poems such as 'Vacillation', where he contemplates the implicit frustration of being caught between responsibility to the spiritual self and responsibility to the greater good:

> Between extremities
> Man runs his course;
> A brand, or flaming breath,
> Comes to destroy
> All those antinomies
> Of day and night;
> The body calls it death,
> The heart remorse.
> But if these be right
> What is joy?[17]

---

16 Yeats, *Yeats's Poetry, Drama, and Prose*, xviii.
17 Ibid. 109.

Here Yeats finds himself yearning for the implicit 'joy' of transcending the 'extremities' between which '[m]an runs his course', a goal that the poem suggests he is ultimately unable to achieve. Other poems point to a similar desire to vanquish the hesitation and doubt that plagues his social position, as in 'Sailing to Byzantium', where Yeats asks that the 'sages standing in God's holy fire … Consume my heart away; sick with desire / And fastened to a dying animal / It knows not what it is'.[18] In this poem, Yeats's frustration with the 'dying animal' represents what he sees as an increasingly violent and materialist cultural and political context. While he idealizes art as that which can transport him from a country where, '[c]aught in that sensual music all neglect / [m]onuments of unaging intellect',[19] he recognizes that such a longing ultimate remains reverie at least for his material self, if not necessarily for his art.

Lowell, equally frustrated with war, violence, and a society that has turned its back on matters or art and spirituality, picks up on Yeats's sense of vacillation in poems such as 'To Peter Taylor on the Feast of the Epiphany,' where he claims

> Peter, the war has taught me to revere
> The rulers of this darkness, for I fear
> That only Armageddon will suffice
> To turn the hero skating on thin ice
> When Whore and Beast and Dragon rise for air
> From allegoric waters.[20]

Here, like Yeats before him, Lowell feels caught between the 'rulers of this darkness' who compel war and violence, and the 'hero skating on thin ice' whose disappearance is always threatened. As in Yeats's 'The Second Coming', Lowell believes that 'only Armageddon will suffice' to awaken the doomed hero, and to begin a process of cultural purification, a line that suggests that, on some level, he welcomes the cataclysmic war compelled by leaders such as Hitler, Mussolini, Hirohito, and Lowell's own domestic nemesis, Roosevelt. For Lowell, this position of vacillation is

18 Ibid. 80.
19 Ibid. 80.
20 Lowell, *Collected Poems*, 80.

one that is held in check by fear. As he writes, 'Fear is where / We hunger'.[21] This apparently contradictory statement suggests that vacillation is more than an experience of personal uncertainty; rather, fear is a politically motivated factor that holds individuals in a position of stasis. This stasis, for Lowell, will persist until, in his military metaphor, the biplanes 'snare / Fear with its fingered stop-watch in mid-air'.[22] As Henry Hart observes, '[t]he fundamental theme of the poem … is fear (a word that appears at the beginning, middle, and end) … His point is that the fear of war is also, paradoxically, its attraction. Although he mocks all daredevils who lust for fear, he confesses that he also reveres what should be feared.'[23] This apparent reverence for the evils of war align Lowell, metaphorically at least, with Yeats insofar as both writers appear to believe that things must get worse before they get better; that profound cultural change cannot take place without apocalyptic rupture.

In these poems of vacillation Lowell inherits Yeats's own unclear political position. Just as Yeats appears to at once condemn the violence of Irish nationalism and praise the 'terrible beauty' that the uprising has created, or as he longs for the 'rough beast' to usher in the beginning of a new historical era, Lowell appears to at once praise and condemn the 'self-destructive will to pursue political ideals that are virtuous as well as vicious'[24] in poems such as 'The Quaker Graveyard in Nantucket' and 'To Peter Taylor on the Feast of the Epiphany'. The spirit of vacillation suggests that Lowell took seriously Yeats's famous claim that 'we make out of the quarrel with others, rhetoric, but of the quarrel with ourselves, poetry.'[25] However, it also seems that this quarrel with the self ultimately provided a means for Lowell to overcome the impasse created by a poetics of vacillation, and to forge a new poetics indebted to understanding the relationship between fear, the self, and the state. While Yeats, in poems such as 'Sailing to Byzantium', exalted the aesthetic realm as a potential means of balancing the forces of the real world and his ideal visions, Lowell instead turned to the self as a

21 Ibid.
22 Ibid.
23 Hart, *Robert Lowell and the Sublime*, 80.
24 Ibid. 83.
25 Yeats, *Yeats's Poetry, Drama, and Prose*, 285.

means of intimately exploring the impact of fear, anxiety, cruelty, and other dark emotions symbolized in earlier poems by figures such as 'the rulers of darkness' and 'Ahab', in order to understand how such political and social realities affected subjectivity. Put more simply, the point at which Lowell's poetry diverges from its indebtedness to Yeats's apocalyptic vision comes with Lowell's reimagining of fear as a determining factor in the experience of everyday life, not merely as a symbol of a larger historical trajectory.

This shift in Lowell's attitude towards fear is linked to the emergence of Cold War culture in the United States. As he writes in a manuscript entitled 'Art and Evil', the years between 1936 and 1956 felt as though 'the earth's surface … sagged and cracked. These have been the years of Hitler, Stalin's purges, Buchenwald, the atomic bomb, the threat of nuclear war. During this period our graver and more high-powered critics have had to attempt a massive reappraisal; they have pretty well agreed that writers can be too healthy for their own good. Today we are all looking for darkness visible.'[26] However, as Lowell concedes, in the early Cold War era that search for darkness was complicated by the fact that the United States suddenly found itself in a period of prosperity and renewal:

> Then a funny thing happened: just as we had labeled our times the Age of Anxiety, and had managed to point out an ample and redeeming shadow of darkness in just about every writer who had ever lived – just at this point we suddenly found we were midway in a second solid, sensible, wealthy, optimistic, child-bearing era, one not unlike the times of Queen Victoria and Prince Albert. Out of the black earth of our evil authors and visions, we have somehow rebuilt our own booming 1870s, '80s, and '90s, complete with their dynasties of Republican Presidents.[27]

In this quote Lowell recognizes a dramatic shift – from the age of anxiety coined by Auden – to an age of excess, one where the fears of the past, and the powerful desire for renewal expressed both by Lowell and Yeats, no longer seemed as relevant. However, the sudden onset of this new, relatively calmer and more prosperous time appears to have compelled, rather than deterred, Lowell to explore in new and vigorous ways the relationship between the fear generated by political interests, and the individual.

---

26 Lowell, *Collected Prose*, 129.
27 Ibid. 130.

Poetry in this new age, as Lowell declaimed in his acceptance speech for the 1960 National Book Award, which he won for *Life Studies*, needs to find more essential ways of responding to its cultural situation:

> Our modern American poetry has a snarl on its hands. Something earth-shaking was started about fifty years ago by the generation of Eliot, Frost and William Carlos Williams. We have had a run of poetry as inspired, and perhaps as important, and sadly brief as that of Baudelaire and his successors, or that of the dying Roman Republic and early Empire. Two poetries are now competing, a cooked and a raw. The cooked, marvelously expert, often seems laboriously concocted to be tasted and digested by a graduate seminar. The raw, huge blood-dripping gobbets of unseasoned experience are dished up for midnight listeners. There is a poetry that can only be studied, and a poetry that can only be declaimed, a poetry of pedantry, and a poetry of scandal.

For the Yeats of the 1920s, the inward turn away from the direct political engagement of poems such as 'September 1913' and 'Easter 1916', was a turn towards the intellectual realm and aesthetic ideals, away from the rawness of ordinary life. Lowell, on the other hand, turned away from the 'cooked' poetry of his New Critical predecessors, and towards a poetry of 'unseasoned experience'. Steven Gould Axelrod has argued that this inward turn owes a debt to Yeats's assertion that poetry is the result of a quarrel with oneself:

> Lowell's method as a poet of social and historical awareness probably owes most to Yeats ... Lowell intentionally turned his social-historical poems of the 1950s, 1960s, and 1970s into quarrels with himself, often by identifying himself with his subject. His adherence to the Yeatsian formula is clear in his remark about including personal elements in 'For the Union Dead' to avoid a 'brazen' tone. The poems may lose prophetic power ... but they gain authenticity. Through turning on themselves, they avoid the dangers of bombast or oversimplification. And whatever their limits, they have found a language that makes a political poetry possible in our time.[28]

While Lowell may have had Yeats in mind when he shifted away from the 'bombast' of his earlier poems, his more 'raw', confessional poetry also breaks from Yeats – most obviously in tone and content, but also in its

---

28   Steven Gould Axelrod, 'Lowell's Living Name: An Introduction', *Robert Lowell: Essays on the Poetry*, eds Steven Gould Axelrod and Helen Deese (Cambridge: Cambridge University Press, 1986), 120.

political response. Lowell built on Yeats's conviction by making his own confessional verse an argument not only with the self, but with the self in the context of the placed upon it by a repressive sociopolitical era.

By the publication of *Life Studies* in 1959, Lowell's political poetry had therefore shifted from a Yeatsian model based on fear, violence, and the desire for renewal, to one based on anxiety, paralysis, and the uncertain status of the subject in an era conflicted by Cold War surveillance and neoliberal affluence. In the United States of the early Cold War era, anxiety was a powerful and pervasive ideological tool. The possibility of nuclear war combined with the aggressive surveillance tactics deployed to root out the communist menace, as exemplified by the McCarthyist witch hunts and House UnAmerican Activities Committee hearings, affected the daily lives of US citizens. In many cases, maintaining a sense of anxiety was a political means of managing affect. The naturalizing campaigns of state agencies such as the Atomic Energy Commission and Civil Defense, for instance, were deployed to help both contain and control the profound epistemological uncertainty born in tandem with the United States' development of atomic – and later hydrogen – bombs. Like the radioactive fallout that posed a physical threat to those living in the shadow of nuclear drift, the anxiety produced by the possibility of a future nuclear disaster hung like a dark, if imperceptible, cloud over the Cold War era (and indeed continues to linger in the present). The Trinity test at Alamogordo in August 1945 therefore seems to have left a wound in the cultural and political psyche of the United States. As Robert J. Lifton and Gregory Mitchell assert, that wound remains a 'raw nerve'[29] that has ached in the American psyche, leading to 'profound conflict and uneasiness, causing us to embrace the weapons that terrify us'.[30]

By exploiting, rather than healing, this profound wound, the Cold War US built a politics predicated upon the uncertainty of future disaster. Such an ideological use of anxiety constitutes what Brian Massumi has labelled the political ontology of threat. According to Massumi, the threat

---

29   Robert Jay Lifton and Gregory Mitchell, *Hiroshima in America: Fifty Years of Denial* (New York: Putnam, 1995), xi.
30   Ibid. xii.

of potential disaster has an enduring impact on affective realities: 'Fear is the anticipatory reality in the present of a threatening future. It is the felt reality of the nonexistent, loomingly present as the *affective fact* of the matter'.[31] In other words, for individuals living in an era where fear manifests itself as a political ontology, threat is not just media hysteria, it is a *'felt quality*, independent of any particular instance of itself, in much the same way the color red is a quality independent of any particular tint of red ... Threat is ultimately *ambient*. Its logic is purely *qualitative*'.[32] When fear becomes an affective reality, ever-present and independent of specific moments of catastrophe, it fractures social solidarity and encourages individuals to guard themselves, their families, and their property against lurking, and often invisible, dangers.

In Lowell's Cold War US, the strategic use of fear as a form of repressive, if invisible, politics was therefore not merely a response to rising geopolitical tensions; it was a carefully calculated ideological manoeuver. Lowell responds to this ideological management of affect by using himself as a model for the conflicted Cold War subject. His poem 'Fall 1961', for instance, describes the sense of estrangement and paralysis he feels as a subject during a time of nuclear anxiety: 'All autumn, the chafe and jar / of nuclear war; / we have talked our extinction to death. / I swim like a minnow / behind my studio window'.[33] Too powerless to shatter the glass that contains him, Lowell's minnow swims aimlessly as it waits to be preyed upon. The image of the minnow, a nervous baitfish separated from its school, implies that Lowell is not alone in his anxiety. Indeed, if 'The state', as Lowell says, 'is a diver under a glass bell,' then the minnows are the powerless subjects contained within its perimeter. This feeling of helplessness registers as a complaint against the state's desire to contain, and render docile, public dissent. It suggests Lowell's understanding that fear of impending catastrophe both conditions an atmosphere of docility and licenses preemptive political action, leaving Lowell feeling helpless

---

31   Brian Massumi, 'The Future Birth of the Affective Fact', *The Affect Theory Reader*, eds Melissa Gregg and Gregory J. Seigworth (Durham, NC: Duke University Press, 2010), 54.
32   Ibid. 62.
33   Lowell, *Collected Poems*, 329.

and anxious, which he makes clear in the poem's assertion that 'A father's no shield / for his child.'[34]

In poems such as 'Fall 1961', Lowell identifies the presence of an American '"affective politics," which preserves only through announcing a threat to life itself'.[35] The conflicting impulse between preservation and threat, between fear and containment, makes locating the ideological impetus behind the threat difficult. Thus in the poem Lowell feels estranged, paralysed, and uncertain rather than, as in his early Yeatsian poems, yearning for profound, even apocalyptic change. Indeed, it is this struggle between the desire to act and the uncertainty of how to do so that marks many of Lowell's political poems in the 1950s and 1960s. In these poems, Lowell seems unclear whether or not this sense of paralysis is the result of state intervention or a personal shortcoming, an inability to live up to the expectations of postwar American exceptionalism. Consider, for instance, 'Inauguration Day: January 1953', where Lowell juxtaposes Eisenhower's inauguration with images of a cold, snowy, and frozen America:

> Ice, ice. Our wheels no longer move.
> Look, the fixed stars, all just alike
> as lack-land atoms, split apart,
> and the Republic summons Ike,
> the mausoleum in her heart.[36]

Unlike earlier poems such as 'The Quaker Graveyard in Nantucket', Lowell does not express a vision of an America driven to the brink of violent collapse by war, greed, and capitalist corruption. Rather he sees the US, in its inauguration of Eisenhower, as a state whose vision and morals have been frozen. The violence of this political congelation, which may for Lowell be a veiled reference to the 'Cold' War, does not take place on the grand, apocalyptic scale of violence that Lowell's early poems inherited from Yeats. Rather, it is a slow and systemic violence, one perpetrated against the individual psyche rather than against society at large.

---

34 Ibid.
35 Sara Ahmed, *The Cultural Politics of Emotion* (Edinburgh: Edinburgh University Press, 2014), 73.
36 Lowell, *Collected Poems*, 117.

Lowell links this subjective violence to nuclear anxiety by suggesting that with the splitting of the atom came a concurrent fragmentation of the individual US citizen, making them 'all just alike / as lack-land atoms, split apart'.[37] This fragmentation occurs for Lowell not within a prosperous and fortunate US, but within a 'lack-land', suggesting that the moral and spiritual hypocentre of his otherwise affluent nation has been displaced in an era of nuclear brinksmanship. It is not, however, the terror of a nuclear holocaust that appears to be Lowell's primary concern in this poem. Rather, it is the impact of the anxiety caused by a Cold War political situation predicated upon an ontology of threat that has, in Lowell's words, put the 'mausoleum' into the heart of the Republic. The image of the mausoleum suggests not only the death of the nation's moral 'heart', it also evokes a cold and lonely space of loss, one signifying a spiritual death that haunts the postwar subject. Thus for Lowell, the spiritual fragmentation of the Eisenhower era, along with anxiety and loneliness that are its consequences, are contained within the 'mausoleum' of the heart, making them difficult to connect to larger political or ideological concerns.

The sense of being both frozen and 'split-apart' during the early Cold War speaks not to a desire for the violent resolution of an avaricious political climate; rather, it suggests a frustration with the management of affect during the Cold War climate. As in 'Fall 1961', Lowell's speaker in 'Inauguration Day: January 1953' feels contained, estranged, and fragmented, but also uncertain about how to overcome those feelings in a climate pitted between Cold War anxiety and the optimism and relative affluence of America's rapidly developing neoliberal economy. Focusing on the impact of this conflicted condition is the true political strength of Lowell's poetry of the 1950s and 1960s. While modelling Yeats may have helped Lowell define his political voice in the 1940s, making his poetry a quarrel with both himself and the ideological conditions that contain that self during the early Cold War period is his own unique contribution to political poetry. By emphasizing the way in which affect is used an ideological instrument aimed at instilling a sense of confusion, anxiety, and even docility within the fragmented postwar subject, Lowell's 'confessional'

---

37 Ibid.

turn identifies the fraught condition of the Cold War American subject. The 'frozen' and paralysed status of this subject, no longer desiring a drastic social renewal, suggests for Lowell the true political danger of Cold War America. As subjects are divided, lonely, and anxious, their political solidarity in the face of true threats is compromised and ineffectual.

The management of affect and its containment of dissent identified by Lowell anticipates what Lauren Berlant has identified as a condition of cruel optimism. As Berlant explains, a relationship of cruel optimism emerges when an individual's attachment to an object or scene of desire directly impacts that individual's ability to thrive:

> where cruel optimism operates, the very vitalizing or animating potency of an object or scene of desire contributes to the attrition of the very thriving thing that is supposed to be made possible in the work of attachment in the first place. This might point to something as banal as scouring love, but it also opens out to obsessive appetites, working for a living, patriotism, all kinds of things, one makes affective bargains about the costliness of one's attachments, usually unconscious ones, most of which keep one in proximity to the scene of desire or attrition.[38]

In Lowell's early Cold War, where containment politics sought to naturalize geopolitical threats and to satiate anxiety by encouraging individuals to literally buy into the neoliberal economy, the situation of cruel optimism is predicated upon the belief that the conventional American values of self-reliance, individualism, freedom, and autonomy will lead to happiness and prosperity. The 'affective bargains' individuals make in this scenario demand, in part, a wilful ignorance of both the nuclear shadow and the repressive surveillance tactics of the Cold War state. They demand, in other words, a stasis or paralysis in the face of political unrest. The cruel part of this affective bargain, as Lowell identifies, is that it leads to a sense of loneliness and fragmentation for the individual subject who waits to be rewarded for believing in the future prosperity of the US and its attendant promises of individual sovereignty and happiness. In other words, buying into the American Dream in the Cold War US is, in its essence, a cruelly optimistic proposition.

---

38 Lauren Berlant, 'Cruel Optimism' in *The Affect Theory Reader*, eds Melissa Gregg and Gregory J. Seigworth (Durham, NC: Duke University Press, 2010), 94.

In some of Lowell's most inward-looking poems, he channels an unnamed anxiety that exacerbates the fraught psychological state caused by this paradoxical relationship between cruelty and optimism. In 'Skunk Hour', for instance, we are told that 'The season's ill' and that the speaker's 'mind's not right'.[39] In 'Eye and Tooth', he uses an aquarium metaphor that recalls the containment metaphors of 'Fall 1961' when he writes '[m]y whole eye was sunset red, / the old cut cornea throbbed, / I saw things darkly, / as through an unwashed goldfish globe.'[40] In 'Night Sweat' this anxiety appears Yeatsian in its apocalyptic fervour as its pervasiveness threatens to overcome the speaker: 'Behind me! You! Again I feel the light / lighten my leaded eyelids, while the gray / skulled horses whinny for the soot of night'.[41] The dark visions and omens that contribute to the speaker's anxieties indicate that he recognizes an illness either within himself or his culture; however, he remains frozen, incapable of acting upon it. His feelings of illness and otherness in these poems is predicated upon the inability to conform to the sociopolitical expectations of Cold War America. At the same time, the fact that he does not see himself in the conformist practices and institutions that dominate his culture is a cause of anxiety, one that suggests the flaw is a personal, rather than a political one. From the perspective of cruel optimism, this helps encourage conformity to Cold War political interests; the problem is not, for Lowell's speaker, the political world around him, it is his illness, a personal failure that generates longing for wellness and stability. Lowell's poems therefore demonstrate how, by changing the focus to problems with the self rather than problems with the political sphere, the Cold War ideological apparatus generated longing for a stable (if fictional) private realm while simultaneously containing dissent for destructive public initiatives. Thus the cruel optimism for Lowell's speaker is generated by his optimism that the 'ill' self may someday be recovered, even when the ideological apparatus that sustains that self is, paradoxically, invested in maintaining its instability. Indeed, as Lowell's poems implicitly recognize, cultivating the tension between fear

---

39 Lowell, *Collected Poems*, 191–192.
40 Ibid. 334.
41 Ibid. 375.

and conformity is Cold War America's most effective means of encouraging docility amongst the population.

In more overtly political poems such as 'Waking Early Sunday Morning', Lowell asserts the connection between the cruel optimism of political threat and the complicity of subjects in their own ruin. Returning to a favourite conceit of Lowell's the poem once again begins with a piscine metaphor:

> O to break loose, like the Chinook
> salmon jumping and falling back,
> nosing up to the impossible
> stone and bone-crushing waterfall.[42]

Recalling the childhood delight of visits to the South Boston Aquarium in 'For the Union Dead', Lowell is fascinated with the fish; however, in this metaphor he identifies with the salmon's struggle against powerful forces of nature, one where triumph is paradoxically equated with death. The salmon that is able to 'clear the top on the last try' is only 'alive enough to spawn and die.'[43] In this ecological metaphor, being 'alive enough' is contingent upon a struggle that is at once natural and necessary for the continuation of the species. Lowell's speaker longs for the stability of this natural order, where his 'body wakes / to feel the unpolluted joy / and criminal leisure of a boy,'[44] and where

> the creatures of the night
> obsessive, casual, sure of foot,
> go on grinding, while the sun's
> daily remorseful blackout dawns.[45]

However, as the poem moves from images of a stark and cyclical nature, Lowell's optimism quickly fades. In the human world he wishes 'that the spirit could remain / tinged but untarnished by its strain'[46] and longs to

---

42 Ibid. 383.
43 Ibid.
44 Ibid.
45 Ibid.
46 Ibid. 384.

be 'anywhere, but somewhere else'.[47] The spirit, according to Lowell, has been coopted and misled, first by religion and then by political ideology. Religious value is replaced by conformity as the 'Bible is chopped and crucified / in hymns we hear but do not read'[48] and each day God 'sees through darker glass.'[49] The inefficacy of religion transformed into docile obedience means that 'His vanishing / emblems' are reduced to 'useless things to calm the mad'.[50] As the poem continues, Lowell suggests that the surveillance and discipline of religion have paved the way for obedience to new, post-industrial military gods 'Hammering military splendor' like a 'top-heavy Goliath in full armor'.[51] Referring to the increasingly hostile foreign policies of a Cold War America caught in the midst of a nuclear arms race, and faced with a complex war in Vietnam, Lowell questions the logic of blindly following destructive and militaristic practices. In the same manner that Louis Althusser positions both religion and politics as ideological state apparatuses that determine 'the imaginary relationship of individuals to their real conditions of existence',[52] Lowell implies that ideology interpellates individuals as docile and disciplined subjects.

Concern about this process of interpellation is expressed as the poem continues:

what if a new
diminuendo brings no true
tenderness, only restlessness,
excess, the hunger for success,
sanity of self-deception
fixed and kicked by reckless caution[53]

---

47 Ibid.
48 Ibid.
49 Ibid. 385.
50 Ibid.
51 Ibid.
52 Louis Althusser, 'Ideology and the Ideological State Apparatus' rpt in *Literary Theory: An Anthology* (2nd edn), eds Julie Rivkin and Michael Ryan (Malden, MA: Blackwell, 2004), 693.
53 Lowell, *Collected Poems*, 385.

The '[h]ammering military splendor' of America, it appears, is an ideological device that breeds only 'restlessness, / excess, the hunger for success'. In other words, it perpetuates a destructive neoliberalism wherein military action is justified by the promise of material excess and comfort on the domestic front. For Lowell, however, this logic exemplifies the cruel optimism that ties individuals to destructive practices, a 'sanity of self-deception'[54] in which violent political action is licensed under the auspice that it will either provide greater domestic security or increased personal prosperity. While Lowell wishes to 'break loose'[55] from this condition, he recognizes the difficulty of doing so when even the president, 'girdled by his establishment', is 'sick / of his ghost-written rhetoric'.[56] The president, in other words, is himself part of the logic of cruel optimism; a figurehead who provides the illusion of freedom and democracy when in fact he is 'girdled' by less visible, if more insidious, ideological forces.

As the poem concludes, Lowell offers 'peace to our children when they fall / in small war on the heels of small / war – until the end of time'.[57] Falling prey to small wars, while conjuring the more immediate notion of proxy wars such as that which was emerging in Vietnam, also implies the small acts of violence performed against the subject by Cold War policies of containment and surveillance. The impact of such interventions, particularly those predicated upon a political ontology of threat, is to leave the modern subject like 'a ghost / orbiting forever lost / in our monotonous sublime.[58] Lowell's connection of the terms 'monotonous' and 'sublime' attests to the nature of sublimity in the nuclear era. While scholars such as Frances Ferguson have argued that nuclear explosions create their own technologically orchestrated feeling of sublime terror, Lowell here refers more ironically to the awe and terror created by Cold War culture's monotonous response to impending ruin. Indeed, that monotony is precisely what leaves them weary and disengaged, like ghosts 'orbiting forever lost'.

54 Ibid.
55 Ibid.
56 Ibid.
57 Ibid. 386.
58 Ibid.

It is the power of biopolitics to construct this 'monotonous sublime', one that estranges individuals from their own political and personal well-being, that is most troubling about Lowell's Cold War America. As Berlant notes, this form of cruel optimism acts as an 'analytic lever' that incites Americans 'to inhabit and to track the affective attachment to what we call "the good life," which is for so many a bad life that wears out the subjects who nonetheless, and at the same time, find their conditions of possibility within it'.[59] This weariness, or sense of being oppressed by anxiety to the point of feeling 'frizzled, stale and small'[60] speaks to an unprecedented management of affect in the interest of political ends. However, the conflation of weariness with desire, particularly that promoted by the consumer culture of neoliberal America, makes weariness a self-perpetuating condition. As Berlant argues, this condition is

> one of the attrition or the wearing out of the subject, and ... the irony that the labor of reproducing life in the contemporary world is also the activity of being worn out by it has specific implications for thinking about the ordinariness of suffering, the violence of normativity, and the 'technologies of patience' or lag that enable a concept of the later to suspend questions of the cruelty of the now.[61]

This weariness recalls Lowell's metaphors of being caught, like a helpless fish, behind the glass of its bowl in 'Fall 1961', or of being static and frozen in 'Inauguration Day: January 1953'. While he sees the attritional violence managing the subject according to a political ontology of threat, he feels powerless to alter that ontology's potentially catastrophic course. It is for this reason that Lowell's poetry emphasizes the abject self as a possible mode of resisting the normalization of affect in an era of heightened anxiety. By demonstrating the ubiquitous, and often damaging, nature of anxiety on the Cold War subject, Lowell draws attention to the fact that 'the season's ill', not just in his mind but in Cold War America at large. His poetry of the 1950s and 1960s makes it clear that by controlling affect, the Cold War state manages human response, or cultivates indifference, to epochal concerns, such as those raised by the spectre of nuclear oblivion.

59   Berlant, 'Cruel Optimism', 97.
60   Lowell, *Collected Poems*, 184.
61   Berlant, 'Cruel Optimism', 97.

Yeats's visions of apocalyptic change and his conflicted, often vacillating positions about what impact that violent change may have on Irish history, helped wrench Lowell away from the cloistered New Critical style he learned from Fugitives such as Tate and Ransom. By positioning poetry as an argument with the self, Yeats may have also shown Lowell the way towards his later confessional verse. While the political poetry of Yeats seems to have inspired Lowell's style, his most effective political poems emerged, almost paradoxically, as his poetry seemed to turn more inward and away from a more pronounced, Yeatsian appeal to the power of a shifting historical gyre. By using the fragmented Cold War self to demonstrate the impact that the political management of affect had on the American subject, Lowell's confessional verse jumped off from the Yeatsian model in order to demonstrate the relationship between a political ontology of threat and the anxiety, stasis, and disengagement that it helped to promote. This cruelly optimistic logic, as Lowell's poems assert, facilitated the growth of a Cold War political ideology that at once promoted the growth of American neoliberalism, and posed a veritable threat to geopolitical security. The sublime, 'terrible beauty' of Yeats shifts, for Lowell, to a critique of the political powers that keep the subject 'frizzled, stale, and small.'[62]

---

62   Lowell, *Collected Poems*, 184.

CALISTA MCRAE

Robert Lowell and Louis MacNeice: Reading Likeness through Elegy

After Louis MacNeice's death in the early autumn of 1963, Robert Lowell wrote to Elizabeth Bishop, asking if she had seen the news: 'I liked some of his poems, more the early ones, very much. Always a smart mind and eye, and a spring to the rhythm.'[1] Lowell also wrote a blank-verse sonnet in memory of the older writer. In *Notebook 1967–68*, he included it – there entitled 'The House-Party' – as part of a section called 'To Summer', a disparate array of eleven poems for or about Theodore Roethke, Eugene McCarthy, Harpo Marx, and Joseph Stalin, among others. When revising the manuscript for the 1973 *History*, however, Lowell took the elegy out of that sequence. He positioned it just after elegies for Eliot, Pound, and Wyndham Lewis, and directly before those for Williams and Frost, a not-quite-chronological move that placed MacNeice among fellow writers.[2]

And yet this sonnet does not wholly fit in among the elegies for other poets. It is particularly subdued, lacking the wildness that characterizes

---

[1] Robert Lowell, *The Letters of Robert Lowell*, ed. Saskia Hamilton (New York: Farrar, Straus and Giroux, 2005), 436.
[2] For an examination of how MacNeice engaged with some of his contemporaries, see Tom Walker, *Louis MacNeice and the Irish Poetry of His Time* (Oxford: Oxford University Press, 2016). On MacNeice's legacy, see *Louis MacNeice and His Influence*, eds Kathleen Devine and Alan J. Peacock (Oxford: Oxford University Press, 1998), especially Richard York's study of MacNeice and Derek Mahon (85–98), Michael Allen on MacNeice and Michael Longley (99–113), and Neil Corcoran, 'Keeping the Colours New: Louis MacNeice in the Contemporary Poetry of Northern Ireland' (114–132). For Lowell's early influences, see Steven Gould Axelrod, *Robert Lowell: Life and Art* (Princeton, NJ: Princeton University Press, 1978).

Lowell's poems. It also seems disjointed, even in a book of disjointed sonnets: it moves between vignettes, anecdote, and aphorism, with references to baroque music and modernist art. Lowell's strategies are not immediately clear: why such a miscellany of facts? Why the long timespan, when so many of his other elegies for poets remember a single moment from the very recent past? Why such a personal poem, for someone Lowell knew relatively slightly; and why its emphasis on fear? A glance at Lowell's earliest responses to MacNeice – followed by a closer examination of how MacNeice is represented in the sonnet – can help answer some of these questions. While Lowell felt a surprising poetic kinship with MacNeice, he saw the older writer as embodying a different approach to self-presentation and to poetry itself.

The two writers enjoyed each other's company, but they did not correspond or meet frequently. In a 1951 letter written from Greece, where MacNeice was on leave directing the British Institute, he remarked that 'Robert American Poet Lowell has just passed through here. Nice. Is he good as a poet? Haven't seen his book.'[3] Though the Northern Irish poet referred to American Poet Lowell in a few later letters, there is little record of what he thought of Lowell's work. Lowell, in turn, wrote relatively little about MacNeice, but a few early references suggest what might have initially struck him.

Lowell had read MacNeice's work since his early twenties: in an early notebook of drafts for *Land of Unlikeness* (1944), he copied out the whole of MacNeice's 'Bagpipe Music'. While it is only one poem among many – he also transcribes Eliot, Yeats, Hart Crane, John Crowe Ransom, and so on – the page is striking. To see anything by MacNeice in Lowell's 'toppling, elephantine' handwriting – as Lowell describes it in his poem 'Grass Fires'[4] – is to see the poets' contrast writ literally large; Lowell's lumpy print looks as if he should be writing out his own grim, enjambed couplets, not the sprightly and menacing work of MacNeice. Generally speaking, MacNeice writes in loose, lilting forms, filled with grace, internal rhyme,

---

3   Louis MacNeice, *Letters of Louis MacNeice,* ed. Jonathan Allison (London: Faber and Faber, 2010), 546.
4   See Lowell, 'Grass Fires' in Frank Bidart and David Gewanter, eds, *Collected Poems* (New York: Farrar, Straus and Giroux, 2003), 796.

and levity. His work is close to song and talk – an opposite to Lowell's harsher fixed forms (like heroic couplets and octaves), jagged free verse, and rough blank verse, each torqued by an aggressively bleak view of the world. The severe, minatory poems of Lowell's *Land of Unlikeness* seem worlds removed from MacNeice's jaunty lines and tumbling rhythms. But the way in which MacNeice's seemingly light verse covers despair and agitation reminds us of an opposite technique in Lowell: a seemingly heavy verse that, on closer inspection, can seem composed of bubbles and clichés, like pumice. And Lowell might have been struck by MacNeice's depictions of chaos and unease, when he himself was beginning to write in the mid- and late 1930s.

A few years later, in an otherwise pugnacious 1946 omnibus review, Lowell singled out MacNeice's work for praise. Although he qualified his admiration (noting a tendency to write moral characters, some 'rambling generalizations,' some 'Audenese,' and occasional lapses into 'solid, competent, mechanical flippancy'),[5] he pointed to MacNeice's *Springboard* (1946) as 'the best book in this group [of eighteen poets] and the best individual poems,' and claimed that MacNeice has 'perhaps the most observant eye in England.'[6] He ended his review by quoting two stanzas of 'Our Brother Fire', giving closing prominence and a considerable amount of space to MacNeice's anthropomorphized, rampaging force of destruction in London.

In concluding with 'Our Brother Fire', Lowell dwells on MacNeice's depiction of frenetic violence:

> Did we not on those mornings after the All Clear,
> When you were looting shops in elemental joy
> And singing as you swarmed up city block and spire,
> Echo your thoughts in ours? 'Destroy! Destroy!'

In both of the poems Lowell notices – 'Bagpipe Music' and 'Our Brother Fire' – the speaker's attitude towards catastrophe is ambivalent. 'Bagpipe Music' finds the new age both exhilarating and troubling, seedy and

---

5 Robert Lowell, 'Current Poetry'. *The Sewanee Review* 54/1 (1946), 152.
6 Ibid. 153.

seductive; as MacNeice seizes on the flotsam, excitement, and ennui of modernity, he captures its energy with slangy, jingly clashes between sound and sense. 'Our Brother Fire', too, hears the pull of fire's song, and sees a joy welded to destruction.

Lowell seems to have liked this side of MacNeice, and shares his attitude towards the modern world's uneasy appeal. Both poets are simultaneously fascinated by and wary of the excesses, power, and threats of urban life, by the vitality and menace of their early twentieth-century cities. They both see a peculiar beauty in what MacNeice called 'this vast organism grown out of us'.[7] MacNeice makes the inorganic seem animate, giving Birmingham's traffic lights the cool, glowing colours of 'crème-de-menthe or bull's-blood'; Lowell brings his cars to life, having them 'nose forward like fish', and sees a snowplough as a 'dragon' with 'thirty gangling feet of angled lights'.

'Our Brother Fire' also reminds us that both poets are attracted to clichés and mixed metaphors – or more precisely, that they revive stock figures of speech that would seem to have had all imagery drained out of them. The fire is 'having his dog's day' in the London blitz. Such figures of speech – see, a few lines later, the idea of 'giv[ing] the dog a bone' – charge the poem with a weird verbal energy. In the same manner, Lowell's colloquial phrases exceed, undercut, and warp their subjects; stones 'fal[l] like a ton of bricks', a whale is 'sick as a dog'.[8] Like MacNeice, the author of 'Homage to Clichés', Lowell uses such phrases not to dismiss them as instances of mindless, repetitive modern life, but as if to let air out of his English, and load it with strangeness. Both poets see clichés more thoroughly than most people do.

Seeing is fundamental to what MacNeice and Lowell share. Their ways of seeing are closer than we have recognized; each has an exceptionally visual mind. And seeing helps illuminate Lowell's later tribute to the older poet, in which MacNeice is represented as a friend. As we turn to the sonnet itself, we can continue to draw out the two poets' visual similarities, which are reflected in the opening of this tribute:

> A dozen children would visit half a dozen;

---

7   Louis MacNeice, *Collected Poems* (London: Faber and Faber, 1966), 35.
8   Lowell, *Collected Poems*, 47, 16.

> downstairs a lost child bullied the piano,
> getting from note to note was jumping rail-ties;
> the black keys showed bruises and turned white.
> The outdoor games the child heard outside and missed
> were as heavily hit and commonplace –
> no need to be Bach to be what we are ...
> Louis, watching his father, the Bishop, wade
> a trout-stream barefoot, for the first time liked him:
> 'What poor feet!' Till thirty, he was afraid
> a woman would roll on him, and smother him.
> A month from his death, we talked by Epstein's bust
> of Eliot; MacNeice said, 'It is better
> to die at fifty than lose our pleasure in fear.'[9]

Although the elegies for the other modernists tend to focus on one meeting between Lowell and the older poet (meeting Eliot in a hallway at Harvard, talking to Pound at the mental hospital, visiting Williams and his mother, awkwardly conversing with Frost), this one goes much further back in time, and then moves forward decades. Instead, the first ten lines begin from childhood memory and imagination. The playfully laboured, emphatically physical piano-bullying of the first quatrain suggests a child's small hands: the move from key to key requires him to aim and jump with effort, across the awkward gap of a railroad tie.

The loss of childhood is felt vividly – and missed, keenly – at the end of MacNeice's 'Soap Suds'. It seems likely that Lowell composed his elegy with this poem in mind. 'Soap Suds' opens MacNeice's final, posthumous book, *The Burning Perch* (1963), and recalls the expanse and proportions of childhood, accessed through a Proustian memory:

> This brand of soap has the same smell as once in the big
> House he visited when he was eight: the walls of the bathroom open
> To reveal a lawn where a great yellow ball rolls back through a hoop
> To rest at the head of a mallet held in the hands of a child.[10]

---

9   Ibid. 538.
10 MacNeice, *Collected Poems*, 517.

The scent of soap causes the present-day room to unfold into the outside world, one that shares the house party and outdoor games of Lowell's elegy. But this palpable remembrance of a croquet game cannot be retained: as the ball rolls through hoop after hoop in the subsequent stanzas, time rushes to the present, and the scene dissolves in the poem's final lines.

Early personal memory returns continually throughout MacNeice's *Collected Poems*; the early 'Autobiography' consists entirely of childhood images – an autobiography, in other words, grounded in the first dozen years of one's life. Terence Brown has noted 'the obsessional degree of MacNeice's preoccupation with a childhood whose traumata he could never fully exorcise'.[11] And as Jon Stallworthy has pointed out, 'memories of childhood [are] mined' with especial frequency in MacNeice's late work, which Lowell would likely have read in the months after MacNeice's death.[12]

Here again Lowell is responding to a kind of likeness: his own childhood was much the same as MacNeice's, with respect to loneliness and to the long shadow it cast over the writer's life. In fact, the 'lost child', so pointedly nameless, might stand in for MacNeice or for Lowell himself. It certainly recalls the times that the young MacNeice hid from family or nurses, in what one poem called 'the long flat hours of my childhood';[13] it was described at length in *The Strings Are False*. Stephen Spender remembered that MacNeice could also tend to isolate himself in adulthood: 'In his personal relations, the opacity of surface resulted in many people finding MacNeice aloof, disdainful, detached and cold'; there were 'patches of reserve'.[14] But this childhood is isolated also in the way Lowell depicts his own in *Life Studies*. The young Lowell 'skulked in the attic', memorizing names of generals, and was once kicked out of the Boston Public Garden for starting a fight with his third-grade classmates; later, at Saint Mark's

11   Terence Brown, 'Louis MacNeice's Ireland', in *Tradition and Influence in Anglo-Irish Poetry*, eds Terence Brown and Nicholas Grene (Basingstoke: Macmillan, 1989), 79.
12   Jon Stallworthy, *Louis MacNeice: A Biography* (New York: W.W. Norton & Co, 1995), 467.
13   MacNeice, *Collected Poems*, 492.
14   Stephen Spender, 'The Brilliant Mr. MacNeice', *The New Republic*, 27 January 1967.

school, he was ostracized.[15] To 'bull[y]' a piano is an intensely Lowellesque thing to do (his aunt, after all, thundered on a keyless piano in *Life Studies*).

The opening vignette, then, sums up both boyhoods. While the similarities between childhood in *The Strings Are False* and in the prose sections of *Life Studies* are striking, MacNeice drafted his book around 1940 and it was not published until after his death, well after the 1959 *Life Studies*.[16] But while neither poet could have seen the other's autobiographical prose, Lowell would later have noted the way MacNeice shared – and anticipated – his use of the odd angles and perspectives of childhood. And MacNeice's autobiographical poetry resonated deeply with Lowell, who was interested in how his own early experiences affected him.

Lowell's sonnet begins by acknowledging how MacNeice himself created a poetry grounded in the sensations and perspectives – and wonder and misery – of his own childhood. MacNeice's poems are shot through with the way that children see the world. Often his poems seek that early world, although it is a site of trouble as well as pleasure. 'Lost child', in Lowell's elegy, is a kind of pun – the child himself has wandered off and gotten lost in the house, and is also 'lost' to the adult he became.

But childhood for MacNeice is not simply a source of nostalgia – it is the source of an aesthetic practice, which Lowell quietly notices. The end of Lowell's first quatrain foregrounds visual experience, imitating MacNeice's distinctly and effectively *childlike* manner of handling figurative language. In Lowell's remark that 'getting from note to note was jumping rail-ties', that verb 'was' is striking: it makes vivid a moment of imagining. It is the same quick act of metaphor, for example, that MacNeice undertakes when he writes that 'When we were children, words were coloured / (Harlot and murder were dark purple)'.[17] It is a slightly rough construction: as a metaphor that separates vehicle from tenor, it puts emphasis on the stative verb itself, so that it feels more like simile. It catches at how children imagine, stating and pretending at once, half-perceiving what is imagined as real.

---

15   Lowell, *Collected Poems*, 172, 117, 800.
16   Stallworthy, *Louis MacNeice*, 286.
17   MacNeice, *Collected Poems*, 214.

The rapid images of the piano keys as rail ties to be jumped, and then as the bruises and pallor of a face, bring out an aesthetic tendency shared by the two poets – and one that Lowell noted in the older poet's work. MacNeice's quick, shifting, half-synaesthetic acts of comparing, which are often at the heart of his metaphors, anticipate Lowell's. When the 5-year-old Lowell sees his uncle's clothes, they seem to glow with life: 'His coat was a blue jay's tail, / his trousers were solid cream from the top of the bottle'.[18] In the same poem, the boy wonders, 'What were those sunflowers? Pumpkins floating shoulder-high?' That *is* a jay's tail, sunflowers *are* pumpkins: these sentences bind one thing to another closely, while reminding us that these images are shaped by the child's perception.

Sometimes the two poets' metaphors overlap uncannily, suggesting that MacNeice's fleeting metaphors stuck in Lowell's head. Consider, for example, the opening image of MacNeice's 1935 'Morning Sun':

> Shuttles of trains going north, going south, drawing threads of blue,
> The shining of the lines of trams like swords [...][19]

And in Lowell's 'Terminal Days at Beverly Farms':

> sky-blue tracks of the commuters' railroad shone
> like a double-barreled shotgun
> through the scarlet late August sumac,
> multiplying like cancer
> at their garden's border.[20]

Tram lines and train tracks reflect the sky and shine like weapons, for both poets. Lowell's scene is more obviously menacing – the sumac grows unchecked, like a mass of cells – but MacNeice's poem also turns from a clear day to intimations of death: in the final stanza, when 'the sun goes out', the day stops being a 'turning page of shine and sound', and grows cold and gray. Death sits behind both poems' bright scenes.

---

18 Lowell, *Collected Poems*, 167.
19 MacNeice, *Collected Poems*, 26.
20 Lowell, *Collected Poems*, 175.

The two metaphors above are notable for how loaded they are: it is a dense, subjective way of seeing. It demonstrates how MacNeice's descriptions differ from that of other poets important to Lowell, such as William Carlos Williams or Marianne Moore. Williams and Moore tend to look deliberately at an object, for a sustained amount of time: they hone in, to strip away, to defamiliarize so as to see precisely and objectively. MacNeice, on the other hand, takes more rapid looks at the world, and is willing to let his own off-kilter, whimsical ideas constantly permeate and shape the thing itself: threads, then swords. Lowell's surroundings, similarly, are charged by the sometimes hectic intensity of Lowell's own gaze: a blue jay's tail, cream from the top of the bottle. Helen Vendler has praised Lowell's 'wonderful photographic eye that roams over many cities in *Notebook*', 'an eye liberated to notice whatever is most salient, from "the hideous concrete dome of MIT" to "the Charles itself, half ink, half liquid coaldust."'[21] As suggested by the lines Vendler quotes, Lowell's eye *roams*, swooping briefly to illuminate and transform a detail, then another detail.

These glances at the actual world vibrate with an abundance of images. MacNeice presents Lowell with an imaginative landscape that seems more lavishly concentrated than the real world and yet expressive of it – it is the kind of nearly synesthetic vision Lowell would go on to develop in *Life Studies*.[22] They saturate their colours, for example, with metaphor and shifting connotation: 'the sky, plum after sunset, merging to duck's egg, barred with mauve', MacNeice writes of an urban sky, while Lowell turns swiftly from the blue of a blue-jay's tail to the cream from a milk-bottle.

Whether or not MacNeice influences Lowell, the ways they see certainly suggest affinity; they are both exceptionally and idiosyncratically visual poets. Lowell admires MacNeice's extravagant, fleeting sketches of the world and its contents; as we have seen, his 1946 review remarked that

21   Helen Vendler, 'The Poet and the City: Robert Lowell', in *Literature & the American Urban Experience: Essays on the City and Literature*, eds Michael C. Jaye and Ann Chalmers Watts (New Brunswick, NJ: Rutgers University Press, 1981), 59.
22   The importance of sight is also underscored in *History*, which pairs the sonnet for MacNeice with one for Wyndham Lewis. The sonnet for Lewis focuses on optics and vision: 'I see non sequitur', Lowell writes (Lowell, *Collected Poems*, 538). MacNeice, like Lowell and Lewis, 'see[s] non sequitur' as well.

MacNeice 'has perhaps the most observant eye in England'. Two decades later, Lowell again spoke of MacNeice's 'smart mind and eye' to Bishop.[23] It's fitting, then, that he begins his sonnet with a quatrain gesturing both toward MacNeice's own ambivalent nostalgia for childhood – specifically, toward how that childhood informs the older poet's aesthetics, especially his visual perceptions.

Although the first half of the poem – a full seven lines – remains with early life, in the second half of the sonnet, time moves forward more rapidly, just as years fly through croquet hoops in MacNeice's 'Soap Suds'. Lowell cuts to fishing in a 'trout-stream', a memory that at first glance seems completely disconnected from what preceded it. It recalls, however, how MacNeice's poems repeatedly link music to fish, through a pun on *scales* and through the quasi-synaesthetic resemblance between chromatics and iridescence. MacNeice's 'Sunday Morning', for example, begins with someone 'practising scales, / The notes like little fishes vanish with a wink of tails'.[24] 'Donegal Triptych' similarly juxtaposes swimming trout and musical notes: 'For now the music will start once more, the trout stream chirp and gurgle'.[25] Lowell's move from the piano to the trout-stream echoes this odd association, a kind of MacNeicean signature.

While this poem reads as if it were composed of what Lowell learned through MacNeice's writing, it also remembers their conversations, especially their last talk at that party. The peculiar note about fearing that a woman would 'roll on him, and smother him' seems to record MacNeice's mother's worry that she would 'overlay' him when she shared a bed with her young son on holiday: MacNeice recorded that memory in *The Strings Are False,* his posthumous autobiography, published in 1965 (which Lowell likely read, perhaps not long before he began work on his sonnets).[26] But as first published in *Notebook 1967–68,* the sonnet initially had MacNeice himself say 'Until I was almost thirty [...] I thought / a woman would roll

---

23   Lowell, *Letters*, 436.
24   MacNeice, *Collected Poems*, 23.
25   Ibid. 447.
26   Louis MacNeice, *The Strings Are False: An Unfinished Autobiography* (1965; rpt London: Faber and Faber, 1982).

on me', suggesting that this remark was made to Lowell himself, through conversation rather than reading.

By the time of *History*, however, Lowell took that anecdote out of direct quotes, and left it unexplained. So too with his initial title, 'The House-Party', which implied that Lowell had absorbed this fragmented biography over an evening's conversation; he subsequently played down this implication, removing the title and replacing it with MacNeice's name and dates. The decision to take an earlier sentence *out* of quote marks fits into the structure Lowell's sonnet makes, one from isolation to a conversation and exchange. While the boy warms to his previously intimidating father, the young man's standoffish uncertainty continues in the recollection of how MacNeice was afraid of being literally smothered by a woman. The adult, finally, speaks quite openly with a friend.

Here we move into the most central way in which Lowell is thinking about MacNeice. I've been drawing out the subdued similarities between the two poets, suggesting that we can make sense of the poem's first few lines by seeing how they relate back to MacNeice's own writing, and by seeing them as a kind of condensed tribute to MacNeice's lifelong subjects and style. But Lowell is also thinking about difference, especially in his seventh line: 'no need to be Bach to be what we are'. Initially, that aphorism seems to come somewhat out of nowhere: it's not initially clear how it relates to the lines that flank it. The declaration seems to offer reassurance that one can simply be oneself, that one does not have to be an unprecedented genius, like Bach. That idea is supported by the next image Lowell cuts to, where MacNeice's father is loved for his 'poor feet' – for his comic vulnerability, not for anything imposing. (The reference to 'the Bishop', in the context of this reflection on greatness and singularity, suggests that Lowell also has in mind Elizabeth Bishop – another poet who achieved the unforgettable without turning to grandeur.)

That seventh line, then, complicates one's reading of the child at the piano: the child's isolation is part of an attempt to find an art that would make him a major, monumental figure, like Bach. His playing, however, is clumsy, 'as heavily hit and commonplace' as the ordinary games played by the ordinary children outside. One could simply be outside playing games, rather than striving to create music.

Here the ambiguity of the 'lost child' – a potential figure for MacNeice or for Lowell himself – becomes more relevant. Lowell had been driven by ambition since he was a teenager, when he sought Pound as a mentor. He had won a Pulitzer when he was 30; by his early forties he had changed the face of modern American poetry with *Life Studies*, and he was continuing to do so in the massive books of sonnets. MacNeice, on the other hand, is less purposefully wild and isolated – less grandiose, less dramatic, less of a personality, less of an ego. While MacNeice's fears and sorrows are subjects in his poetry, he tends to talk about them more lightly, casually, and understatedly, and he situates himself in less extreme isolation. He pictures his reader as 'an ideal *normal* man who is an educated member of his own community and is basically at one with the poet in his attitude to life',[27] a marked contrast to the highly self-conscious, apparently solipsistic dramas that Lowell stages. Lowell recognizes, quietly, that MacNeice does not set himself up as a solitary creative personality as wilfully and strainedly as he himself has done: he knows that the self that MacNeice presents in his poetry is more relaxed, more willing to 'be what' it is, to present itself as ordinary.

This sonnet, then, sustains two readings – one of kinship and one of difference – within itself, at once. The opening seven lines, describing an unspecified young boy, can be read as both a sketch of MacNeice's solitary childhood, or as a recollection of Lowell's own unhappy childhood and deliberately isolated adolescence. Their attitudes seem to differ, however, in their poems. While Lowell depicts MacNeice as a solitary child, he does not suggest that he is a solitary genius, like Bach or the bust of Eliot: this sonnet is explicitly to a poet often labelled minor. The bust of Eliot, besides which MacNeice and Lowell talk in Lowell's sonnet, also relates to this implicit meditation on poetry. Eliot makes an appearance here as an undeniably major poet, complete with a bust cast by a prominent Modernist sculptor. Eliot's 'What Is Minor Poetry?' appeared in 1946, in the same issue of *The Sewanee Review* that included Lowell's reviews of contemporary poetry (including that of MacNeice, as

---

27 Louis MacNeice, *Modern Poetry: A Personal Essay* (New York: Haskell, 1969), 34. Emphasis added.

we've seen). Eliot's essay, 'concerned to dispel any derogatory association connected with the term "minor poetry"', suggested that we should not seek to identify a feeling of 'greatness or importance' in poetry, but rather 'an awareness of *genuineness*'.[28] This is an idea rather similar to the idea of not needing to be Bach, of instead 'be[ing] what we are'. It is also an idea that was important to MacNeice himself, so often compared to and ranked below Auden: his scepticism about greatness is articulated at length in a 1946 poem, 'Elegy for Minor Poets', where he declared he would 'praise these in company with the Great'.[29]

Both MacNeice and Lowell, trying to find their way after Eliot and the dictates of modernism generally, gravitated towards quite personal poetry (think of the laidback, intimate *Autumn Journal*; think of *Life Studies,* or *Notebook*). But MacNeice's personal poetry evades the intense circling around that self that can sometimes seem to define Lowell's. While MacNeice is quite candid about his fears, desires, delights, and aversions, his handling of those emotions is at a remove from Lowell's self-baring and self-staging persona. He doesn't dwell on himself, and generally seems conversational rather than stentorian – a conversational manner borne of restraint, and some amount of indirection. We see this in the end of the poem, where MacNeice speaks of death rather openly, and makes it not about himself but about people in general, with the first-person plural.

Thus this sonnet considers MacNeice on two planes: it presents MacNeice as a model of a less self-aggrandizing kind of poetry, and it simultaneously sketches MacNeice's development as a person. It begins with images of a standoffish boy and young man. As we've seen, a sense of troubled isolation emerges from the first half of Lowell's sonnet, evoked by the 'lost child', 'bullied' piano and 'bruised' keys. But while the poem begins with an opposition between the dozen-and-a-half children and the solitary child, it closes in a moment of intimate conversation, with MacNeice using the plural possessive, speaking of 'our' pleasure, willing to speak for a collective.

---

[28] T.S. Eliot, 'What Is Minor Poetry?' *The Sewanee Review* 54.1 (1946), 1.
[29] MacNeice, *Collected Poems*, 231.

One of the sonnet's chief questions lingers unanswered: why foreground fear? The word *afraid* ends the tenth line, and *fear* is the last word of the poem; it's a strange note to strike repeatedly in such a brief elegy. First and most saliently, anxiety suffuses MacNeice's work: a number of his poems position everyday pleasures – sensory, commonplace, familiar pleasures –against fear, and especially the frightening encroachment of time. One 1937 poem would have resonated with Lowell for its depiction of how dread physically permeates the mind: 'The taut and ticking fear / That hides in all the clocks / And creeps inside the skull'.[30] In the same poem MacNeice refers to 'the bell / that tolls and tolls, the monotony of fear',[31] suggesting again a fear of time passing. MacNeice's 'Autobiography' ends with the speaker similarly frightened and isolated: 'When my silent terror cried, / Nobody, nobody replied … I got up; the chilly sun / Saw me walk away alone.' *The Burning Perch* is 'taken up with death' in Peter McDonald's words.[32] For MacNeice, fear seems to centre on *time,* on the way it slides forward, as clocks tick and bells toll; loneliness – that 'nobody, nobody replie[s]' – serves to heighten fear.

It is poignant, then, that Lowell ends by having MacNeice address mortality and fear in the same quick sweep. Lowell's sonnet recognizes the extent to which MacNeice's body of work addresses and is informed by fear – especially the fear of time and death. The aphoristic sentence that ends the poem is an answer to the implication of the title Lowell gave the final version of his sonnet, 'Louis MacNeice, 1907–1963': although MacNeice lived a short life, and although fear about time running out had been a constant in his poems, he seems to respond calmly to death. He is almost affirmatively resigned. (Lowell does not include birth and death dates in his titles for Eliot, Pound, Williams, or Frost, though he does for Roethke, a few pages earlier – 1908–63, dates as short as MacNeice's.)

That it is better 'to die at fifty than lose our pleasure in fear' is grammatically ambiguous. The most obvious meaning is that 'it's better to die before one's pleasure is overwhelmed by fear'; but one can also, like Jay

---

30   MacNeice, *Collected Poems*, 27.
31   Ibid.
32   Peter McDonald, 'Louis MacNeice: *The Burning Perch*', in Neil Roberts, ed., *A Companion to Twentieth-Century Poetry* (Oxford: Blackwell, 2003), 499.

Martin, read it as saying, 'it's better to die before losing the pleasure that fear can give.'[33] The ambiguity is apt for MacNeice, whose work – think of his unnerving nursery rhymes and the nightmares of *The Burning Perch* – continually transforms fear into a source of pleasure. Lowell seems to perceive that both possibilities exist in MacNeice's poems: fear sits behind the poem's aesthetic and actual pleasures, giving them depth; it can also wipe out pleasure completely.

This last aphorism, like the earlier line about Bach, considers how to reconcile the self to its plight: one should be what one is, one should also admit one's fright and mortality. By making these two aphoristic sentences the backbone of his sonnet, Lowell raises two points that are central both to MacNeice and to his own writing: he brings up the terms on which the self can be memorable or appealing or moving (rather than great), and that self's capacity for delight or solace in the face of transience. His sonnet's disparate materials suggest what might take the place of trying to 'be Bach': to 'be what we are' is to be composed of sensitive feet, of phobias, of parties and friendship, and of the odd ability to see piano keys as rail-ties.

In *Notebook 1967–68,* the last words were slightly different: there the sonnet ended, 'to die at fifty than lose my pleasure in terror,' with a singular 'my' evoking the utter isolation of MacNeice's 'Autobiography' and ending on the obliterating intensity of *terror*. In the final version, Lowell has moderated that terror, and has MacNeice use the plural *our*, reaffirming that the total isolation of the poem's beginning has vanished. It's significant that both of these aphorisms use *we*, the first-person plural that can be both reserved and communal: it's the pronoun with which MacNeice often speaks. To speak with a *we* is both to efface one's self and to express one's place in a group. And it's interesting that Lowell – a famously dramatic, ostensibly self-absorbed writer – can turn the volume down here, can focus on the minute verbal and personal tendencies of another writer.

Lowell has read MacNeice with more care than his brief references in letters might suggest: he knows that this writer is drawn to music, to colours,

---

33 Jay Martin, 'Grief and Nothingness: Loss and Mourning in Lowell's Poetry', in *Robert Lowell: Essays on the Poetry*, eds Steven Gould Axelrod and Helen Deese (New York: Cambridge University Press, 1986), 39.

to fishing and fish, to trains. Lowell weaves such subjects into his sonnet. He also entwines references to two of the people who haunt MacNeice's poetry: he has noted how MacNeice pictures his father in an elegy, 'Carrying his boots and paddling like a child'.[34] Although MacNeice's elegy declares that 'no sign // Remains of face or feet when visitors have gone home', those bare feet are also remembered in Lowell's poem. 'Louis MacNeice, 1907–1963' becomes poignant through these pieces of noticing: it commemorates another person's private, otherwise forgotten memories. While the poets did not know each other well, Lowell evidently felt a kinship arising from their surprising connections.

In showing us what Lowell saw in MacNeice, the elegy shows us another side of Lowell – one marked by reticence and close attention. Stepping far back in time to trace the arc of MacNeice's short life, Lowell stays somewhat at a distance, as if to acknowledge that he himself did not know MacNeice well, and to mark the sense of estrangement that MacNeice's poems came from and sought to mend. While Lowell avoids having an explicit presence in the poem, he is there as a contrast, as a listener, and as a careful reader: the two poets are quietly represented as being in conversation.

---

34   MacNeice, *Collected Poems*, 226.

KARL O'HANLON

Rebels in Formal Dress: Robert Lowell, Denis Devlin and their Transatlantic Literary Network

In a 1948 letter to Elizabeth Bishop, Robert Lowell explains the writing on the verso: '[it's] something Ezra Pound wants sent to 13 writers: me, Randall, Allen, Williams, Cummings, Wyndham Lewis, Auden, Spender – I forget the rest – "action within twenty-four hours" whatever that means'.[1] The missive *ex cathezra*, sent from St Elizabeth's Hospital, is an impenetrable rant, and contains the usual programme for frenetic action:

> Jarrel/Tate/Spender? Discuss: Brooks Adams, Frobenius, Gesell, essentially Loeb/ Ford. W.L. to Tate. Barry Domville 'Admiral to Cabin Boy' Has Tate anything of Devlin's/ or has L? what anyone else know of him.[2]

As this chapter will uncover, it is significant that Pound, modernist marketeer and networker *par excellence*, writes to Lowell, the future of American poetry, enquiring about Denis Devlin, an Irish modernist poet beginning to gain a readership in US poetry. With an eye to the complex literary networks Pound alludes to in his letter, and taking his enquiry whether Allen Tate or 'L' have any of Denis Devlin's work in hand rather less literally, we might well wonder if Tate and 'L' – Lowell himself – *have anything* of Devlin, if they bear the mark of his influence.[3]

---

1   Robert Lowell to Elizabeth Bishop, 25 February 1948, *The Letters of Robert Lowell*, ed. Saskia Hamilton (New York: Farrar, Straus and Giroux, 2007), 86.
2   Pound, on verso of the letter to Bishop, in *The Letters of Robert Lowell*, 694, n97. Erratic punctuation and spelling is Pound's own.
3   Saskia Hamilton suggests that 'L' refers to Wyndham Lewis, but the gnomic obtuseness of the letter permits my reading.

As John Montague wrote in his 1973 essay 'The Impact of International Modern Poetry on Ireland', 'the great interest of Denis Devlin is that he is the first poet of Irish Catholic background to take the world as his province.'[4] Devlin spent the early 1930s shuttling between Dublin and Paris, where he had been a close associate of Samuel Beckett, Thomas MacGreevy, and Brian Coffey. His first full collection, *Intercessions*, was published by the Parisian publisher Europa Press in 1937, and in addition to French Surrealism (André Breton and Paul Eluard), was heavily influenced by high modernism (particularly T.S. Eliot and Hart Crane).[5] It was while he served as a diplomat during the 1940s as first secretary to the Irish legation in Washington, DC, that he met Allen Tate, Robert Penn Warren, and almost certainly, Tate's protégé, Robert Lowell. Examining the intricate connections between Lowell and Devlin, this chapter will locate both poets within a complex transatlantic literary milieu, spanning from Washington, DC, to Rome. I will explore how Devlin's artistic career in the states suggests a belated transmission of Irish poetic modernism to US poetry, and trace the emergence of a new key in his work profoundly influenced by Allen Tate and the New Critics. Tate and his associates were similarly seminal in the powerful entry of Robert Lowell onto the scene of American letters. This chapter argues that by situating Lowell and Devlin within a specific periodical network, we are able to uncover a transatlantic, cross-cultural aesthetic profoundly shaped by New Criticism and, above all, Allen Tate.

It would appear that the first review of Robert Lowell's work by an Irish writer was by Denis Devlin in *The Sewanee Review*; some five years would elapse before Austin Clarke would dismiss the 'spiritual excesses' and 'strenuousness' of Lowell's poetry in the pages of *The Irish Times*.[6]

---

4   John Montague, in *The Figure in the Cave and Other Essays*, ed. Antoinette Quinn (Dublin: Lilliput Press, 1989), 212. 'Catholic' is a necessary qualifier in light of the career of W.B. Yeats, but as we shall see, Catholicism is not irrelevant to that internationalism.
5   See Alex Davis, *A Broken Line: Denis Devlin and Irish Poetic Modernism* (Dublin: University College Dublin Press, 2000), 28. Davis's book is the only book-length study of Devlin's work to date, and indispensable as an introduction to his poetry.
6   Austin Clarke, 'Scalping the Muse', *The Irish Times*, 30 September 1950: 6.

Devlin reviewed Lowell's first volume *Land of Unlikeness* (printed in only 250 copies) for the 1946 summer issue of the Tennessee journal, which was edited by Allen Tate from the 1944 autumn issue, with the issue carrying Devlin's review being the last Tate would edit. In the 1940s, the journal was paying relatively close attention to Irish writing, with reviews of Devlin, W.B. Yeats and W.R. Rodgers, and essays on George Bernard Shaw and James Joyce. In Tate's autumn 1945 issue, Louis MacNeice contributed translations of Louis Aragon, while the January–March 1946 issue carried a review of a new MacNeice volume by Lowell. There is also an intriguing article in the autumn 1950 issue, 'Agrarianism in Exile' by Richard M. Weaver, which argues that Southern Agrarianism of earlier decades is 'rich in correspondences' with contemporary Ireland in terms of religiosity, agricultural economy, and mythopoeia.[7] It is clear that *The Sewanee Review* was invested in Irish writing, and it seems probable that Devlin's review would have had a select readership in Ireland. Devlin certainly sent Thomas MacGreevy copies of reviews of his *Lough Derg and Other Poems*, published in New York by Reynal and Hitchcock the same year, and he may have sent the Lowell review on to friends.[8] The piece discreetly situates the precocious achievement of Lowell's *Land of Unlikeness* against Irish religious and literary contexts. Devlin implicitly compares the book with W.H. Auden's *For the Time Being: A Christmas Oratorio*, in which Auden's spiritual concerns suffer from the comparison:

> [*For the Time Being*] releases [the poet's] anxiety, whose object is the terrorising Unknown, into a modest optimism of waiting whose reward is certainty, God: all in a fable which expresses the central assumptions of neo-Protestantism, occupied as it has been, in recent years, with self-renewal through a return to its theological origins in the Reformation.[9]

Devlin's chief criticism of Auden is that his work is theological apologetics, and not poetry; like 'an intellectual Paulist', his 'methods and

---

7   Richard M. Weaver, 'Agrarianism in Exile', *The Sewanee Review*, 58.4 (October–December 1950): 586–606 (603).
8   See the Thomas MacGreevy papers, Trinity College, Dublin, TCD MS 8112/17.
9   Denis Devlin, 'Twenty-Four Poets', *The Sewanee Review*, 53.3 (summer 1945): 457–466 (457).

purposes' are 'those of the orator', and the poem therefore 'lives on one plane without resonance'.[10] Note as well the criticism of 'certainty', an important feature of New Critical poetics, as shall become apparent.

By contrast, Devlin hails Robert Lowell's book as 'a remarkable poetic apparition':

> [*Land of Unlikeness*] will irritate the humanist descendants of Erasmus and shock devout Christians. He is a rebel in formal dress; he apostrophizes the Virgin and the Redeemer with the rude but reverent familiarity of a medieval goliard ... Though he comes near to being the reincarnation of a lost Metaphysical poet, his personal, contemporary use of their conceits, their word-play and their witty passion, frees him from that archaicisation. Closer reading, indeed, reveals a wide allusiveness: a Websterian colouring, a quaint eighteenth-century Mars, even an affinity with the sardonic comic of Joyce.[11]

The short review of Lowell provides insight into how Devlin assimilates Lowell's poetry to his own critical frames of reference. He carefully situates Lowell's poetry as antagonistic to both 'devout Christians' and humanists; nevertheless, there is an implicit preference in Devlin's characterization 'medieval goliard' for the riotous, carnal Catholicism of Lowell's verse, as against the 'intellectual Paulist' strains of Auden's neo-Protestantism. The assertion of contemporaneity with which Lowell imbues models derived from sixteenth- and seventeenth-century Metaphysical poetry is suggestive of Devlin's awareness of the influence of New Critical aesthetics on Lowell's early poetry, its modern and self-aware retrieval of Elizabethan and Jacobean poetic form. Lowell himself later reflected of the late 1930s through the 1940s:

> [both Allen Tate and I] liked rather formal, difficult poems, and we were reading particularly the sixteenth and seventeenth centuries ... It seems to me we took old models like Drayton's Ode ... I think both Tate and I felt that we wanted our formal patterns to seem a hardship and something that we couldn't rattle off easily.[12]

---

10 Devlin, 'Twenty-Four Poets', 458.
11 Ibid. 459–460.
12 Frederick Seidel, 'An Interview with Robert Lowell', in *Robert Lowell: A Portrait of the Artist in His Time*, eds Michael London and Robert Boyers (New York: David Lewis, 1970), 266.

Finally, Devlin's review notably detects 'an affinity with the sardonic comic of Joyce', notwithstanding the fact that Lowell, like his contemporary and friend John Berryman, betrayed clear debts in his early poetry to – and later openly acknowledged the mastery of –the great founder of what came to be seen as the rival tradition in Irish literature, W.B. Yeats.[13] The reference to Joyce, to the necessary (and counterintuitive) exclusion of Yeats, is evidence of the way in which Devlin views Lowell through his own lens of Irish modernism, and a subtle, but instructive glimpse of cross-cultural maps of reading and reception in mid-century US poetry.

Devlin's review of Lowell, then, may be read as an oblique précis of the manner in which Devlin was consciously negotiating the dominant aesthetic of postwar American poetry. It betrays his determination to locate elements of consanguinity between Lowell's poetry and the Irish modernist experimentalism of his own early verse in the preceding decade, while signalling that his own mature poetry was developing under the aegis of New Critical precepts.[14] Of this process of cross-aesthetic, cross-cultural navigation, several facets demand particular attention: interest in a vexed expression of religious belief, a contemporary handling of difficult traditional forms, and the perhaps surprising suggestion of affinities between Irish modernist experimental verse of the 1930s and the New Critical–influenced formalism of mid-century US poetry.

An account of Devlin's entrance into transatlantic literary networks in which Lowell also operated sheds further light on their explicit connections, their milieu (and the dominant New Critical aesthetic attached to it), and the literary cross-currents between Ireland and the US. In 1939 as war broke out, Devlin was posted by neutral Ireland first to the Consulate General in New York, then in 1940 as first secretary to the Irish legation in the nation's capital. Devlin wasted no time in forging literary connections: in

---

13   See Steven Matthews, *Yeats as Precursor: Readings in Irish, British, and American Poetry* (London: Macmillan, 2000), 170–175. Matthews asserts that Tate's influence was the most potent factor in the centrality of Yeats to Lowell's generation.

14   Alex Davis's study contains an admirable section on Devlin's poetry in the mid-1940s as conforming to 'an autotelic construct of ambivalent, but not indeterminate, meaning that is the hallmark of the New Critical "verbal icon"' (58); see *A Broken Line*, especially 55–59.

New York, he made contact with Norman Macleod, a left-wing poet and director of the Poetry Center at the Young Men's Hebrew Association, 92nd St and Lexington Avenue, New York. Devlin read at the YMHA on 6 April 1940.[15]

It is an open question to what extent Irish modernism, outside of Joyce, had made any serious inroads into American poetry, but Devlin's career in the early 1940s surely holds the answer. In the March 1935 instalment of Joseph Hone's 'A Letter from Ireland' in *Poetry*, Yeats's future biographer described for an American audience the furore following the August 1934 publication of 'Recent Irish Poetry' in the *Bookman* by Samuel Beckett, writing as 'Andrew Belis'.[16] The review essay starkly divided Irish poetry into the 'antiquarians' and 'others', those content in 'delivering with the altitudinous complacency of the Victorian Gael the Ossianic goods', and those aware of 'the new thing that has happened ... namely the breakdown of the object, whether current, historical, mythical or spook'.[17] Hone reports that 'some of those who meet with [Belis's] approval are hardly known outside Ireland', shrewdly noting in passing that Beckett's name is absent from the list, which includes Blanaid Salkeld, Percy Ussher, Brian Coffey, and Denis Devlin. Hone writes: 'the poems of Denis Devlin in particular ... have aroused an interest that has not been confined to the extreme partisans of the modernistic school and the anti-celticists.'[18] It is significant that as early as 1935, in a major, and relatively widely circulated US poetry journal, a correspondent on Irish poetry was enshrining the debate in the terms set by the modernist young Turks, albeit attempting to retrieve Devlin from the extreme partisans of that camp. Hone's transatlantic intervention flies in the face of several public statements Devlin made in the wake of Beckett's *Bookman* piece, including a radio broadcast on the Irish Free State's national station, 2RN, on 4 October 1935 entitled 'A Reply to F.R. Higgins', in which Devlin resolutely throws in his lot with the innovators; the broadcast ends with an excerpt from a poem by

15 'News and Notes', *Poetry*, 56.1 (April 1940), p. 55.
16 Joseph Hone, 'A Letter from Ireland', *Poetry*, 45.6 (March 1935): 332–336.
17 Samuel Beckett, 'Recent Irish Poetry', *Disjecta: Miscellaneous Writings and a Dramatic Fragment* (London: John Calder, 1983), 70.
18 Hone, 'A Letter from Ireland', 334.

Hart Crane, another indication of the transatlantic inflections of Devlin's modernism.[19] In January 1941, again in *Poetry*, Devlin himself would seek to apprise the American readership of the internecine Irish poetry wars of the previous decade. The 'News and Notes' section reports:

> An interesting note on the Irish poets comes from Denis Devlin of the Irish legation at Washington, one of the younger Irish poets. Mr Devlin says that a shift is taking place in Irish poetry, which in recent years has been dominated by a group which might be called the agricultural poets. These poets, following certain phrases of Yeats's work, have been interested in the sophisticated ballad, in the Irish country rather than the city, and in the assonance and lighter movement of Gaelic meters transferred into English verse. A new group of younger poets, of which Mr Devlin himself is one – others are Samuel Beckett, Donagh MacDonagh, Niall Montgomery, and Brian Coffey – is now, however, winning a hearing in the leading magazines. Their work is urban and sociological in emphasis.[20]

Alongside poems in Macleod's 1940 anthology of YMHA readers, *Calendar* (published by James A. Decker's Prairie City-based press), *The New Republic* (28 October 1940), and *Poetry* (February 1941), Devlin's note announces the presence of a self-consciously modernist Irish poet on the American scene. It is perhaps no exaggeration to say that in the early 1940s, Devlin was in some sense not only a diplomat to the US for Ireland, but for Irish modernism.[21]

In Washington, DC, as the complex diplomatic negotiations with the Roosevelt administration surrounding Ireland's neutrality increased Devlin's workload, he began to move in the same literary circles as the young Robert Lowell. It seems likely that Devlin met Allen Tate, Lowell's mentor, at some point in the early 1940s. In a memorial issue of *Éire/Ireland*,

---

19   I have identified this piece (from among Devlin's papers in the National Library of Ireland) as the script of the broadcast; see my forthcoming article, 'The Case for Irish Modernism: Denis Devlin at the League of Nations and 1930s International Broadcasting' in *Modernism/Modernity*.
20   'News and Notes', *Poetry*, 57.4 (January 1941): 282.
21   Beckett saw fit to pass to Devlin (on leave from the Irish legation at some point in the 1940s) a typescript copy of *Watt* to try the US market; in the event, it would not appear until 1953, when it was published in Paris by Olympia Press.

the weekly bulletin of the Department of External Affairs published after Denis's untimely death in 1959, Robert Penn Warren recollected:

> It was Denis Devlin's poem 'Lough Derg' that began our acquaintance. Unless my memory fails me, Allen Tate was responsible for its being offered to *The Southern Review*, of which I was one of the editors. I thought it a beautiful poem, calm and poised but glowing with feeling. It stood in a peculiar contrast to much of the poetry of that period, outside of schools and trends.[22]

'Lough Derg' was published in the penultimate issue of *The Southern Review*, in the spring of 1942, so Tate would have had to pass it to Warren at some point in the previous year. Devlin and Tate were moving in the same literary and social circles in the heady atmosphere of the wartime capital, including soirées hosted by poet and patron Katherine Biddle (née Garrison Chapin), the wife of Francis Biddle who served as Attorney General in the Roosevelt administration, and the novelist Katherine Anne Porter, who in 1944 was a house guest of Marcella Comès Winslow, ex-officio portraitist to the Poet Consultant at the Library, and a cousin through marriage of Robert Lowell. It was at one of Katherine Anne's parties that Devlin would meet Warren for the first time in 1944.[23] Another key individual in this literary milieu was Saint-John Perse (Alexis Leger), an exile from Vichy France working as an adviser in the Library of Congress since January 1941; Devlin's authorized translations of Perse would begin to appear in *The Sewanee Review* (during Tate's editorship) from late 1944.

Tate, and his profound inheritance and transmission of the criticism of T.S. Eliot, was undoubtedly the linchpin in any aesthetic overlap between Devlin and Lowell. At the behest of sometime-adversary Archibald MacLeish, then Librarian of Congress, Tate became the first Consultant in Poetry at the Library in August 1943; he would be followed in the role by

---

22 Robert Penn Warren, 'Denis Devlin: A Recollection', *Éire/Ireland* 4935 (September 1960): 6.
23 See Warren, 'Denis Devlin: A Recollection', 6, and Joan Givner, *Katherine Anne Porter: A Life* (London: Jonathan Cape, 1982), 330–335.

Warren.[24] Ensconced in the close-knit literary-bureaucratic milieu of wartime DC, Tate and Warren would become passionate advocates of Devlin. During Warren's Consultancy, the Irish diplomat-poet read to the Writer's Club of the Library of Congress on 3 January 1945 (reading Yeats's 'Long-Legged Fly' and 'Under Ben Bulben' alongside his own poetry). Devlin dedicated his late opus 'The Passion of Christ' to Tate, who returned the favour by dedicating his sequence 'More Sonnets at Christmas' to the memory of Devlin. In addition to the review already discussed, Tate also published Devlin's translations and original poetry in *The Sewanee Review* during his tenure as editor from 1944 to 1946 (in an issue that included a poem from Lowell, as I discuss later).

Tate and Warren presumably had something to do with the publication of Devlin's *Lough Derg and Other Poems* in 1946; Albert Erskine, who had been married to Katherine Anne Porter and worked with Warren on *The Southern Review*, was at the time an editor at Reynal and Hitchcock; in addition to Devlin's poems, Reynal and Hitchcock published several notable works by writers affiliated with the New Criticism, including Cleanth Brooks's seminal *The Well-Wrought Urn: Studies in the Structure of Poetry* (1947). After Devlin's death from leukaemia while serving as Irish ambassador to Italy, Tate and Warren canvassed for the establishment of the Denis Devlin Memorial Award, and co-edited his *Selected Poems* in an edition published in 1963 by Holt, Reinhart and Winston. In the Preface, they rank Devlin's poem 'Lough Derg' along with Wallace Stevens' 'Sunday Morning', T.S. Eliot's 'Gerontion', and Hart Crane's 'The Broken Tower':

> In all these poems, the poets are exploring the difficult region where doubt and faith have been conducting an inconclusive dialectic since the middle of the last century ... ['Lough Derg'] is composed of nineteen six-line stanzas, rhymed *ababcc*, a modification of rhyme royal, or perhaps an adaptation of the stanza, *aabccb*, of 'Le cimetière marin'. In other ways the poem suggests a derivation from, but in no sense an imitation of, Valéry. [T]here is little that to an American ear sounds like Irish idiom; and there are almost no traces of Yeats's 'romantic Ireland' of the Celtic Twilight. Devlin

---

24 For a comprehensive account of Tate's time in the role, see Thomas A. Underwood, 'A Bard Among Bibliographers: Allen Tate's Washington Year', *The Southern Literary Journal* 24.2 (spring 1992): 36–48.

was one of the pioneers of the international poetic English which now prevails on both sides of the Atlantic.[25]

Almost twenty years after Devlin's review of Robert Lowell's *Land of Unlikeness*, Tate and Warren commend in Devlin's body of poetry some of the aspects he himself highlighted in Lowell's early work, including an adaptive attitude to the classic forms of poetic forebears, and the 'inconclusive dialectic' between doubt and faith. In casting Devlin as a pioneer of 'the international poetic English which now prevails on both sides of the Atlantic' – a plaudit that one could easily imagine being given to Lowell – Tate and Warren are canonizing an aesthetic that they shaped and institutionalized as editors, taste-makers, and pedagogues of the postwar era.

It would be hard to overstate Allen Tate's role in Lowell's poetic development. In April 1937, Lowell drove out from Nashville to Benfolly, the home that Tate shared with his novelist wife, Caroline Gordon. Failing to detect Tate's ironic courtesy when he insisted that there was only room for a tent on the lawn for their impromptu visitor, Lowell duly drove into town and bought a Sears & Roebuck olive green umbrella tent, and proceeded to pitch it on the Tates' lawn for three months.[26] Decades later, Lowell would describe Tate's influence on his early poetry: 'every other day, I turned out grimly unromantic poems – organized, hard, and classical as a cabinet.'[27] Lowell soon followed Tate's friend John Crowe Ransom to Kenyon College, eventually re-joining the Tates at their new home in Monteagle, Tennessee, in the early 1940s, where he worked on *Land of Unlikeness*. Lowell would later reflect on his poetic formation, 'the kind of poet I am was largely determined by the fact that I grew up in the heyday of New Criticism ... preoccupied with technique, fascinated with the past,

---

25 Allen Tate and Robert Penn Warren, 'A Preface by Allen Tate and Robert Penn Warren', *Selected Poems by Denis Devlin* (New York: Holt, Rinehart and Winston, 1963), 13–14.
26 See Paul Mariani, *Lost Puritan: A Life of Robert Lowell* (New York: W.W. Norton and Co., 1994), 60–61.
27 Robert Lowell, *Collected Prose* (London: Faber and Faber, 1987), 60.

and tempted by other languages.'[28] Those New Critical preoccupations were increasingly crucial to Devlin while in the States. Where Lowell came of age in the New Criticism and would slough off much of its influence with his ground-breaking volume *Life Studies* (1959), Devlin's poetry found its mature expression under the aegis of his New Critic champions.

Robert Lowell's debut, *Land of Unlikeness* – which as we have seen was reviewed by Devlin in Tate's *Sewanee Review* – was published in September 1944 in a print run of 250 by the Cummington Press, one of the few presses putting out new work despite wartime scarcity.[29] Allen Tate provided a glowing introduction to the volume:

> T.S. Eliot's recent prediction that we should soon see a return to formal and even intricate metres and stanzas was coming true, before he made it, in the verse of Robert Lowell ... in a young man like Lowell, whether we like his Catholicism or not, there is at least a memory of the spiritual dignity of man, now sacrificed to mere secularisation and a craving for mechanical order.[30]

The parallels with the preface to Devlin's *Selected Poems* almost twenty years later are striking, particularly the praise for Lowell as an intricate formalist, and the subtle suggestion in the phrase 'at least a memory of the spiritual dignity of man' that Lowell's Catholic poetry, rather than devotional verse, is inexorably caught in that same 'inconclusive dialectic' between faith and doubt that Tate and Warren insisted was an exemplary feature of the best poems of the twentieth century, including Devlin's 'Lough Derg'.

Both Lowell and Devlin contributed to the winter 1944 issue of *The Sewanee Review*, the first to appear during Tate's short tenure as editor. The issue saw the first publication of one of Devlin's authorized translations of Saint-John Perse, 'Rains', alongside one of his own poems, 'Meditation at Avila'. Lowell's poem 'Colloquy in Black Rock, Connecticut' immediately follows Devlin in the issue. Other contributors to the issue worth

---

28 Lowell, in Stanley Kunitz, 'Talk with Robert Lowell', in *Robert Lowell: Interviews and Memoirs*, ed. Jeffrey Meyers (Ann Arbor: University of Michigan, 1988), 85.
29 See Mariani, *Lost Puritan*, 104.
30 Allen Tate, 'Introduction', in Robert Lowell, *Collected Poems*, eds Frank Bidart and David Gewanter (New York: Farrar, Straus and Giroux, 2003), 859–860.

mentioning include Devlin's New York ally, Norman Macleod (steering clear of left-wing themes, the object of censure in Tate's editorial), an essay-epistle from the Catholic philosopher Jacques Maritain to Jean Cocteau on the relationship of art to sanctity, a short story from Katherine Anne Porter, and papers from Wallace Stevens, Marianne Moore, and other participants in a summer 1943 US reboot of the famous Entretiens de Potigny, organized by Free French intellectuals at Mount Holyoke College, Massachusetts. John Crowe Ransom also added to the now considerable body of his own writing on New Criticism in an essay entitled 'The Bases of Criticism'.

In addition to providing a platform for New Criticism, the common threads in the issue include a celebration of European, specifically French culture, and both critical and poetic explorations of Catholicism to which Tate was increasingly attracted. His conservative editorial, 'The State of Letters', excoriated Marxist critics, and a broader tendency among liberals to subject literature to 'democracy and nationalism, the wonderful union of which will probably become the religion of the next age.'[31] The editorial rallies in defence of Eliot, under populist attack from Carl Sandburg for his religious anti-democratic conservatism. Tate frets over the 'official literature' that seems to be coming into force in the patriotic fervour of war (and implicitly laments his own culpability as first Poet Consultant); the editorial ends by dedicating *The Sewanee Review* to keeping alive 'the humane imagination'.[32] The general thrust is conservative, but pitches itself as a resistance to totalitarianism: 'THE SEWANEE REVIEW will oppose, when it is necessary for a literary review to consider politics, the democratic or any other state, if like the fascist state it shall make an all-engrossing demand for our loyalty and shall thus become the national religion.'[33] On the basis of this, one might detect in that New Critical interest in an 'inconclusive dialectic' between doubt and faith in modern poetry a political subplot that is conservative and anti-totalitarian, sceptical of false closures: a politics that has much in common with Eliot's editorial predilections in *The*

---

31 Tate, 'The State of Letters', *The Sewanee Review*, 52.4 (October–December 1944): 608–614 (611).
32 Ibid. 611, 613–614.
33 Tate, 'The State of Letters', 611–612.

Criterion.[34] Not everyone was on board: Evelyn Scott complained in a 1938 letter to Lowell's novelist first wife Jean Stafford, 'All that Tate-Ransom crowd has to revive the "mysteries," in their worst meaning, in order that Tate-Ransom may be sure of dictatorial officiation at the altar.'[35] Similarly, Katherine Anne Porter, while mentioning in passing that 'awful black mean [soul], Lowell, lumps "elegant" Denis Devlin with Saint-John Perse and – the source, perhaps, of the problem – T.S. Eliot, who conjure an image of 'a pack of mournful hounds' howling about 'religious mysticism … myth, the voice of the blood, the will of man to be deceived'.[36]

It is crucial to stress the store set by Allen Tate and his New Critical confreres on control of a journal as a platform and community for their specific intellectual and aesthetic agenda. In 1936, Tate has published in essay 'The Function of the Critical Quarterly' in Warren's *The Southern Review*, which stressed the periodical as the home of 'a critical program', and the promotion of a 'moral and intellectual order' whether or not society was interested or not.[37] As Robert Buffington has examined, Tate had long harboured notions of capturing *The Sewanee Review* since his Agrarian period, and when *The Southern Review* was closed abruptly due to the war, Tate's manoeuvres gathered pace, so that by autumn 1943 he had been offered the editorship, beginning in July 1944. The fact that Tate gave so much space in his first issue to Devlin and Lowell (ten pages of the Perse translations, three to Devlin's original poem, and one to Lowell) suggests that they exemplified the 'critical program' and the aesthetic wing of his envisioned 'moral and intellectual order' as set out in the editorial.

---

34 As Jason Harding writes, the caricature of *The Criterion* that sees it as proto-fascist fails to respond to 'Eliot's editorial determination not to oversimplify difficult and complex areas of politico-cultural exchange'; *The Criterion: Cultural Politics and Periodical Networks in Inter-War Britain* (Oxford: Oxford University Press, 2002), 177.
35 Quoted in Mariani, *Lost Puritan*, 74.
36 Katherine Anne Porter to Glenway Wescott, 19 March 1947, in *Letters of Katherine Anne Porter*, ed. Isabel Bayley (New York: Atlantic Monthly Press, 1990), 335.
37 Quoted in Robert Buffington, 'Allen Tate and the *Sewanee Review*', *The Sewanee Review*, 123.2 (Spring 2015): 240–251 (241).

Even in their titles, Devlin's 'Meditation at Avila' and Lowell's 'Colloquy in Black Rock Connecticut' are strikingly similar: both wed specific places (in Europe, and the US) to co-opted forms drawn from Counter-Reformation Catholic spirituality; Devlin's 'meditation' is suggestive of the contemplative prayer outlined by Saint Theresa of Avila in *The Interior Castle* (1577), while Lowell's 'colloquy' is reminiscent of the personal, intimate imagined conversations with the persons of the Trinity or the Virgin Mary in Saint Ignatius of Loyola's seminal Jesuit treatise, *The Spiritual Exercises* (1522–4). Both poems share remarkable thematic consanguinity, and exemplify, each according to their own lights, a mid-century aesthetic shaped by Tate and New Criticism.

> Magnificence, this terse-lit, star-quartz universe,
> Woe, waste and magnificence, my soul! ...
>
> Dance, the shellfish eaten, dance, the stertorous heels,
> Sensual asseveration of bare thigh:
> I stored her joy in my breast against the future.
> Good night, the husband stands, savouring a well-turned jealousy; the wife
> Goes to him, sleepy and reluctant
> Contempt falls like a shadow between us ...
>
> Nothing between
> Rock and sky.
> Santa Teresa
> Her choirs of leaf-faced monks
> Quavering like plainchant
> Chanting to God to down
> The devil, his works and pomps.
> The blue, absolute blow
> of linear Castilian night
> Cleaves earth and heaven,
> God being star-froze heaven
> And Devil, fluent earth.
> O Santa, Santa Teresa,
> Covetous, burning virgin!
> Scorning to nourish body's
> Farmlands with soul's
> Modulating rains ...[38]

[38] Denis Devlin, 'Meditation at Avila', *The Sewanee Review*, 52.4 (October–December 1944), 530–533. There are small amendments and variances in the version in Tate

Formally, Devlin's poem seems less akin to the rhymed stanzas and concision of 'Lough Derg' extolled by Tate and Warren in the Preface to the *Selected Poems*, and rather owes more to the flexible *vers libre* he had been writing in the 1930s in poems like 'Communications from the Eiffel Tower'. In his radio broadcast 'A Reply to F.R. Higgins' on 4 October 1935, Devlin had stated, 'Poetry is not to be strangled and noosed in rhymes,' a sign of how far the New Critical line had come to influence his work by the early 1940s.[39] Nevertheless, if the lack of end rhymes, and shifts between loose, quasi-alexandrines ('Good night, the husband stands'…) with terse, dactylic trimeter in 'A Meditation at Avila' suggest Devlin's residual modernist tendencies in terms of a *vers libre*, other aspects of the poem more readily exemplify New Critical aesthetics.

The poem's Counter-Reformation theology is sensual and simultaneously remote, so that the 'Castilian night', in that punning aural *traductio* favoured by the New Critics, transforms its 'blue' into 'absolute blow', a violent apprehension of divinity through the natural world's assault on the senses. This force 'cleaves earth and heaven': the word 'cleave', is a Miltonic word that means the opposite of itself, simultaneously 'to cut in two', and 'to cling to or fasten'. As John Leonard points out, Milton's usages of 'cleave' aptly conform to the definition of irony supplied by William Empson, that fellow traveller of New Criticism, in *Some Versions of Pastoral* (1935): 'An irony has no point unless it is true, in some degree, in both senses'.[40] Seventeenth-century wordplay meets New Critical wit in Devlin's use of 'cleave'; he suggests that the 'linear Castilian night' in its sensuous violence holds earth and heaven together, at the same time as the horizon is the point at which the two are cloven apart; by extension, since God is cast as 'star-froze heaven' and the Devil as 'fluent earth', there is a tension – arguably Manichean in both its significances – between a stark division of carnal and spiritual, or their mutual dependence. Thematically,

---

and Warren's *Selected Poems* and subsequent appearances of the poem in collected volumes. Elisions in square brackets indicate my excerpts. Line breaks as in *The Sewanee Review*.
39 See note 19 above.
40 See John Leonard, 'Self-Contradicting Puns in *Paradise Lost*', in *A Companion to Milton*, ed. Thomas N. Corns (Oxford: Blackwell, 2001), 394.

the poem plays on baroque conventions of divine eros and the sensuality of Saint Teresa's religious ecstasy, interweaved with a seamy suggestion of extra-marital *frisson* conducted over shellfish and dancing; Devlin had spent three weeks in Spain in spring 1932 with a friend, the US journalist Sam Pope Brewer, and the 'bare thigh' seems to be a memorized detail rather than mere fancy.[41] At the level of wordplay as well as overarching thematic content, Devlin's poem conducts that 'inconclusive dialectic' between faith and disbelief that Tate found aesthetically (and perhaps politically) appealing.

Lowell's 'Colloquy in Black Rock Connecticut', in contrast to Devlin's prosody which suggests both Irish modernist free verse and elements of Spanish mystical verse, is a frenetic Hopkinsian tour de force:

> *Black Mud*, a name to conjure with: O mud
> For watermelons gutted to the crust,
> Mud for the mole-tide harbour, mud for mouse,
> Mud for the armoured Diesel fishing tubs that thud,
> A year and a day, to wind and tide; the dust
> Is on this skipping heart that shakes my house,
>
> House of our Saviour who was hanged till death.
> My heart, beat faster, faster. In Black Mud
> Martyre Stephen was broken down to blood:
> Our ransom is the rubble of his death.
>
> Christ walks on water. In Black Mud
> Darts the Kingfisher. On Corpus Christi, heart,
> Over the drum-beat of St. Stephen's choir
> I hear Him, Stupor Mundi, and the mud
> Flew from His burning wings and beak, my heart,
> The blue Kingfisher dives on you through fire.[42]

---

41 For the biographical context of the poem, see Brian Coffey, 'Of Denis Devlin: Vestiges, Sentences, Presages', *Poetry Ireland Review* 75 (Winter 2002/3): 82–100 (85).

42 Robert Lowell, 'Colloquy in Black Rock Connecticut', *The Sewanee Review* 52.4 (October–December 1944): 534. Lowell subsequently revised the poem for its appearance in *Lord Weary's Castle*.

Here, Lowell's favoured canzone rhyme scheme, that plays a *rime riche* ('death', 'Mud', 'blood') recurrent throughout the poem off the stanzaic rhyme schemes, operates within a much stricter form and iambic metre than Devlin. The poem compounds Christian martyrology with rhythmic effects and symbolism adopted from Gerard Manley Hopkins (especially 'As Kingfishers Catch Fire'), charged by Lowell's personal circumstances as a 'fire-breathing Catholic C.O.', as he puts it in a later poem, 'Memories of West Street and Lepke'. Lowell has just finished his sentence for draft resistance ('a year and a day' in the poem is a nod and a wink to that sentence, with the extra day making him a felon in the eyes of the law). After his release, he worked as an orderly in a Catholic cadet nurses' dormitory in Black Rock, where the mud flats gathered nearby St Stephen's Catholic Church.[43] The poem elevates Black Rock's working-class Hungarian reverence of Saint Stephen into a Joycean celebration of the suffering artist: 'I, the stunned machine of your devotion, / Clanging upon this cymbal of a hand, / Am rattled screw and footloose'. While Lowell affected in a letter to Babette Deutsch that 'Colloquy' was 'the only poem that came to me Wordsworthian-wise – walking', the intricacy of the rhyme and the rhythmic mimesis suggest painstaking labour.[44] Mariani writes 'it is a poem of pain and exultation which threatens to explode beyond its formal restraints at any moment'.[45] It is perhaps this mixture of strictness and inebriation that Lowell's poem shares with the latent Irish modernist tendencies of Devlin's poem being channelled into a newfound interest in the formalism of mid-century US poetry.

Like 'Meditation at Avila', 'Colloquy at Black Rock Connecticut' conducts a grim, ambiguous polka around whether faith redeems life's detritus, or whether the poet is circumscribed by mortal flesh and, like Saint Stephen, doomed to be 'broken down to blood'. If its rhythms dare to 'explode beyond its formal constraint', it remains within New Critical precepts on unity, autonomy and the poem as 'a complex of attitudes'.[46] Tate

---

43 See the notes to the poem in Lowell, *Collected Poems*, 1007.
44 Quoted in Mariani, *Lost Puritan*, 116.
45 Ibid.
46 The phrase is from Cleanth Brooks, *The Well Wrought Urn: Studies in the Structure of Poetry* (1947; rpt London: Dobson, 1949), 175.

accepted both poems as centrepieces for his maiden issue, as each in its own way (as I have endeavoured to show) closely adheres to a mid-century US poetic that was being formulated and consolidated through the auspices of the poet-editors and teachers associated with New Criticism. The 1944 winter issue of *The Sewanee Review* may be seen as a key moment in the development of both Devlin and Lowell, a point of convergence after which they would increasingly diverge: Devlin, the Irish modernist whose mature work would increasingly conform to a New Critical aesthetic, although not without a backward glance to the experimentalism of his youth, while Lowell was the youthful poster-boy whose precocious success would consolidate the arrival of New Criticism's pre-eminence for only a brief while before he came to see it as inhibiting and passé.

'Colloquy' was one of a handful of poems from Lowell's forthcoming second collection *Lord Weary's Castle* (which carried several over from *Land of Unlikeness*); Lowell would win a Pulitzer for the book in 1947. Randall Jarrell admired the poem enough that even though it had already appeared in *The Sewanee Review*, he would publish it with a clutch of new poems from the forthcoming collection in *The Nation*, which he had taken up the reins of editing after his discharge from the army.[47] Reviewing *Lord Weary's Castle* in that magazine, Jarrell commended 'Colloquy' for 'some of the most successful kinaesthetic effects in English', adding: 'Mr. Lowell's poetry is a unique fusion of modernist and traditional poetry, and there exist side by side in it certain effects that one would have thought mutually exclusive; but it is essentially a post- or anti-modernist poetry, and as such is certain to be influential.'[48]

Jarrell's tentative designation of Lowell's poetry as 'post-modern' never quite struggles out of the shadow of his earlier statement, that *Lord Weary's Castle* weds modernism and traditional poetry, a fusion that Tate had made his poetic embassy. Nevertheless, the ghost-phrase shows the depths of Jarrell's critical intuition. Lowell's subsequent development into what many critics consider his major work in *Life Studies* and subsequent volumes

---

47 Mariani, *Lost Puritan*, 135.
48 The review is reprinted in Randall Jarrell, *Poetry and the Age* (1955; rpt London: Faber and Faber, 1973), 194.

witnessed a repudiation of the wracked formalism and religious fervour of his early poetry. The albatross label 'Confessionalism' that came to be so readily identified with Lowell's work nevertheless indicated the extent to which he seemed, all of a sudden, to eschew masks and the mediating presence of historical density, and deal nakedly with the troubling matter of his personal life. In fact, the break was never so decisive; at any rate, it was arguably a blend of the tight formalism, his way with violent history in the early poetry with the brash confidence in facing the personal and quotidian in his mature work that made the greatest impact on the generation after him, which included the Northern Irish poets, Seamus Heaney, Michael Longley, and Derek Mahon. Meanwhile, the field of Irish poetry at large remained ignorant of Denis Devlin, whose *Collected Poems* edited by Brian Coffey was published by Dolmen Press in 1964 to little fanfare outside the small avant-garde circle associated with Michael Smith and Trevor Joyce's New Writers' Press.[49]

There remains but a brief postscript to this sketch of a mid-century New Critical milieu and aesthetic that encompassed Devlin and Lowell, one that picks up that other key strand besides formalism and the value placed on a vexed articulation of religious faith: namely, Devlin and Lowell being 'tempted by other languages'. In the early 1950s, Lowell and his second wife Elizabeth Hardwick would travel extensively throughout Europe. They spent considerable stretches of this three-year-long grand tour in Rome, which after the war had become an 'open city' for American writers, with both Warren and Tate visiting for extended periods from the late 1940s onwards. He visited the agnostic-Catholic philosopher George Santayana, whom he described in a memoir as 'gentle, sceptical, faithless, he might have recognised the metaphysical feudal Virgin of Henry Adams.'[50] In a letter to Peter Taylor several years later, Lowell would recall with fondness 'an all-Irish New Years at Denis Devlin's'.[51] 'As the Italian novelist Ignazio Silone wrote after Devlin's death, the Embassy in Ireland during the 1950s 'had become a pleasant meeting-place where various Italian writers and poets

49 See Davis, *A Broken Line*, 126–135.
50 Lowell, *Collected Prose*, 206.
51 Robert Lowell to Peter Taylor, 31 October 1958, in *The Letters of Robert Lowell*, ed. Saskia Hamilton (New York: Farrar, Straus and Giroux, 2005), 329.

could come together', attracted there by 'the human personality of Denis Devlin'.⁵² Lowell's friend, Theodore Roethke, dedicated an unpublished poem to Devlin after a visit in July 1956 that manages to capture the atmosphere of the Embassy at that time and Devlin's magnetism: 'The Dancing Man (In Memoriam: Denis Devlin, poet and Irish Minister to the Italian Republic, after an evening in which he outdanced everyone)'.⁵³ Such an environment could only have proven fertile inspiration for the ambitious Lowell to delve further into European poetry, a course of reading that would result in his idiosyncratic processes of translation and adaptation in both *Life Studies* and *Imitations*.

Lowell also stayed for ten days with Princess Caetani at her castello in the Latium hills; born Marguerite Chapin in the US, Caetani was the half-sister of Katherine Biddle, and like her, a patron of literary arts. The Princess edited an influential new bi-annual journal *Botteghe Oscure*, named after the arched street in Rome where medieval apothecaries sold wares from windowless shops, and where its editorial office was based. Like its predecessor *Commerce*, Caetani's postwar journal was staunchly internationalist, emphasized work in translation, and subscribed to Madame de Staël's apothegm 'the commerce of ideas is the one that grants most certain profit.'⁵⁴ In a letter to Elizabeth Bishop on 24 April 1951, Lowell mentions his visit to the Princess, 'a mad, sympathetic aristocratic Mrs. Ames ... she thinks of nothing except her magazine – like an only child, a simile I understand so well.'⁵⁵ It would be 1959 before Caetani published Lowell's poetry in *Botteghe Oscure*, having turned down his poem on Ford Madox Ford despite, as he told Ezra Pound, 'begging me for five years for anything, anything.'⁵⁶

---

52 Ignazio Silone, untitled tribute, *Éire/Ireland* 493 (5 September 1960): 4.
53 See James Richard McLeod, *Theodore Roethke: A Manuscript Checklist* (Kent, OH: Kent State University Press, 1971), 65.
54 In writing this essay, I have been indebted to an excellent article on Caetani and the *Botteghe Oscure*: Lorenzo Salvagni, 'The Caetani-Mathews Papers: Introducing René Char to the American Readership', *altrelettre*, 28 May 2014, DOI: 10.5903/al_uhz-20. Quoted on page 10. Accessed 30 January 2018.
55 Lowell to Bishop, 24 April 1951, in *The Letters of Robert Lowell*, 171.
56 Lowell to Pound, 25 March 1954, in *The Letters of Robert Lowell*, 227.

Lowell has a brief cameo in the Princess's US ambitions that once again draws him into connection with Devlin. In the tenth volume of the journal published in autumn 1952, there appeared a long section of the lapidary poetry by the French poet René Char alongside an English translation by Devlin and Jackson Mathews, a professor at the University of Washington. From an extensive study of both the Caetani and Mathews papers, Lorenzo Salvagni has convincingly argued that Caetani acted as an enthusiastic 'agent in the collaboration between Mathews and Char'.[57] At some point after the autumn issue, Devlin was side-lined from further projects involving Char, a fact that Salvagni deals with briskly: 'the American [Mathews] was more suited to the task, given his deep knowledge of French poetry and his previous work in the field of French-English translation'.[58] Nevertheless, as so often with slights in the literary world, the fallout seems to have been more complicated. According to Salvagni, Mathews, with the backing of Caetani (and presumably Char), adopted 'a two-pronged attack' to secure an American publisher for a volume of Char's poetry translated by Mathews: Caetani would forward offprints of the Devlin and Mathews' translations in *Botteghe Oscure*, and Mathews would follow up with a letter to editors.[59] They first approached Lowell's publisher, Robert Giroux. On 12 January 1953, Mathews wrote:

> Dear Mr. Giroux, You will perhaps have received from Princess Caetani an offprint of Botteghe Oscure, containing a selection of poems by the French poet René Char translated by Denis Devlin and myself. I hope you may also have seen Genêt's 'Letter from Paris' in The New Yorker for January 10th, which speaks of Char's leadership of living French poets. I am at present translating with the help of Char and Signora Caetani a good-sized volume of his work, and we wish to propose that Harcourt Brace publish it.[60]

---

57 Salvagni, 'The Caetani-Mathews Papers', p. 15. Salvagni suggests in a footnote that Allen Tate probably introduced Caetani and Mathews, and, grand old actor-manager that he was, it seems likely that if it wasn't Katherine Biddle or Saint-John Perse, Tate may have put Caetani in touch with Devlin, 'The Caetani-Mathews Papers', 29n16.
58 Ibid. 15.
59 Ibid. 15–16.
60 Ibid. 16.

What Mathews conveniently glosses over in the letter is the relationship of his earlier collaborative translation with Devlin to the proposed US volume. Roger Little, the editor of Devlin's translations in English, notes that all nineteen of the translations for *Botteghe Oscure*, on the evidence of Devlin's papers in the National Library of Ireland, are Devlin's work with little or no input from Mathews; further, he quotes an unfortunately undated letter from Mathews to Caetani (which Salvagni neglects to mention): 'I thought you'd have seen the *New Yorker* article, so didn't send it yesterday. Devlin will be more furious yet – or perhaps he won't mind? I was a bit taken aback myself – he'll never speak to me.'[61]

The New Yorker piece is almost certainly the 'Letter from Paris' review article by Jean Genet, published 10 January 1953, of Volume X of *Botteghe Oscure* that Mathews alludes to in the Giroux letter. Genêt writes of the 'considerable animation in poetry circles on seeing the first big selection of Char's work for foreign consumption – thirty-five pages, half in French, half in spirited English translation by Professor Jackson Mathews, of Washington State University ... in the autumn issue of *Botteghe Oscure*'.[62] Might Genêt have been sent an offprint as part of Caetani and Mathews' US operation, and his oversight in failing to mention Devlin as a collaborator – indeed, if Little is correct, sole translator – follow their lead?

Mathews would remain fidgety about his role in manoeuvring Devlin out of the picture; when Giroux turned down the project, he approached David McDowell at Random House, who was enthusiastic, although the deal dragged on for several years. As late as March 1956, the year that the volume, entitled *Hypnos Waking*, was finally published by Random House, Mathews was shilly-shallying in a letter to McDowell over Devlin's role in the translations:

> All the poems published in Botteghe X were translated by Denis Devlin and me in collaboration. I have so completely re-worked the translations, changing the titles of three in English, that I am sure Denis Devlin would not want his name attached and they can be considered original translations. But I don't know whether one can

---

61 Quoted in Denis Devlin, *Translations into English*, ed. Roger Little (Dublin: Dedalus Press, 1992), 327.
62 Jean Genet, 'Letter from Paris', *The New Yorker* (10 January 1953): 62–67 (66).

properly say they were published in Botteghe X. It is a bit of a dilemma, don't you think?[63]

Robert Lowell had broached the 'dilemma' with Mathews three years earlier. Mathews' initial approach to Giroux had enlisted the bona fides of both Tate and Lowell, who was fresh from his stay with Princess Caetani. In an uncollected letter to Mathews (dated 'March 3rd 1952', but given the chronology, a certain typo, written in 1953), Lowell writes that he has sent a note of support to Giroux, advising that Mathews try to secure an introduction by Saint-John Perse. At the end of the letter, he writes:

> Didn't you think the Princess was a bit lofty with Denis Devlin? She'd been urging him to do some translations for years, what he did was certainly a labour of love. He's quite offended, not at you, but at her. I thought the poems read pretty well in English. There's a certain vibrance and concision in the French, that I would imagine untranslatable.[64]

In the most diplomatic way, Lowell seems to be taking the cause of the side-lined Devlin, praising his translations as good English versions, measured against the 'untranslatable' qualities of the original. In this casual defence of his friend, the older Irish modernist who had studied so intently the European poetic tradition, one may detect the inchoate principles by which Lowell – as he had already demonstrated in poems such as 'The Ghost (after Sextus Propertius)' – would set about his incredible 1961 volume *Imitations*, which subjected classical and European models to a process of poetic, rather than merely linguistic, translation. As he wrote in his Introduction: 'Boris Pasternak has said that the usual reliable translator gets the literal meaning but misses the tone, and that in poetry tone is of course everything.'[65] His letter to Mathews, couched

---

63   Jackson Mathews to David McDowell, 7 March 1956, in the Jackson Mathews Papers, the Southern Historical Collection, the Wilson Library, University of North Carolina, Chapel Hill, 4012 3.3.1/79.
64   Robert Lowell to Jackson Mathews, 3 March 1952 [1953], in the Jackson Mathews Papers, the Southern Historical Collection, the Wilson Library, University of North Carolina, Chapel Hill, 4012 3.3.1/76.
65   Robert Lowell, 'Introduction', *Imitations* (London: Faber and Faber, 1962 [first published 1961]), xi.

in courtesy, suggests that the Princess has missed the *tone* of Devlin's achievement.[66]

In their attraction to European poetry (and comparable approaches to translation), their complicated developments in terms of poetic form, and the highly charged grappling with Catholicism that informs their poetry, Devlin and Lowell exemplified the literary currents of a specific transatlantic literary milieu (with Washington, DC, and Rome as centres). Their publications in Tate's *The Sewanee Review*, and the suggestive affinities between their work in the mid-1940s, mark what was simultaneously a watershed and the high-point of a rampant New Critical aesthetic, a literary network that had managed to enlist a young tyro of American letters, and a doyen of Irish modernism.

---

[66] This is not to argue that Devlin is inattentive to the literal; Roger Little writes of 'the fine balance of modesty and creativity' in Devlin's translation; in 'Saint-John Perse and Denis Devlin: A "Compagnonnage"', *Irish University Review* 8.2 (autumn 1978): 193–200 (195).

STEPHEN GRACE

'thudding in a big sea': The Oceanic Ecologies of Robert Lowell and Seamus Heaney

In his memorial address for Robert Lowell, Seamus Heaney praised his American forebear's 'amphibious ability to plunge into the downward reptilian welter of the self and yet raise himself with whatever knowledge he gained there out on to the hard ledges of the historical present, which he then apprehended with refreshed insight and intensity.'[1] More than just an eloquent tribute, Heaney's comments sketch out the poles, of self and history, within which both he and Lowell have often been read: Lowell as the bearer of a famous American name, an archetypal public poet declaiming on the great issues of his times, but also as the author of *Life Studies*, that key foundational text of 'confessionalism'; Heaney as the poet of the Northern Irish Troubles and representative voice of Catholic Ulster, but also as the poet of rural childhood. What I want to suggest is that, in addition to self and history, we can read both Lowell and Heaney in terms of ecology. More specifically, and picking up on the aqueous drift of Heaney's metaphor, we can read them in terms of an oceanic ecology. By drawing in particular on Steve Mentz's book *Shipwreck Modernity*, I will argue that 'the downward reptilian welter' is less a mark of the self, and more the trace of an unsettlingly alien, radically non-human environment; or, to put it more precisely, the complex, shifting, unstable, and asymmetrical hybrid environment that is constituted by the human and the non-human. In what follows

1 'On Robert Lowell', *The New York Review of Books* (9 February 1978), available online at <http://www.nybooks.com/articles/1978/02/09/on-robert-lowell/> (accessed 10 October 2017).

I will consider how this hybrid environment is not only described by Lowell and Heaney, but also embodied in their poetic forms.

In *Shipwreck Modernity*, Mentz argues for the centrality of the ocean to our concept of the environment, for a blue ecology, in contrast to the more familiar green ecologies. This has obvious practical relevance, both now and in the past. As Mentz notes, the ocean 'cover[s] more than two-thirds of the earth', 'worldwide blue-water trade routes became essential to European economies' from the fifteenth-century onwards, and 'Oceangoing ships and voyages generated the global ecology in which all material things in the world – animals, plants, viruses, cultures – were distributed around the globe'.[2] Focusing on the period 1550–1719, Mentz argues that although the ocean is bound up with the human institutions and practises of sea-faring and trade, this period of 'early globalization was fundamentally ecological in nature'; that is to say, human engagement with the ocean gave out on to a radically non-human environment.[3] Ocean journeys did not just bring geographically dispersed human populations in to contact, but also, as Mentz points out, 'animals, plants, viruses' and other non-human life.[4] Furthermore, the sheer size and scope of the ocean disrupts human scales of measurement and value, and can be threatening to human bodies. The precarious position of the human in the non-human furnishes Mentz with the shipwreck of his title, and he argues that '[t]he threat of shipwreck makes the ocean itself an essential actor in this historical drama [...] the inhospitable sea represents the most powerful nonhuman actor in world history. Attending to the global force of the sea applies posthuman ecological pressure to the historical experiences of globalization'.[5] The ocean is not simply space to be traversed, but has a certain degree of resistance, and perhaps even agency, that runs counter to human motives and actions. It is an 'actor', even if the agency it possesses is not quite the same as a human agency and, in fact, might require us to rethink the concept of agency. In addition to its literal meaning, Mentz's

2   Mentz, *Shipwreck Modernity: Ecologies of Globalization 1550–1719* (Minneapolis: The University of Minnesota Press, 2015), 2.
3   Ibid.
4   Ibid.
5   Ibid.

shipwreck also has metaphoric resonances, and he suggests that the experience of immersion in a disorderly, confusing, and alien element models our lived sense of time, both as individuals and collectives, or what Mentz calls 'the suddenness of lived experience [...] the thrown-into feeling of entanglement within an always moving historical now [...] That fluctuating and recurring *now* marks the polyepochal time of shipwreck'.[6] The experience of being in history, then, is like the experience of being immersed in the ocean.

Mentz's sense of ecological history can be contrasted with more human-oriented accounts of the ocean. In the introduction to their essay collection *Sea-Changes: Historicizing the Ocean* Bernhard Klein and Gesa Mackenthun invoke Derek Walcott's poem 'The Sea is History'. They argue that Walcott's 'poetic metaphor works to restore the sea to the dynamics of the historical process, energizing it for the task of re-imagining, re-writing, and re-membering the past as a complex and polysemic dialogue, a meeting place of different cultures rather than solely the battleground of antagonistic forces'.[7] This multi-sided, multi-voiced ocean is historical and cultural. It is defined in terms of human processes – re-imagining, re-writing, dialogue – and resists earlier, non-historical, constructions of the sea as either 'a demonic and anti-human principle' or 'an atemporal figure of forgetting and oblivion'.[8] Though Klein and Mackenthun are surely right to interrogate mythologized accounts that render the ocean 'demonic' and 'atemporal', their insistence on the ocean's historicity is an insistence on human historicity. It overlooks the non-human environment. Mentz's notion of 'ecological pressure', however, makes space for these 'non-human actor[s]', such as the ocean, and in doing so offers a fuller understanding of history.

Klein also alludes to Walcott's 'The Sea is History' in his observations about the changing nature of Heaney's historic imagination. Noting the shift in Heaney's work from the violence of his earlier bog-poems, which meditate on historical atrocities, to his later, more reconciliatory writing,

---

6   Ibid. xi.
7   Bernhard Klein, and Gesa Mackenthun, eds, *Sea Changes: Historicizing the Ocean* (London: Routledge, 2004), 2.
8   Ibid. 1–2.

Klein describes the bog as 'an uninhabitable space, a realm of the dead not of the living' whose chief attribute is stasis: 'there is preservation, no end of preservation, only no change'.[9] Heaney's post-bog poems, Klein goes on to say, have

> more or less renounced his poetic desire to stare at the dead in awe and fascination in favour of the much more difficult task of dialogue. This Dantesque dialogue with the dead – which dominates collections such as *Field Work* (1979) and *Station Island* (1984) – is frequently set in a self-consciously liminal, intermediary or transitional location, far away from the bog: the beach, strand, or coast.[10]

He goes on to compare Heaney's later, post-bog work with 'Derek Walcott, whose poetic historiography takes the sea as its paradigmatic figure of history – in poems such as "The Sea is History" – thus championing a space in which memory sinks to the ground and is forgotten […] and which privileges the fluidity of change over the historian's demand for preservation'.[11] To an extent, this is a well-worn critical narrative, with the 1979 collection *Field Work* at its heart. That book was written in the years in which the friendship between Lowell and Heaney was at its closest, critics such as Henry Hart, Neil Corcoran, and Stephen James have identified it as Heaney's most Lowellian volume, and Heaney suggests that Lowell's influence on his work was strongest at that point: 'Lowell didn't make his presence felt in the way I wrote until […] the blank-verse sonnets started to avalanche down upon us out of *History* and *The Dolphin* and the book *For Lizzie and Harriet*'.[12] What I intend to argue is that Lowell's presence complicates the prevailing arc of Heaney's career, that *Field Work* is permeated by an oceanic ecology that comes out of Lowell's influence, and that this ecology is closer to Mentz's in- or post-human ocean than Klein's historicized one.

---

9   Klein, *On the Uses of History in Recent Irish Writing* (Manchester: Manchester University Press, 2007), 139.
10 Ibid.
11 Ibid.
12 Dennis O'Driscoll, and Seamus Heaney, *Stepping Stones: Interviews with Seamus Heaney* (London: Faber and Faber, 2009), 147.

'a deep no sound': The Inhuman Ocean

Lowell was a great poet of the ocean. His sense of personal and collective history is deeply conditioned by the Atlantic, and his work is replete with ships, swells, squalls, and shore-lines. His signature early work, 'The Quaker Graveyard in Nantucket', is a poem of shipwrecks, and immerses its readers in the shock of a non-human otherness, an alien environment, that Mentz attributes to the ocean:

> Sailors, who pitch this portent at the sea
> Where dreadnaughts shall confess
> Its hell-bent deity,
> When you are powerless
> To sand-bag this Atlantic bulwark, faced
> By the earth-shaker, green, unwearied, chaste
> In his steel scales: ask for no Orphean lute
> To pluck life back. The guns of the steeled fleet
> Recoil and then repeat
> The hoarse salute.[13]

Ostensibly about Warren Winslow, Lowell's cousin who died when his Naval destroyer suffered an explosion and sank in New York harbour during the Second World War, 'The Quaker Graveyard' also takes in the story of Ahab and the *Pequod* in *Moby-Dick,* and the historical voyages of Quaker and other nineteenth-century whalers. These narratives so thoroughly saturate 'The Quaker Graveyard' that it is difficult to find a foothold from which to try and make sense of it. This is as much a matter of form, as content. Nick Halpern argues that the poem is 'turbulent' and 'joltingly expressive', and that such disorientation is a consequence of Lowell's line breaks: 'The enjambment is relentless: neither the end of the line nor the end of the stanza can impede the poetic line. Neither can any reservation, emotional or intellectual: if the poet feels hesitations or second thoughts, they find no place in the poem.'[14] The relentlessness of

---

13 Lowell, *Collected Poems* (London: Faber and Faber, 2003), 14.
14 Nick Halpern, *Everyday and Prophetic: the Poetry of Lowell, Ammons, Merrill, and Rich* (Madison: University of Wisconsin Press, 2003), 52.

the enjambment is mimetic of the ocean, in that it creates and heightens chaos and confusion. So too is another Lowell trademark, the adjectival run ('green, unwearied, chaste'). Adam Kirsch writes that 'nothing is more characteristic of his work than his largesse with adjectives, often dispensed three at a time', and, in the context of this largesse, notes that Lowell in later life recalled himself as being 'full of Miltonic, vaguely piratical ambitions' and argues that the '"piratical" – a heedless energy, a doubtfully heroic violence – is the most commanding element in Lowell's poetry, from beginning to end. It is this rhythmic and linguistic energy, more than even the most personal subject matter, that makes his poems immediately recognisable'.[15] Lowell's adjectives and enjambment, then, are continuous with such piratical impulses, and give expression to the ocean's chaotic and tumultuous energies. They model the experience of shipwreck.

Lowell attributes the piratical impulse to himself, and the clamour of 'The Quaker Graveyard' could be read as continuous with the poet's state of mind, rather than any external environment. Whilst some of the violence in 'The Quaker Graveyard' can be attributed to this self-aggrandizement, there are also aspects of the poem's language that seem to run beyond the control of its speaker, and stem from the ocean, rather than the sailors attempting to master it. These sailors are presented as 'powerless', and the tolling adjectival list 'green, unwearied, chaste' is applied to 'the earth-shaker', to the ocean itself, and not to humans. Those adjectives, for all that they reveal about Lowell himself, also point to what eludes him. Their excess implies an inability on the part of form to match content, implies that some aspect of the 'real' world always remains outside the poem and the poet, who must then continually generate more and more language in an effort to snare that reality. Heaney, writing of 'The Quaker Graveyard', said that 'It is thrilling to put out in these conditions, to feel what Yeats called "the stirring of the beast", to come into the presence of sovereign diction and experience the tread of something metrical, conscious and implacable'.[16]

15 Adam Kirsch, *The Wounded Surgeon: Confession and Transformation in Six American poets: Robert Lowell, Elizabeth Bishop, John Berryman, Randall Jarrell, Delmore Schwartz, and Sylvia Plath* (New York: W.W. Norton & Co, 2005), 3–4.
16 Heaney, *Finders Keepers: Selected Prose 1971–2001* (London: Faber and Faber, 2002), 208.

The majority of Heaney's terms here imply an agency beyond that of the poet. Language is 'sovereign' and 'implacable', so that when Heaney also describes it as 'conscious' the consciousness is not that of the poet, but of something else, of 'the beast' stirring beyond Lowell's control.

For all that he admires 'The Quaker Graveyard', this is a sound that Heaney seems to want to get away from, preferring, in 'Lowell's Command', the 'self-denial' and 'readiness *not* to commandeer the poetic event' of later poems such as 'Fall 1961' and 'Epilogue'.[17] Heaney frames this transition as the kind of narrative arc through which his own career has been understood, and in one sense his account of Lowell is an account of how he would like to read. He notes 'the not uncommon spectacle of a poet with just such a dear-won individual style facing into his forties and knowing it will all have to be done again,'[18] and praises Lowell's ability to re-invent himself. While the non-human, oceanic environment changes, however, it never really goes away. This non-human activity continues to occur throughout Lowell's work, though not always as loudly as in 'The Quaker Graveyard', and even in those quieter poems that Heaney most praises. The ocean's peculiar immersive shock can still be heard in Lowell's poems, even when they seem to have left saltwater tumult far behind. The late poem 'Epilogue', for example, has Lowell

> Pray for the grace of accuracy
> Vermeer gave to the sun's illumination
> stealing like the tide across a map
> to his girl solid with yearning[19]

We might read this graceful accuracy as a move out of the sea entirely, from a destructive immersion in the oceanic elements to an orderly re-imagining of those elements in the artistic representation of Vermeer and Lowell himself. And yet that welter, with its strange, non-human energies, recurs here too. Lowell's piratical impulses are not completely silent but rather they have become quieter: a little earlier in the poem Lowell writes that 'sometimes everything I write /…/ seems a snapshot, / lurid,

---

17   Ibid. 217.
18   Ibid. 208
19   Lowell, *Collected Poems*, 838.

rapid, garish, grouped',[20] again employing his signature adjectival run, and whilst 'solid' seems well-weighed it quickly gives out on to the more restless 'yearning'. Perhaps most telling of all, the locution 'stealing like the tide' reintroduces the transgressive, commandeering aspect of Lowell's writing, equating artistic representation to an act of appropriation that is explicitly connected to the sea. This is all deftly and subtly done, unlike the big, booming cadences of 'The Quaker Graveyard', but it demonstrates that Lowell's oceanic tang, the flavour of the non-human, never really left his writing.

Something of the ocean's non-human, ecological presence can be seen in Heaney's 'Elegy' for Lowell, in which he imagines Lowell as

> helmsman, netsman, *retiarius*.
> That hand. Warding and grooming
> and amphibious.
>
> Two a.m., seaboard weather.
> Not the proud sail of your great verse …
> No. You were our night ferry
> thudding in a big sea,
>
> the whole craft ringing
> with an armourer's music
> the course set wilfully across
> the ungovernable and dangerous.[21]

Henry Hart rightly notes Heaney's ambivalence in the poem, writing that 'Enthralled by Lowell, he identifies with the other Irishmen "enthralled" by imperial conquerors and distrusts his reverence. Lowell and his art appear as a figurative ship mastering the "ungovernable" Irish sea, a sea that Heaney has historical reasons to fear.'[22] For Heaney the ocean is a source of 'fear' because it enables the contact with those conquerors who despoil indigenous peoples of their homes and lands. Such conquest is understood as being continuous with Lowell's imperious expansion of

20 Ibid.
21 Heaney, *Field Work*, 32.
22 Henry Hart, *Seamus Heaney: Poet of Contrary Progressions* (Syracuse, NY: Syracuse University Press, 1992), 124–125.

self, and the former potentially has its roots in the latter. Approached in this way 'Elegy' becomes an 'allegory of invasion and conquest',[23] as Hart puts it.

Such a reading places Lowell, Heaney, and the Irish sea, in an explicitly postcolonial context, in which the predominate relationship is that of colonizer and colonized, and whilst this a prominent aspect of the poem, it overlooks the non-human oceanic presences that ghost through the language. Stephen James, in commenting upon this poem, suggests that 'helmsman, netsman' 'seem to step from the pages of "The Quaker Graveyard in Nantucket"',[24] and, though not adjectives, the tripartite list has something of Lowell's Atlantic clamour about it, a whiff of salt-water tumult. Similarly, the enjambment drives the poem on so that its rhythms come to sound 'wilful', and even potentially 'ungovernable'. Lowell himself, though ostensibly downsized to a 'night ferry', is still imagined as 'thudding in a big sea', a suitably forceful verb, even if it is shorn of glamour and grandeur.

In another poem, one of the celebrated 'Glanmore Sonnets', Heaney similarly looks to control and harness the wilder Lowellian energies:

> Dogger, Rockall, Malin, Irish Sea:
> Green, swift upsurges, North Atlantic flux
> Conjured by that strong gale-warning voice,
> Collapse into a sibilant penumbra.
> Midnight and closedown. Sirens of the tundra,
> Of eel-road, seal-road, keel-road, whale-road, raise
> Their wind-compounded keen behind the baize
> And drive the trawlers to the lee of Wicklow.
> *L'Etoile, Le Guillemot, La Belle Hélène*
> Nursed their bright names this morning in the bay
> That toiled like mortar. It was marvellous
> And actual, I said out loud, 'A haven,'
> The word deepening, clearing, like the sky
> Elsewhere on Minches, Cromarty, The Faroes.[25]

---

23   Ibid. 124.
24   Stephen James, *Shades of Authority: The Poetry of Lowell, Hill and Heaney* (Liverpool: Liverpool University Press, 2007), 174.
25   *Field Work*, 39.

This sonnet, one of the wettest in *Field Work*, is set in the heart of Lowell country, in the 'North Atlantic flux', and Lowell himself seems to lurk somewhere behind 'that strong gale-warning voice'. Indeed, Heaney's 'whale-road' echoes, among other sources, Lowell's own use of that phrase in 'The Quaker Graveyard', and the positioning of the verb 'raise' at the end of line 6, marked off by a heavy caesura, recalls similar manoeuvers in Lowell's writing ('chaste' and 'faced', in the passage quoted above, for example'). The opening line, too, employs a kind of incantation whose repetitions are similar to those of Lowell's adjectival lists, and its potent, forceful rhythms anticipate the 'Green, swift upsurges' that follow in the rest of the poem.

Or, at least, that follow in the rest of the sonnet's octave. Following the turn in line 9, another incantation, in French this time, Heaney lightens – or dries – the poem's sestet, whose procedures are closer to a poem like 'Epilogue' than 'The Quaker Graveyard'. Modifiers like 'bright', 'marvellous', and 'actual' are more in the spirit of the finely tuned adjectives used in that later Lowell poem. Similarly, Heaney's listing is less piratical, and more sonorous. In 'Feeling into Words' he suggests that his poetic sensibility '[might have] began with the exotic listing on the wireless dial: Stuttgart, Leipzig, Oslo, Hilversum. Maybe it was stirred by the beautiful sprung rhythms of the old BBC weather forecast: Dogger, Rockall, Malin, Faroes, Finisterre'.[26] These listings do not have quite the recklessness of a Lowellian adjectival chain, or the headlong plunge of some of his enjambments. Then again, not every Lowell poem employs adjectives and enjambment in this manner, and if Heaney's language is usually more controlled and balanced, it too retains the capacity to open out on to strange and potentially unsettling perspectives. This 'exotic listing' is incantatory, and has the power to conjure strange and distant places, so that 'the Faroes' at the conclusion of 'Glanmore VII' unexpectedly and uncannily conjures the presence of Ancient Egypt on the Irish coast.

The incantatory energies that permeate 'Glanmore VII' also occur in the sequence's opening sonnet, the poem that immediately follows 'Elegy' in *Field Work*:

---

26 *Finders Keepers*, 17.

> The mildest February for twenty years
> Is mist bands over furrows, a deep no sound
> Vulnerable to distant gargling tractors.
> Our road is steaming, the turned-up acres breathe.
> Now the good life could be to cross a field
> And art a paradigm of earth new from the lathe
> Of ploughs.[27]

Though this is Heaney at his most richly pastoral, this sonnet is importantly ghosted by the presence of the ocean, and an oceanic ecology, a ghosting that revolves around the phrase 'a deep no sound'. The primary meaning of 'deep', when used as a noun, refers to the deep parts of a river or sea, a usage that predates its terrestrial equivalents, while 'sound' refers to a strait or large inlet of an ocean. These two words are complicatedly separated by 'no', and its status is difficult to place. When first reading the poem I thought 'no' modified 'sound', and was to be contrasted with the nounal 'deep', a relationship that would become apparent in the subsequent lines: a deep no sound could fill, or a deep no sound approaches, or some other syntactic variety in which a verb specifies the particulars of the connection between the two nouns. What Heaney offers in place of that verb is an adjective, 'Vulnerable', which forces us to look back at the preceding phrase and read it not as two contrasted nouns, 'deep' and 'sound', but rather as a single noun phrase, 'a deep no-sound', in which what had looked like a noun ('deep') becomes an adjective, and what had seemed to be an adjective ('no') forms a compound noun ('no-sound'). In the process, 'no' acquires significantly more emphasis than it would have carried had Heaney used a more syntactically predictable structure: as a modifier for 'sound', 'no' might have borne a little extra weight, but as the first part of a newly fashioned compound, it seems to actively demand a heavy stress, to invite being read as '*no*' rather than just as 'no'.

Heaney's language here stages the elusive agency of the non-human environment. The oceanic undertones of 'a deep no sound' are significant. Heaney's 'deep no sound' is continuous with the more landed 'mist bands over furrows', which are themselves identified with 'The mildest

---

27 Heaney, *Field Work*, 33.

February for twenty years'. This is landed, terrestrial poetry. Not only is Heaney in an explicitly rural setting, but both 'mildest' and 'twenty years' imply human scales of value. February is mild from the perspective of the farmers for whom it is usually an unproductively harsh month, and twenty years is a significant length of time to individual humans. The 'deep no sound', however, has a harder ring. In its sense of vast scale and emphatically voiced negative, the phrase unsettles the sonnet's otherwise comfortingly human frames of references. Tellingly, this unsettling is accomplished by variants on two signature Lowellian strategies: forceful enjambment, and adjectival listing. It is by breaking the line before 'vulnerable' Heaney generates the unsettling revision of 'no', whilst the piled up chain 'deep no sound', if not adjectival, has some of the vigour of Lowell's early listings. Lowell's ocean, then, ghosts some of Heaney most apparently peaceable, pastoral poems, disturbing and de-centring their human-centric perspectives.

'a diver under a glass bell': Human Technologies and Non-human Environments

Heaney's 'deep no sound' is heard, at least partially, against the backdrop of 'distant gargling tractors', and the voicing of the line depends on the peculiar relationship between these two things, in which the former is 'vulnerable' to the latter. This relationship highlights the connection between human and non-human worlds, the technological and the 'natural', and that the environment is a product of both. In 'Glanmore I' this is a mostly benign hybridity, but that is not always the case. 'Glanmore IX', for example, picks up where 'Elegy' leaves off, under the 'bay tree':

> Did we come to the wilderness for this?
> We have our burnished bay tree at the gate,
> Classical, hung with the reek of silage
> From the next farm, tart-leafed as inwit.
> Blood on a pitchfork, blood on chaff and hay,
> Rats speared in the sweat and dust of threshing –
> What is my apology for poetry?

> The empty briar is swishing
> When I come down, and beyond, your face
> Haunts like a new moon glimpsed through tangled glass.²⁸

Though 'burnished' the 'bay tree' is also marked with the presence of industrial processes and produce, the 'silage' whose 'reek' serves a reminder that farming is a mechanical and not just a 'natural' process. Similarly, 'pitchfork' and 'threshing' are reminders of the low-level technologies used by humans for centuries in their interaction with the environment. That Heaney should describe the scene as 'Classical' implies a degree of knowingness on his part, that he is aware that idealized rural landscapes stage their pastorals.

More complicatedly, 'Glanmore IX' obliquely alludes to a Robert Lowell that is concerned in a very specific way with the precarious balance between humans, technology, and the environment; 'Fall 1961'. In that poem, written at a moment of acute Cold War tension when wholesale nuclear conflagration seemed imminent, Lowell imagines that

> Our end drifts nearer,
> the moon lifts,
> radiant with terror.
> The state
> is a diver under a glass bell.²⁹

Unlike Heaney's limited 'reek of silage', Lowell's poem is about the most sophisticatedly modern – and destructive – technology, about machines capable of initiating instantaneous and wholesale catastrophe. Nevertheless, these two poems share, I think, a similar atmosphere. Lowell's moon combines the apparent antonyms radiance and terror much as Heaney's moon both 'Haunts' and is 'new', eerily blending death and beauty in the same figure. In the opening stanza of 'Fall 1961' Lowell describes the 'back and forth' and 'the tock, tock, tock / of the bland ambassadorial / face of the moon / on the grandfather clock'.³⁰ The moon becomes an emblem of time about to run out, a strangely posthumous

---

28 Heaney, *Field Work*, 41.
29 Lowell, *Collected Poems*, 329.
30 Ibid.

sense of time in which destruction seems certain, but has yet to actually take place. 'Fall 1961' embodies a sense of inertia, of agent-less action that seemingly proceeds of its own accord. In place of the reckless superfluity of energy in 'The Quaker Graveyard', Lowell articulates torpor, whilst the poem's abstract nouns – 'Our end', 'the moon', 'The state' – and simple present tense verbs – 'drifts', 'lifts' – elide specific human action and responsibility. There is also a feeling of inertia around the strange image of the state as a diver in a glass bell. As the institution that most commonly funds, develops, and deploys nuclear weapons, the state is best placed to assume responsibility for the crisis the poem outlines. Lowell, however, imagines the state as itself imperilled, as having dived into the deep with glass for protection, as being dangerously exposed to the surrounding oceanic environment. In his essay 'Robert Lowell and the Cold War' Steven Gould Axelrod suggests that the state is 'danger-seeking',[31] as though the US and Soviet governments were engaged in some kind of destructive thrill-seeking, but I think the poem's overall sense of drift works against the notion of active 'seeking', imagining instead that the prospective nuclear conflagration is something that just happens.

This is, of course, not true, but it speaks to the ways in which technologies quickly pass beyond the control of those who invent them, the ways in which they pass from human governance into the non-environment. When Mentz describes the 'Oceangoing ships and voyages' that 'generated the global ecology in which all material things in the world – animals, plants, viruses, cultures – were distributed around the globe'[32] he implies that a large amount of this ecology was generated without conscious design, that the processes of trade and exploration that initiated the global ecology did not run according to an intended plan (even if such a plan had ever been devised), and that it had substantial unforeseen consequences. The development of nuclear weapons is in some way an extension of this process: the first generation of US and Soviet strategic missile submarines, carrying nuclear warheads, entered active military service in the late 1950s and early 1960s, at the time that Lowell was writing his poem. If the global

---

31 Axelrod, 'Robert Lowell and the Cold War', *New England Quarterly* 72. 3 (1999): 339–361; 352.
32 Mentz, *Shipwreck Modernity*, 2.

ecology was haphazardly generated by oceangoing ships and voyages, then it might have been (and may yet be) haphazardly destroyed by oceangoing, missile-bearing submarines.

When read in this light, 'Fall 1961' sounds a long way from Heaney's 'Glanmore IX', but his poem too meditates on the partial, blundering, ineffectual and ultimately violent interventions human beings make in the environment, the 'Blood on a pitchfork' and 'Rats speared in the sweat and dust of threshing'. Heaney's question, 'Did we come to the wilderness for this?', poses again the precarious position of humans in a non-human environment, and is asked in the 'oracular rhetorical'[33] manner that, as Corcoran observes, is another Lowellian trait taken up in *Field Work*. A similarly rhetorical question occurs a little later in the poem when Heaney asks 'What is my apology for poetry', implying a degree of guilt for, and culpability in, the violence he sees around him. This is not a direct and immediate sense of guilt, but rather a more diffuse feeling of complicity that the poet is powerless to avoid or change. It is a feeling encapsulated in the lines that Heaney quotes from 'Fall 1961' in 'Elegy' – 'A father's no shield / for his child'[34] – and also in Lowell's compelling image of the state as 'a diver in a glass bell',[35] whose unsettling power is picked up by Heaney's strangely oxymoronic closing phrase, 'tangled glass'.[36] Oxymoronic, because glass is not usually thought capable of the kind of movement that 'tangled' implies. By describing it in these terms Heaney gives the perceptions in his sonnet an otherworldly, dream-like aspect that combines motion and stasis, culpability and inertia, in a similar manner to 'Fall 1961'. To say that 'The state / is a diver under a glass bell' is to further equate this condition to being submerged in water, and indeed a little earlier in his poem Lowell pictures himself as 'a minnow / behind my studio window'.[37] Though Heaney's 'Glanmore IX' does not directly mention water, or Lowell, its buried allusions to 'Fall 1961', and manner of description conjure the sensations of

33 Neil Corcoran, *The Poetry of Seamus Heaney: A Critical Study* (London: Faber and Faber, 1998), 84.
34 Lowell, *Collected Poems*, 329.
35 Ibid.
36 Heaney, *Field Work*, 41
37 Lowell, *Collected Poems*, 329.

being submerged, as though the speaker of the poem were exposed to an alien element and incapable of escape.

Lowell's self-accusations continue, and continue to be cast in oceanic terms, in 'For the Union Dead'. Nuclear weapons feature here too, but this time the main focus of his critique is, as Helen Vendler says, 'a new, commercialized history'.[38] Boston's historic sites, including the statue of Civil War hero Colonel Shaw and the old Aquarium that Lowell remembers visiting as a child, are the bearers of 'an old ethical'[39] past that has been displaced by a contemporary commercialism, embodied in the poem's last stanza as 'Giant finned cars' that 'nose forward like fish; / a savage servility / slides by on grease'.[40] Although Vendler is right to point to a narrative of decline in the poem, in which Boston's current citizenry – including Lowell himself – neglect their inheritance, the Aquarium and the fish complicate this narrative. Though Lowell remembers these fish as 'cowed, compliant' in the Aquarium, he also says that he 'often sigh[s] still / for the dark downward and vegetating kingdom / of the fish and reptile'.[41] That adjectival triad 'dark downward and vegetating' imbues the fish with something akin to the inhuman energies of 'The Quaker Graveyard', imputing to marine ecologies a non-human life that is then drained away by the Aquarium. This energy then returns, frighteningly, in the 'savage servility' of the poem's end, as though what the Aquarium had tried to hubristically control and tame has erupted with renewed force in the 'Giant finned cars'.[42] As with 'Fall 1961', the human occupies a fraught and precarious position within the non-human environment, a precariousness partly created and exacerbated by technological interventions such as the aquarium and the car. These interventions are less dramatic than nuclear weapons, but no less influential. The car, in particular, functions as a symbol of those modes of production and consumption that lie behind so much human-driven climate change. Tellingly, Lowell switches his attention from the geo-political Cold War conflict

38 Helen Vendler, *The Given and the Made: Strategies of Poetic Redefinition* (Cambridge, MA: Harvard University Press, 1995), 15.
39 Ibid.
40 Lowell, *Collected Poems*, 378.
41 Ibid. 376.
42 Ibid. 378.

to more nebulous – and hence, more inexorable – economic processes. Again, Lowell is acutely aware of his compromised position in all of this, his 'confessed participation in the degradation he so scathingly observes',[43] as Vendler puts it, and again his figure for the participation is aqueous.

Heaney is no stranger to self-accusation and self-reproach, but these are usually, and understandably, pre-occupied with the conflict in Northern Ireland. In 'Oysters', however, his self-criticisms, like Lowell's in 'For the Union Dead', are economic, as he worries about the 'privilege' associated with certain modes of consumption:

> Over the Alps, packed deep in hay and snow,
> The Romans hauled their oysters south to Rome:
> I saw damp panniers disgorge
> The frond-lipped, brine-stung
> Glut of privilege
>
> And was angry that my trust could not repose
> In the clear light, like poetry or freedom
> Leaning in from sea. I ate the day
> Deliberately, that its tang
> Might quicken me all into verb, pure verb.[44]

As Bernard O'Donoghue observes, the poem's 'pleasant social gathering [...] is spoilt by the association with the exploitative, imperialist Romans' and 'The inability to enjoy freedom without such principled reflections makes the speaker angry'.[45] Tellingly, these anxieties focus on the ocean, presented as a possible site of freedom, but also the source of the 'ripped and shucked and scattered'[46] oysters whose transportation provokes the poet's ire. If, in 'Elegy' Heaney tries to resist Robert Lowell's imperial pretensions, then here he unwittingly adopts them, and finds himself unable to break free from them. Anger makes Heaney eat 'the day / Deliberately', but the desired outcome is only provisional – 'its tang / *Might* quicken

---

43 Vendler, *The Given and the Made*, 16.
44 Heaney, *Field Work*, 11.
45 Bernard O'Donoghue, *Seamus Heaney and the Language of Poetry* (Hemel Hempstead: Harvester Wheatsheaf, 1994), 78.
46 Heaney, *Field Work*, 11.

me'[47] – and, in any case, that word, deliberately, accrues an unwelcome grandiosity later in *Field Work* when Heaney imagines Lowell 'promulgating art's / deliberate, peremptory / love and arrogance'.[48] This is Lowell-as-emperor, and his imperiousness is bound up with his deliberateness, a willed and wilful exertion of power that Heaney may find overbearing, but that he also finds himself replicating.

O'Donoghue also argues that 'The imperialism implicit in the Roman parallel in "Oysters" means that, like several other Dedalus-like bids for freedom in Heaney, it will be frustrated by a regard for public responsibility',[49] suggesting that there is no artistic or poetic space free from such public responsibilities. We can amend this argument to say that there is no space free from ecological responsibility. A late poem, 'Desfina', the last of the 'Sonnets from Hellas' in 2001's *Electric Light* sees Heaney again in the act of consumption:

> we wolfed down horta, tarama and houmos
> At sunset in the farmyard, drinking ouzos,
> Pretending not to hear the Delphic squeal
> Of the steel-haired cailleach in the scullery.
> Then it was time to head into Desfina
> To allow them to sedate her. And so retsina,
> Anchovies, squid, dolmades, french fries even.
> My head was light, I was hyper, boozed, borean
> As we bowled back down towards the olive plain,
> Siren-tyred and manic on the horn
> Round hairpin bends looped like boustrophedon.[50]

Lacking the explicit imperialism of 'Oysters', Heaney here indulges his appetites. There is a relish about the way he lists exotic and exciting foodstuffs, but tension too. The poem's listing of foods comes to seem excessive and greedy, and the poet himself overbearing and over-privileged as he over-indulges his appetites, especially with cries of distress in the

---

47   Ibid. Emphasis added.
48   Ibid. 31.
49   O'Donoghue, 81.
50   Heaney, *Electric Light* (London: Faber and Faber, 2001), 43.

background. Heaney's posture here – 'siren-tyred and manic on the horn' – recalls that of Lowell in 'Elegy', when he drinks 'America like the heart's iron vodka', and 'rid[ing] on the swaying tiller / of yourself ... what was not within your empery?'[51] The car, too, suggests the 'Giant-finned' vehicles of 'For the Union Dead', those symbols of a debased commercialism, and [the] relish of [the] food is undercut to an extent by a Lowellian adjectival run – 'I was hyper, boozed, borean'. The excitement of the holiday is shadowed by an undercurrent of anxiety, that in even undertaking this excursion Heaney too has adopted Lowell's imperious demeanour, and that his unfettered consumption is a form of exploitation. Though not invoked explicitly, as in 'Oysters', the sea is an important off-stage presence, implied by the 'anchovies' and 'squid', but also, more complexly, by 'french fries'. These fries migrate to Greece from vernacular American culture, with a nod to their French origins, carried over the Atlantic by a late twentieth-century Americanized globalization. The process by which 'Oceangoing ships and voyages' that Mentz argued had 'generated the global ecology' by circulating 'animals, plants, viruses, cultures' are on-going (though it is of course possible that the ocean is now traversed by aeroplane, and not ship). These processes allow Heaney to travel to Greece and try the local cuisine, but they also bring other, less anticipated things.

Another late poem 'In Iowa', from 2006's *District and Circle*, also employs the ocean as a figure for unexpected inter-connections. Heaney sees an 'abandoned' tractor (or 'mowing machine'), 'each spoked wheel with a thick white brow' of snow that 'took the shine off oil in the black-toothed gears'.[52] This isolated vehicle, sighted in 'a slathering blizzard' out on the prairie, brings with it intimations of distant times and places: 'In Iowa once. In the slush and rush and hiss / Not of parted but as of rising waters'.[53] Secluded amongst a community of pious 'Mennonites', Heaney sinisterly replaces a vision of religious salvation with one of environmental disaster. The Israelites crossing the Red Sea becomes the contemporary reality of

---

51   Heaney, *Field Work*, 31.
52   Heaney, *District and Circle*, 52.
53   Ibid.

rising sea levels as a consequence of global warming, itself a consequence of economic dependency on fossil fuels like the oil Heaney sees on the tractor. Even though the tractor is not being used, and even though Heaney is in Iowa, thousands of miles away from any shore, the sight of the vehicle still summons those menacing 'rising waters'. Like the French fries and oysters in earlier poems, the tractor becomes a marker of compromised privilege, whose occluded costs and consequences are rendered visible by the sea.

The ocean's ostensibly marginal place in these poems points to its submerged position in the contemporary imagination, just as its moments of sudden re-emergence point to its continuing importance. It continues to be profoundly, powerfully influential, even when its presence is not obvious, or especially visible. Such an off-centre, out-of-kilter influence disrupts the complementary balance that Heaney attributed to Lowell when he described him as being able to 'plunge into the downward reptilian welter of the self and yet raise himself with whatever knowledge he gained there out on to the hard ledges of the historical present, which he then apprehended with refreshed insight and intensity'.[54] In his memorial Heaney imagines the ocean is available to poets as a resource to be mined, but the ocean as it appears in his poems – and as he inherited it from Lowell – is less predictable, and possesses its own non-human agency, flashes of which can be seen both Lowell's and Heaney's language. This agency is often complicatedly, and destructively, intertwined with human inventions and technologies, which have a tendency to pass in to [into?] the environment and out of human control, thus smearing and obscuring 'the hard ledges of the historical present',[55] and whatever insight may be found there. This can be bleak, but also refreshing. As a radically non-human environment the ocean opens poems up to unexpected perspectives and sensations, to salt-water's invigorating 'slush and rush and hiss'.[56]

---

54 'On Robert Lowell', *The New York Review of Books* (9 February 1978), available online at <http://www.nybooks.com/articles/1978/02/09/on-robert-lowell/> (accessed 10 October 2017).
55 Ibid.
56 Heaney, *District and Circle*, 52.

GERALD DAWE

Waiting for the New Life: Reading Robert Lowell in Bangor, Co. Down, in the 1970s

I

Robert Lowell and his poetry are indelibly associated in my mind with Bangor, a County Down town on the southern shores of Belfast Lough in Northern Ireland. Though I didn't realize it at the time when I started to read him in the late 1960s and early 1970s, his New England villages and communities were being channelled in my mind through that coastline of Helen's Bay, Ballyholme Esplanade, Groomsport, Ballymacormick Point and the Copeland islands. The trawlers berthed in the little harbour in Bangor – now an extensive marina – carried distant family resemblances in 'Water':

> Remember? We sat on a slab of rock.
> From this distance in time,
> it seems the color
> of iris, rotting and turning purpler,
>
> but it was only
> the usual gray rock
> turning the usual green
> when drenched by the sea.[1]

There was also the wry, sardonic modern twist of Lowell's 'English' that found a deep echo in the young private lives we were living then, spreading our wings in North Belfast and picking out from the school anthologies

---

1   Robert Lowell, *Collected Poems*, eds Frank Bidart and David Gewanter (New York: Farrar, Straus and Giroux, 2003), 321.

the new poetry of Americans like Lowell and those who, at one point or another, had come under his influence such as Sylvia Plath. Donald Hall's third edition of Michael Roberts's ground breaking anthology, *The Faber Book of Modern Verse*,[2] was the set text for A Levels and from that book the Americans emerged supreme, catching a mood of exhilaration that spread out from the American late 1950s into the transatlantic 1960s, bringing great music in its wake but also the anxieties and challenges of Vietnam and the nuclear arms race:

> Burnished, burned-out, still burning as the year
> you lead me to our stamping ground.
> The city and its cruising cars surround
> the Public Garden. All's alive –[3]

But it wasn't solely this supercharged and hip modernity which Lowell caught as the mood of the moment. Reading Lowell also provoked a certain kind of local resonance, a complex and un-explicated sense of the puritan inheritances of Northern Protestantism; a familial feeling that pervades *Life Studies*, *For the Union Dead* and *Near the Ocean*.

I certainly would have been barely conscious of this at the time but the social proprieties which Lowell anatomizes in '91 Revere Street'[4] and picks out with such chastening detail elsewhere in *Life Studies* in his portraits of his mother, father, grandfather and others, carried a marked similarity to the anecdotes and handed-down family stories of the delayed postwar world I had known in the drawing rooms and front rooms of ancient 'aunts' whose one and true love had perished in one of the world wars:

> Born ten years and yet an aeon
> too early for the twenties,
> Mother, you smile
> as if you saw your Father
> inches away yet hidden, as when he groused behind a screen

---

2   Michael Roberts, ed., *The Faber Book of Modern Verse* (1936; London: Faber and Faber, 1965).
3   Lowell, 'The Public Garden', *Collected Poems*, 341.
4   Lowell, *Collected Poems*, 121–150.

> over a National Geographic Magazine
> whenever young men came to court you
> back in those settled years of World War One.⁵

And of course for any young boy or girl growing out of adolescence into that northern industrial society with its 'suburban factories'⁶ at the very heart of its major city, the contrasting civic landscape of Lowell's statues in 'New England greens'⁷ might also have found a strong local resonance. Firstly in the very sense of commemoration with the public display and ongoing rites of marking the state's identification with the sacrifice of two world wars:

> The stone statues of the abstract Union Soldier
> grow slimmer and younger each year –
> wasp-wasted, they doze over musket
> and muse through their sideburns …⁸

Church cenotaphs, military monuments, regimental flags, this was the very stuff of our immediate lives which Lowell strangely helped us to see. But he also prompted in his poems a critical edge which opened up the background of social life and urged his readers to see another story, the *actual* society:

> When I crouch to my television set,
> the drained faces of Negro school-children rise like balloons.⁹

By the time *For the Union Dead* was published in Britain in 1965, Northern Irish society was on the edge of its own political turmoil which would lead into civil unrest and eventually widespread violence:

> I swim like a minnow
> behind my studio window.

---

5   Lowell, 'During Fever', *Collected Poems*, 182.
6   Lowell, 'The Mouth of the Hudson', *Collected Poems*, 328.
7   Lowell, 'For the Union Dead', *Collected Poems*, 377.
8   Ibid. 377.
9   Ibid.

> Our end drifts nearer,
> the moon lifts,
> radiant with terror.
> The state
> is a diver under a glass bell.[10]

Lowell's crucial example could show how it was possible to have a poetic response to a political situation. But also he revealed how a society can contain inside it contradictory cultural pulses and ideological pressures, stability, conventions, ways of life which seem unchanging but are in fact on the point of transition, sometimes radical transition.

There was much in those early books that passed me by. As with songs of the time, the 'boardwalks' and 'sidewalks', 'levees' and Chevy's, the argot of consumerist and vernacular America was repeated but without really knowing what it was all about; except for the provocatively individualistic urban energy that contained a shadowing, questioning, shriving sense of uncertainty:

> Everything had been swept bare,
> furnished, garnished and aired.
>
> Everything's changed for the best –
> how quivering and fierce we were,
> there snowbound together
> simmering like wasps
> in our tent of books.[11]

Simmering 'like wasps' remains as stunning as the 'two cops on horseback' who 'clop through the April rain' in 'The Drinker',[12] checking 'the parking meter violations', 'their oilskins yellow as forsythia'. *Forsythia*? Marrying these local details to the 'man ... killing time', the *Herzog*[13]-like living space as the cheese 'wilts in the rat-trap, / the milk turns to junket

---

10   Lowell, 'Fall 1961', *Collected Poems*, 329.
11   Lowell, 'The Old Flame', *Collected Poems*, 324.
12   Lowell, 'The Drinker', *Collected Poems*, 349.
13   Saul Bellow, *Herzog* in *Novels 1956–1964* (New York: Library of America, 2007), 731–734.

in the cornflakes bowl' and the Melvillean ancestral images ('the whale's warm-hearted blubber, foundering down/leagues of ocean, gasping whiteness'),[14] was, is, simply reality-changing. This was the kind of electric stuff that knocked a young reader (and his much older self) into a reverie of desire. 'I want to write like that' but then reality checks in. So back to Bangor.

II

Like thousands of other Belfast families Bangor represented the summer. It was to Bangor during the 1950s that we went for a month's holiday, renting a house in which lived my mother, sister, grandmother and which several of their friends visited from time to time. Occasionally my uncle and his pal dropped by but outside of some time spent on the beach at Ballyholme their minds were fixed on the bars and dancehalls.[15]

A taxi took us to the North Eastern station. The train journey from Belfast to Bangor was a ceremonial affair of expectation that was only ever complete by entering the station in Bangor, stepping into the main street and looking down towards the McKee clock tower, the Mine and the rattling chains of coal buckets or the spinning wheel of the little Fair.

We stayed in comfortable redbrick houses with tidy gardens and small backyards. The houses were full of heavy furniture and carpets, stairways and cubby-holes, shadowy back bedrooms and craft-worked etchings of the Mourne Mountains, Helen's Bay or some well-known 'place of interest' like the Mull of Kintyre or Portpatrick. The few books around were miscellanies; Saturday Bedside anthologies. The hearths were covered by fire screens and tables of one sort or another popped up out of comers, at bay windows, between doors.

---

14 Lowell, 'The Drinker', *Collected Poems*, 349.
15 This section draws upon the present writer's contribution to *The Bangor Book: Writing from and about Bangor and North Down*, compiled and edited by Kenneth Irvine (Bangor: Ards and North Down Borough Council, 2016).

We had connections in Bangor, friends of my grandmother's. One had a shop in the main street and we visited there for tea, enviously eyeing their son, a tanned and athletic young man who worked his summers on the pleasure boats. Another friend of my grandmother's, whom I was intrigued by with her quiet manner and marvellous 'country' accent, lived in Prospect Road and had fostered our dog when we moved from suburban Belfast to one of the busy arterial roads on the city's north side. She and her sister passed 'snaps' of men and women I knew nothing about between themselves and smiled a lot. We went from their house into Ward Park to look at the big Gun, flower beds, and Bowling Green and then took in the last of the evening sun. There was something hurt about the sisters.

From time to time my grandmother's Belfast friends dropped in on day visits or even stayed a night or two by way of offering her diversion. Their 'real' holidays were spent in the Isle of Man or Bournemouth and she also went to visit her sister in London. I fell in love with one of those friends at the age of 6 or 7. She had flaming red hair and adoring eyes and smoked 'plain' cigarettes.

On deck-chairs we would sit facing the sea. The Ice Cream shop on the promenade was like a little bunker and up above it stood tall silent Guest Houses. Most afternoons beyond Pickie Pool,[16] and throughout Sundays, songs were sung and although we never took part, we would listen and move on:

> Each little flower that opens,
> Each little bird that sings,
> He made their glowing colours,
> He made their tiny wings:
>
> The purple-headed mountain,
> The river running by,
> The sunset and the morning,
> That brightens up the sky.[17]

---

16 See Derek Mahon 'A Long Sunset', *Olympia and the Internet* (Oldcastle: Gallery Books, 2017), 42.
17 Cecil Frances Alexander, 'All Things Bright and Beautiful', *Hymns for Little Children* (Philadelphia, PA: H. Hooker, 1850), 27–28.

There's always somewhere that holds a special place in one's memory of childhood and growing up. Lowell's poems are filled with such recollections of times and New England places he grew up in and revisited from his Boston base. A place that is set in the backroom of the mind with its landscape and sound and smells and a kind of elusive reality. For many Belfast people Bangor fulfilled that elsewhere life. Bangor provided an intimate and alluring hold on generations of ordinary people long before the cheap flights sent folk off in every global direction imaginable.

For the 1960s generation, Bangor provided a summer of day-trip possibility – dancing, meeting girls, hanging out on the sea front, being cool at the 'sea side'. We hitched there. And for a couple of summers we stayed there overnight, in a friend's family chalet-cum-bungalow, played our music. For those who went before us – like those in the 1940s awaiting the D-Day embarkation to liberate Europe,[18] or before that, in the hazier days of the 1930s between the wars, the place seemed to stay unchanged and unchangeable.

When I think of Bangor today it is through the viewfinder of both a late 1960s pleasure ground, but also as a very young lad going down with my own family on holiday in the 1950s, staying in rented houses off Dufferin Avenue. Or a little later as a boy scout on an endurance test pitching up in the Clandeboye estate and rising in the dewy morning to the sound of cattle breathing over the tiny tent.

Bangor was also a home-from-home for my late mother and stepfather, their last harbour in the new century. Walking along Ballyholme, strolling up above Pickie Pool, sitting down in Ward Park, looking across to the tall houses of Prospect Road where those grand 'aunts' had moved to from postwar Belfast, Bangor really was an imagined neighbourhood as much as a real place.

But throughout it all, Bangor wasn't associated in my mind at least with cultural history or the ecclesiastical tradition such as it actually held. Not at all. Ignorance blossomed in the mood music of my time. Beside the bedside annuals of the 1950s there was Riesling and Bob Dylan in the 1960s. It was also about leaving on trains and buses home to a dusky north

---

18 See <https://wwiini.org/place/the-eisenhower-pier-bangor> (accessed 30 November 2017).

Belfast when it was already lightening-up time and the inevitable question about when next we'd head back down.

All along that coast, there is the magic and mystery of where the land meets the sea. People foregathered where their spiritual guides had established monasteries since 555.[19] The inducements and energies of life there remain strong and empowering. I can still feel the mood take hold of excitement when I recall stepping out of the railway station and still look down Main Street to imagine the coal boats clanking. Hear the gulls cry. As in 'Returning' to the 'sheltered little resort, / where the members of my gang / are bald-headed, in business',[20] Lowell provides no wiggle-room for the nostalgia of self-deceit. This might well be one of his greatest poetic legacies for a time such as today that praises easy sentiment and the comfort of instant response:

> Yet sometimes I catch my vague mind
> circling with a glazed eye
> for a name without a face, or a face without a name,
> and at every step,
> I startle them. They start up,
> dog-eared, bald as baby-birds.[21]

When Lowell goes further back to the Sunday dinners he endured as a small boy in Revere Street, Boston, we can identify the sense of anxiety and the strain of the young boy seeking, through the older poet's recollection, 'out'. As he recalibrates his father's delayed life in the wonderful memoir in *Life Studies* there is a powerful feeling that Lowell's manic energy was born, first and foremost, of frustration with 'waiting for the new life' he wanted to grab with both hands for himself:

> Perhaps I exaggerate their embarrassment because they hover so greyly in recollection and seem to anticipate ominously my father's downhill progress as a civilian and Bostonian. It was to be expected, I suppose, that Father should be in irons for

---

19 Irvine, *The Bangor Book*, 4–8.
20 Lowell, 'Returning', *Collected Poems*, 347–348.
21 Ibid. 348.

a year or two, while becoming detached from his old comrades and interests, while waiting for the new life.[22]

III

In 1969 I sat my A Levels and wrote on poetry in the English examination. I had read A. Alvarez's *The New Poetry* which further underlined the opening-up of the 'English' canon to American poets – as those contemporary American poets included in the *Faber Book of Modern Verse* re-appeared.[23] In May the following year I was invited to a dress dance at Queen's University. A friend's girlfriend wanted me to go on a blind date with *her* friend. So off the four of us went – me the younger in dress suit, swallowing Bushmills whiskey; and a friendship bloomed. I would meet the girl, and we would attend classical recitals in the Ulster Hall. In that brief time we spent together, barely a summer, she quoted Robert Lowell and from the house she shared with her family in Bangor, produced his books, such as the hardback of *Near the Ocean*. I heard in that contemporary ironic voice nuances and inflections close to those I knew but had not really *heard* before as poetry, certainly in the Belfast out of which I was growing increasingly more impatient to be gone.[24]

While I had been reading a lot and trying to assimilate all this work into some kind of coherence, I can see now looking back that it was the figure of Robert Lowell, whose poetry had, from that early age, such a deep

22   Lowell, '91 Revere Street', *Collected Poems*, 147.
23   A. Alvarex, *The New Poetry* (rev. edn; Harmondsworth: Penguin, 1966).
24   Robert Lowell had connections with Bangor through his third wife, the novelist Caroline Blackwood who was born and brought up in Clandeboye Estate in County Down and whose collection, *For All That I Found There* (London: Gerald Duckworth & Co. 1973), contains reminiscences of her local life: 'All the Bangor streets were so dismal', she remarks in a memoir of her nurse-maid Betty and her short-lived romance with a locally stationed GI during World War II, 'and grey and deserted that she [Betty] felt that they might have both found it gayer to have taken a walk around a cemetery', 127.

impression on me, and proved creatively troublesome, to say the least, to assimilate.

In her thought-provoking reassessment of Lowell's posthumous reputation with the publication of the massive *Collected Poems* in 2003, Marjorie Perloff asks why Lowell's 'star plummeted in the decades following his death?' She replies:

> [I]t may well be that the poetry community recognized that, despite his undeniable place in postwar America, Lowell's poetry was, in the end, flawed. Far from being too confessional, he became, to my mind, too glibly public. Poets do not, of course, need to be nice people or have the 'right' political opinions [...] but I believe readers assume that, whatever their quirks, they should load every rift with ore, avoiding sarcasm, easy caricature, and 'clever' one-liners. Once Lowell had become famous, he seems to have fallen in love with his own public persona and, all too often, allowed that persona simply to indulge itself.[25]

When I look at my own efforts over the years since the early 1970s to the present it's clear that my debt to Lowell goes very much deeper that I'd previously thought. The division between past and present, and the *violent* sundering of that continuity out of which one's cultural identity, memory and tradition emerges, alongside the developing of an individual voice, led me to the blunt, almost physical realization that there is an inevitability about change; it is simply the principle by which we make life valuable and renewing. Robert Lowell taught that lesson both in personal but more significantly in social and political terms through those poems of his which were simply unflinchingly of their time.

25 Marjorie Perloff, 'The Return of Robert Lowell' *Parnassus: Poetry in Review* 27.1/2 (January 2003): 25.

MICHAEL HINDS

Name and Shame: 'Identification in Belfast'

Marjorie Perfloff's *agon* with the reputation of Robert Lowell persists throughout her work. It begins with her reviewing of him in the early 1970s, which prompted Elizabeth Bishop to huff supportively in a letter to Lowell that 'Miss Perloff – whoever she is – does some very bad far-fetched interpreting'.[1] Despite this, it would be hard to argue with the formalist scruple of Perloff's work that carried over into her 1973 study, *The Poetic Art of Robert Lowell*; and yet this book is where Perloff makes a decisive break, adopting a scepticism about Lowell's claim on canonicity which still persists. In 1983's influential essay-review '*Poètes Maudits* of the Genteel Tradition', Lowell is confidently designated by Perloff as *arrière* rather than *avant garde*, representing 'the end of an era rather than the beginning of one'.[2] More recently, in her aside in *21st-Century Modernism* on the 'fabled' post-modernism of Lowell,[3] she also denied him a designation that had first been ventured by Randall Jarrell in his review of *Lord Weary's Castle*: 'it is essentially a post- or anti-modernist poetry, and as such is certain to be influential.'[4] As Perloff has taken on the role of epochal critic, mapping out the history of American and Transnational poetry and poetics, Lowell has

---

1   Thomas Travisano and Saskia Hamilton, eds, *Words in Air: The Complete Correspondence Between Elizabeth Bishop and Robert Lowell* (New York: Farrar, Strauss and Giroux, 2008), 753.
2   Marjorie Perloff, '*Poètes Maudits* of the Genteel Tradition', *The American Poetry Review* 12.3 (May–June 1983): 38.
3   Marjorie Perloff, *21st-Century Modernism: The 'New' Poetics* (Oxford: Wiley-Blackwell, 2002), 164.
4   Randall Jarrell, 'From the Kingdom of Necessity', reprinted in *Poetry and the Age* (London: Faber and Faber, 1973), 194.

become less and less significant, a minor symptom rather than a major cause. It is an evident compliment to the force of his one-time reputation that Perloff should feel obliged to clear him out of the way; if a poet appears on the front cover of *Time* magazine, maybe it is true that they have become too powerful. Every icon demands iconoclasm, and Perloff does that necessary labour.

To take specific issue with Perloff's dismissals of Lowell's poetic significance, I want to look at the poem that most directly represents the traumatic politics of late twentieth-century Ireland, 'Identification in Belfast'. Lowell is at least gesturing there towards a mode of poetic experiment which Perloff has increasingly championed, namely the Bartlebyism-as-copyism of Kenneth Goldsmith. In books such as his *Seven American Deaths and Disasters*, and in the particularly controversial instance of 'The Body of Michael Brown', where Goldsmith reproduced what he termed 'the autopsy report' of Brown after his killing by police in Ferguson, Missouri, documentary accounts of violence and trauma become both the raw and cooked material of the poem.[5]

Perloff has been particularly energized by what she calls the 'moving of information' in Goldsmith, his poetics of direct citation from either official documentation or media coverage. That said, one of the issues with the Brown poem was that it was not direct, but actually re-processed by Goldsmith, which evidently undermines the radicalism of his experiment. When he was challenged about the ethics of his Brown poem, Goldsmith took to Facebook and sought refuge in a time-honoured defence that you can say anything in a poem and no one will mind:

> I altered the text for poetic effect; I translated into plain English many obscure medical terms that would have stopped the flow of the text; I narrativized it in ways that made the text less didactic and more literary. I indeed stated at the beginning of my reading that this was a poem called 'The Body of Michael Brown'; I never stated, 'I am going to read the autopsy report of Michael Brown.'[6]

---

5 'Something Borrowed,' a good account of this controversy by Alec Wilkinson, appeared in *The New Yorker* (5 October 2015).
6 Posted by Goldsmith on Facebook, 15 March 2015.

Perloff's excitement about an aesthetic in which the poet transcribes, transports or translates the words of others seems to be in part (or maybe in full) an answer to the question that Lowell famously posed in 'Epilogue': 'Yet why not say what happened?'[7] Out of this, Lowell can be considered as signalling a potential practice for Goldsmith to emulate (and paradoxically for Perloff to hail, despite her reservations) in 'Identification in Belfast', which first appeared in *History*. 'Identification in Belfast' uses the method of apparently direct quotation from documentary source into free sonnet form that would become so notorious in *The Dolphin*'s borrowing of private correspondence.[8] It is also a poem drawn mostly from a TV interview, and therefore an anticipation of Goldsmith's method in *Deaths and Disasters*. So the poem is not based on official documentation, as in the poem based on Lieutenant William Calley's court-martial testimony for the My Lai massacre, 'Women Children, Babies, Cows, Cats', which immediately precedes 'Identification in Belfast' in the sequence of *History* and forms an instructive pair in terms of Lowell showing what can and cannot be done with the citation practice.

Perloff's most rigorous exploration of citational practice takes place in *Unoriginal Genius: Poetry by Other Means in the New Century* (2010), a book that begins with a re-evaluation of T.S. Eliot's *The Waste Land* in citational terms, indicating its representation of found materials and fragments. Lowell typically receives the briefest of attention in the book, firstly when reference is made to correspondence between Bishop and Lowell which reveals their miscomprehension about the citational poetics of Brazilian concretists, and then in the familiar terms of describing *Life Studies* as a return to 'the Romantic lyric paradigm.'[9] It is a curiosity that no attention is paid by Perloff to aspects of Lowell's work that are far less Romantic and integrated. It should also be noted straightaway that the exemplary combination-poetics of Pound and Eliot's poem found their way into Lowell's work from an early stage, as in 'The Quaker Graveyard in

---

7   Robert Lowell, 'Epilogue', *Collected Poems*, eds Frank Bidart and David Gewanter (London: Faber and Faber, 2003), 838
8   Robert Lowell, 'Identification in Belfast', *Collected Poems*, 596.
9   Marjorie Perloff, *Unoriginal Genius: Poetry by Other Means in the New Century* (Chicago: University of Chicago, 2010), 56.

Nantucket', a poem that rises and falls on Miltonic and Melvillean rhythms. More than that, it should be noted that much of *Life Studies* is conversant with the method of *The Waste Land*, notably in 'Beyond the Alps', and also in the strange connection of Schopenhauer epigraph and poem in '"To Speak of Woe That Is in Marriage"' which began as a translation of Catullus and then found its way through Chaucer. This method finds a very peculiar focus in 'Skunk Hour', however, which both presents direct citation and different voices to the degree that it can be regarded as Lowell's thorough reversion of the modernist prototype.[10] As in *The Waste Land*, there is quotation from literary and musical sources, canonical and otherwise. It also defines a choric voice of civic disapproval in describing 'Our fairy decorator', then culminates with an apparently straightforward first-person narrator. At first, though, the poem is presided over by a third-person voice, part-Hawthorne, part-Dickens, who presides satirically over the anecdote of 'Nautilus Island's heiress'. Quotations from Milton and the blues standard 'Careless Love' can also be read as running degrees of interference on those other attitudes of voice, but taken as an entirety, it can also be seen as indicative of a poem that understands the self as citational, something contingent upon being expressed in somebody else's language. The quote from Milton is not any more alien and alienating than what appears to be direct utterance. 'Skunk Hour' is therefore both personal and impersonal; read as a demonstration of the poet (or nihilist) as hero, the poem's distinctive voices and citations can be cited as evidence of Lowell's orchestration, expressing both his genius for the power of synthesis, and his will to discover it. Contrarily, however, it can be argued that language is composing itself around and through Lowell, and he works to find a lid to put on it, to discover a craft ('an eel-net', even) with a purpose, just as the 'fairy decorator' re-designates the tools of workmen as artisanal artefacture for his own uses, however ironically. Everybody in 'Skunk Hour' is some kind of artist, creating some kind of spectacle or text; in this context, Lowell is in fact engaged in the work of seeing himself as unexceptional, which takes exceptional work on his part.

---

10   Robert Lowell, 'Skunk Hour', *Collected Poems*, 191–192.

Lowell was always something of an unoriginalist, as Peter Davison has pointed out: 'Lowell's favourite poem was "Lycidas"; during his periodic mental breakdowns he would sometimes adopt Milton's poem as his own and rewrite it.'[11] In an interview, Lowell wrote about Milton's poem that confirmed that part of its intrigue for him lay in how citation generated a radical unoriginality: 'it's a very personal poem in a queer way, but it [...] this armor of convention is incredible. So whole sections of it won't seem original at all except verbally.'[12] This insight is something that Perloff comes curiously close to sharing in her regard for the new unoriginalists: 'Paradoxically, this new citational and often constraint-bound poetry – a poetry as visually and sonically formalized as it is semantically-charged – is more accessible, and, in a sense, "personal", than was the language poetry of twenty years earlier.'[13]

Lowell's sonnet 'Identification in Belfast' is based upon a TV interview with the Reverend Joseph Parker, a Church of Ireland chaplain whose son Stephen was killed along with ten others in multiple explosions across Belfast on 21 July 1972, which came to be known as Bloody Friday. Parker appeared on TV on Wednesday 26 July, then again in November of that year, and it is not entirely clear which broadcast Lowell would have seen, but what certainly did happen is that Parker tended to produce a remarkably consistent account of his ordeal on the day, across formats and time. This is a transcription of the relevant segment of the November interview, in which he recalls identifying the body of his son:

> My wife waited outside. The body was very badly ... his face, head was very badly, you know, well, disfigured. But it wasn't possible to recognize him as my son. I felt sorry for the man in the mortuary. He came up and said: 'I don't think that's your son.' I said, 'look in the pockets'. Of course, he pulled out a box of safety matches

---

11 Peter Davison 'The Poetry of Heartbreak', *The Atlantic* (July/August 2003), available online at: <https://www.theatlantic.com/magazine/archive/2003/07/the-poetry-of-heartbreak/302757/>, accessed 8 May 2019.
12 Jeffrey Meyers, ed., *Robert Lowell: Interviews and Memoirs* (Ann Arbor: University of Michigan Press, 1988), 36.
13 Perloff, *Unoriginal Genius*, xi.

and I looked and Stephen had fooled me two nights before. He was always buying these trick games and so on: joke matches.[14]

At this point, it should be added that Parker's words have been represented by many more writers than Lowell. In this respect, Parker was given a role of exemplary sufferer in 1972, in part because of his frankness and preparedness to speak directly to the media about his grief, but also because of his expressions of forgiveness for the perpetrators of the bombings (which were attributed to, and eventually admitted to by, the Provisional IRA). Parker also features prominently in the 'Victims' section of Jill and Leon Uris's *Ireland: A Terrible Beauty*, basically a coffee-table book of the Troubles that became an unlikely best-seller in the mid-1970s. Uris includes what again appears to be a transcript of Parker's original words to the media, resembling the ones that found their way into Lowell's poem:

> When I got the mortuary I knew there was a boy, the body of a boy there. I looked immediately for someone with fair hair. I was somewhat relieved that the hair was dark, but, of course, it was singed and burnt dark with the heat of the explosion. I thought immediately, though: it's not Stephan. And then I looked quickly again. I recognized the shirt as similar to the one Stephan had been wearing, but again it had been affected by the explosion. The belt was a Scout belt: he was a Scout, and a few days ago he put these studs all round in the belt and he stood there getting me to admire them; he was very clothes conscious. I asked one of the men: would he look in the pockets. I wanted to be absolutely sure. Anyway, he looked in the pockets and found this box of matches- trick matches that Stephan had used that evening before to fool me. And I saw they had no proper maker's label. But I wanted to be sure again-you cling onto everything-so I asked if anybody had a box of safety matches so I could strike one. The police were wonderful; they had found somebody in the road and they came in. I struck one, and then I tried it on the other. Then I knew it was Stephan.[15]

Uris continually misspells Stephen Parker's first name as 'Stephan', an error perhaps only explicable by his mishearing of Parker's accent. Errors of a different kind appear in the Merseybeat poet Roger McGough's poem 'Identification', which appeared in his 1973 volume, *Gig*. In his

---

14 A recording of the interview was presented again in a 2002 BBC Northern Ireland Documentary, from which the transcription was made.
15 Jill and Leon Uris, *Ireland: A Terrible Beauty* (London: Corgi, 1975), 262.

autobiography, *Said and Done* (2006), McGough talks about the cautious genesis of the poem, which 'took me seven months to write.' He emphasizes his care by drawing particular attention to comparisons between his own poem and Lowell's, particularly on their points of difference in detail. Yet McGough's autobiography is like that of many other people, as he has scores to settle, with uncomprehending critics and lucky poets that he reckons have got more attention than himself, which accounts for the sour note at the end of the passage:

> *Gig* is divided into two sections, *On the Road* and 'At the Roadside', and in the second is a poem that took me several months to write called 'The Identification.' The television news on the evening of 4 March 1972 reported yet another bombing in Belfast, at the Abercorn Restaurant filled at the time with shoppers and children. And after all the horrific scenes of carnage, there followed an interview with the father of one of the young victims. He was a Presbyterian minister and the dignity of the man almost transcended his grief, as he described the harrowing process of having to identify the body of Stephen, his son. The American poet Robert Lowell seems also to have been moved by the interview because the same incident is described in a collection of his called *Notebooks*, although in his poem the father recognises the body by a book of 'toy matches' in the child's pocket. In my version, there are no matches, but the father is puzzled by a packet of cigarettes:

> *Pockets. Empty the pockets.*
> *Handkerchief? Could be any schoolboy's.*
> *Dirty enough. Cigarettes?*
> *Oh this can't be Stephen.*
> *I don't allow him to smoke you see.*
> *He wouldn't disobey me. Not his father.*
> *But that's his penknife. That's his alright.*
> *And that's his key on the keyring*
> *Gran gave him just the other night.*
> *So this must be him.*

> *I think I know what happened ... about the cigarettes*
> *No doubt he was minding them for one of the older boys.*
> *Yes that's it.*
> *That's him.*
> *That's our Stephen.*

> I think it's a poem that works and I rather suspect that the critics at the bottom of my paperweight thought so too, because none of them referred to it in their petulant reviews.[16]

For all his pretentions to accuracy and care, McGough's memory fails him here or rather he commands it to fail him. Anyone familiar with 'Identification in Belfast' will know that it is in *History* not *Notebook*, and definitely not a collection called *Notebooks*. Anyone also familiar with the history of the Troubles will also know that a bombing in the Abercorn restaurant did take place on 4 March 1972, killing two women and injuring 130 people in total, but then they should remind themselves that Stephen Parker was in fact killed four months later on Bloody Friday, and that his father was not a Presbyterian minister, but a Church of Ireland chaplain. So despite his reliance on a documentary resource, McGough is highly susceptible to error, or even a negative form of wishful thinking. Once such a sense of hazard is introduced into a discourse, it begins to feel like every assertion should be prefaced with a 'Correct me if I'm wrong.'

I refer to these other rewritings because it raises the problems inherent in the concept of identification – problems that relate to the entirety of not just Lowell's concept of history, and its 'language of imperfection,' but any conceptualization of history. The tension between error and decision is precisely what must be recognized in all these texts. McGough points out that he changed Stephen Parker's toy matches to cigarettes, which performs the feat of turning him into a different kind of naughty boy to what his father described. It is remarkable to note here that McGough did not register Lowell's own radical alterations, changing Stephen's name to Richard, and conjuring with his religious designation by referring to him attending mass (which has the effect for an Irish reader at least of converting the boy to Catholicism). These conscious alterations and unconscious idiocies are what apparently separate Lowell's practice from the concept of direct citation which Goldsmith (sometimes) practices. Yet in a very obvious sense, they all might be viewed as highly conventional examples of poetic practice, a factually disinterested fashioning of material into the sublime object called

---

16   Roger McGough, *Said and Done* (London: Arrow, 2006), 282–283.

a poem. Perloff might argue that this is exactly what might have been expected of an *arrière gardiste*: take the spoken testimony, and then wrangle it into a reliably familiar structure like Lowell's (tautological) free sonnet. This is very much like Goldsmith's defence of his alterations to the Michael Brown text, however; and it can be argued that Lowell's poem in fact can be read in a more productively problematic way, one that is accountable to the problematics of identification in history. This thinking, which takes us into error upon error, nevertheless generates an aptly damaged sense of what happens when accountabilities to poetry and history coincide.

Lowell's poem makes no sense. Misidentification and dis-identification are as much part of his process as what his title promises; they act here as devices of alienation but also shame, preventing the reader from achieving a sentimental complacency with the predicament of Parker. There is evidently a violent irony in a poem called 'Identification in Belfast' that concludes with the mis-naming of its historical subject. The pathos of Parker's real situation is unignorable, of course; but it is also unimaginable, and the dis-identification of Stephen does not represent the denial of his history, rather its necessary prevention, so that Parker's particular suffering remains at least partially obscured. All of these rewritings can be seen as attempting to do the work of sorrowful recuperation which Walter Benjamin attributed to the angel of history; however, they all botch the job, not least because Joe Parker had already done the job so exemplarily.

The reason why Uris and the poets latched onto Parker's words was that they were so moving to anyone who heard or read them, of course; they also allowed for the construction of super-narratives that sought to convert his suffering into optimism (as in Uris's assertion that '[t]here is something Godlike about Joe Parker' (263)). Parker himself founded an pro-reconciliation organization named Witness for Peace, which seems to confirm that he chose a similar path, attempting to make Stephen's death mean something. At the same time, this was not a matter of achieving bromidical consolation; Parker's way of arguing for peace was in itself a matter of bodily agony, which saw him go on a hunger strike 'for sanity' on Thursday 21 September 1972. This public suffering was more intolerable for his own society than it was for himself, and he emigrated to Canada in 1974. Parker's life is properly tragic, therefore, an outcast not only because of his wretched grief, but his refusal to deal with it quietly. This story demolishes whatever pretensions a poet might have to making it feel worse than it is already, and exposes any attempt to do so as not only wishful, but brutal, thinking. Lowell's poem understands this better than the other representations of the death of Stephen Parker, even if this understanding might not necessarily make it a good poem.

Adorno's unbearably rigorous paragraph from 'On Commitment' articulates the shamefulness that ought to be attendant upon the representation of suffering:

> The so-called artistic representation of the sheer physical pain of people beaten to the ground by rifle butts contains, however remotely, the power to elicit enjoyment out of it. The moral of this art, not to forget for a single instant, slithers into the abyss of its opposite. The aesthetic principle of stylization, and even the solemn prayer of the chorus, make an unthinkable fate appear to have some meaning; it is transfigured, something of its horror is removed. This alone does an injustice to the victims; yet no art which tried to evade them could stand upright before justice. Even the sound of despair pays its tribute to a hideous affirmation. Works of less than the highest ranks are even willingly absorbed, as contributions to clearing up the past. When genocide becomes part of the cultural heritage in the themes of committed literature, it became easier to continue to play along with the culture which gave birth to murder ... There is one nearly invariable characteristic of such literature. It is that it implies, purposely or not, that even in the so-called extreme situations, indeed in them most of all, humanity flourishes.[17]

Lowell did not know about Joseph Parker's effective banishment when he wrote 'Identification in Belfast'; the point of the whole poem is what Lowell does not know. Through the apparently wilful inaccuracies, a ban on over-identification with the grieving father is established, so that the fantasy of flourishing humanity is not allowed to emerge. Lowell's hesitations in the face of his raw material acknowledge the unresolved nastiness of that which 'has happened', too much for a poem to encapsulate; at the same time, the poem can suggest the grotesqueness of the event, and the nausea of what is having to be experienced, whether the 'real' subject is known or not. In this, the poem is able to perform the role of being

---

17   Theodor Adorno and Francis McDonagh, 'On Commitment: Part Two', *Performing Arts Journal* 3.3 (Winter 1979): 60.

necessarily inadequate to the reality of the event. As Slavoj Žižek argues in *On Violence*, this is precisely where poetry can address 'the unbearable' by not even pretending to be up to the job: '[P]oetry is, by definition, "about" something that cannot be addressed directly, only alluded to. One shouldn't be afraid to take this a step further and refer to the old saying that music comes when words fail.'[18]

'Identification in Belfast' begins with identification as explanation, the demand that Northern Irish violence always requires contextualization. This is provided with increasing complication; the title is politically neutral, if such a thing was or is possible in Belfast. Then a parenthetical sub-title, '*(I.R.A Bombing)*' identifies the type of event that is being described (practically unprecedented in *History*); but an IRA bombing is not simply an IRA bombing (it is worth remarking that the Provisional IRA only officially admitted responsibility for Bloody Friday thirty years after the event). Calling a bombing an IRA bombing is in itself a gesture of misrecognition in the context of 1972, as it was a matter of considerable significance whether you were talking about the Official IRA or the Provisional IRA at that time. It is tempting to say that would not matter to an external viewer like Lowell, but then the opening three lines make clear that it did. Making reference to the British Army carrying guns with live ammunition for 'the Provisionals,' while they have ones that shoot 'rubber rabbit-pellets' at children. These lines sound like Lowell in classic mode, stirring an infernally cartoonish vision of institutionalized thuggery that is both arbitrary and horribly practical; the man-killing and child-wounding soldiers of the state feel sure to become the consuming subject of the poem, but then they disappear. Even at that, the detail of the 'rabbit-pellets' is odd, rather minimizing the size of the rubber bullets which the Army had employed since 1970. The urge to alliterate was evidently irresistible, but it also gives an indication of how removed Lowell is from the reality of the situation. He knows what he has heard, and what he sees on television; but the question remains about what of that exactly amounts to. Someone referring to 'the Provisionals' is evidently in the know, but someone referring to 'rabbit pellets' is not.

18   Slavoj Žižek, *On Violence* (London: Profile Books, 2008), 4.

The poem then moves into the adaptation of Parker's words, and its revelation of the body of 'Richard' (or anyone-but-Stephen). This asks the reader to leap from contemplating the Provisionals and children as potential victims of the British Army to thinking of children as victims of the Provisionals, although the poem does not make this entirely explicit. These words do not overrule the potential terrors of the soldier-thugs from the beginning of the poem (who are carrying over their work from My Lai in 'Women Children, Babies, Cows, Cats'), but countermand them; the result is a stalemate between Parker's denuded decency and two killing machines. McGough risks turning the atrocity into *kitsch* with 'Our Steven'; Lowell's poem runs the same risk, but in its failure to name its real subject, it directs us away from the poem into the complex and error-strewn historicity which we have here uncovered. That is exactly what Michael Hofmann has indicated as the overall problem of Lowell's *History*, 'that it is unsatisfactory, over-revised, even preposterous. It is Lowell's Brasilia or his Disneyworld.'[19] *History* is both a modernist folly and a *pomo* debacle, with its slippage of events into error and waste, and this represents an understanding which had already appeared in Lowell's appendix to *Notebook 1967–68*: 'Dates fade faster than we do. Many in the last two years are already gone; in a year or two, most of the rest will slip.'[20] *History* is a book-poem with an Ovidian trajectory from the beginning of the remembered to the horrors of the present, one where your mother can become Clytemnestra. This is indeed grotesque. It is a fuse lit with joke-matches. Everyone is provisional. One of the terminal ironies attendant upon 'Identification in Belfast' is that its aesthetics of shame show the very scruple which Lowell was suspected of not having when he incorporated Hardwick's letters into *The Dolphin*; notoriously, Bishop admonished him, writing 'Art isn't worth

---

19 Michael Hofmann, 'His Own Prophet' in *London Review of Books* (11 September 2003): 3–8, available online at: <https://www.lrb.co.uk/v25/n17/michael-hofmann/his-own-prophet> (accessed 8 May 2019).
20 Robert Lowell, *Notebook 1967–68*, ed. Jonathan Galassi (London: Faber and Faber, 2009), 163.

that much.'[21] In the self-admonishing citational poetics of 'Identification in Belfast', about suffering, Lowell agrees.

Responses to specific incidents in Northern Ireland by native poets at this time were no less confused. In the face of Ulster's catastrophes, Seamus Heaney's impulse was often to find a way to let the dead speak rather than himself, or to give himself the task of imagining how they might speak if they could; the vital citational source for this is Dante, as in *Field Work* and *Station Island*, but that inevitably means that he gets caught up in a vision of judgement which is (and is not) his own. So in the celebrated 'Casualty' from *Field Work,* the poem exists to do the Lycidian work of motivationally rebuking the poet as much as memorializing the dead fisherman. Even as the poem seeks to respond adequately to the depredations of the political, it cannot forget its desire to remain a poem, nor can its poet relinquish the role of poet. That makes the poem more vivid, even as it jeopardizes its claim to moral (if not artistic) authority. A very Lowellian bind. Other poets were more strident in providing a moral judgement without such citational filtration; various poems on specific incidents produced culminatory verdicts which in effect represent the poet assuming a choric voice of common law. So in James Simmons' ballad of response in 1974 to the bombing at Claudy – 'Meanwhile to Dungiven the killers have gone / And they're finding it hard to get through on the phone'[22] – or in Michael Longley's 'Wounds', where 'a shivering boy' utters a startlingly inadequate apology to the wife of a man that he has just shot: 'I think "Sorry Missus" is what he said.'[23] Here Northern Irish poets adopt variously subtle and unsubtle methods of response to atrocity, and they do so out of a confident sense of moral agreement; they are speaking out of outrage, and trying to measure it in rhyme. They assume their right to the choric voice, laying claim that the values which they express are pre-eminent. Lowell has no access to such assumptions in 'Identification in Belfast', where the answer to his own question 'Why not just say what happened?' can only be met with other questions. What has happened? What did happen? How can

---

21   Elizabeth Bishop, 'One Art', *Poems, Prose and Letters* (New York: Library of America), 167.
22   James Simmons. 'Claudy', *Poems 1956–1986* (Loughcrew: Gallery Press, 1986), 126.
23   Michael Longley, 'Wounds', *Poems 1963–1983* (Loughcrew: Gallery Press, 1985), 86.

you say that if you do not understand the dimensions of what you have experienced? Critically for him in particular, how can you judge if you are only an American spectator?

It should be said here that even if Lowell makes use of citation, he could never be really citational in the thorough sense which Perloff advocates, namely because he can never be disinterested enough (but neither can Goldsmith). So Lowell could not write the 'non-expressive poetry' that Craig Dworkin describes, for example, with its rejection of 'self-regard of the poet's ego'.[24] For Perloff, Lowell acts to represent the poet-as-ego, and there is evidently much in his poetry to justify such a verdict; but no ego exists in isolation, and it does not necessarily prevail. Against that formidable will-to-power in Lowell, there is something less familiar but equally active, and it comes to the fore dramatically when he adopts the ironic constraint of the free sonnets of *History* and *Notebook*. In these poems, form is nearly arbitrary in terms of its ability to process Lowell's raw materials. The risk of slackness and banality attends everything, radically channelling Lowell towards misconstruction and misunderstanding. As this happens, Lowell becomes more compelling as a poet of injury, waste and shame, a garbage-sifting sniffer of air.

Christopher Ricks' comment on the dustjacket of Lowell's *Collected Poems* about the American poet having a 'technical mastery that is inseparable from imaginative mastery' must be complemented with an inference of an equally complacent relationship between technical and imaginative failure, one that is ever present both in the work of Lowell and his contemporaries. Failure in Jarrell and Berryman's work is a perversely vital presence, for example, and it is also vital to cite the presence of failure during generic discussions of Bishops's mastery as a technician, as if art redeemed every failure she ever made of her life. It might be more productive to say that failures can be so overwhelming that it takes a heave of effort to make them at least bearable. That is a different kind of mastery to that which we might attach to the arts and acts of a supremo. We all know how Bishop writes that the 'Art of losing isn't hard to master', and duly get the joke, yet

---

24   Quoted in Perloff, *Unoriginal Genius*, 17.

at the same time mastery is then reduced to a state of zero potential.[25] Who would want to be able to write a direfully ironic line of such command?

Nobody has ever written about 'Identification in Belfast' in terms of mastery; in fact, hardly anybody has ever written about the poem at all. Nevertheless, it is compelling to cite as a poem where Lowell practically surrenders mastery, both technical and imaginative. What this in turn generates is a mode of query that is above all moral, even as that might be an embarrassing discourse to countenance. Lowell's poem still compels because it energizes a moral response, the rewriting implies a wronging; above all, the poem generates a disgust in its reader, or a series of disgusts. Firstly, there is the sheer wretchedness of the father's situation; but then there is the potential for offense that is discovered when the peculiarity of Lowell's alterations comes into play. That said, the alterations practically call themselves to the reader's attention. There is no struggle about this, rather a resignation to the idea of being fated to do the wrong thing. This can indeed exasperate, and might sound like the 'bullshit eloquence' which Adrienne Rich heard in the epitaphic announcements of *The Dolphin* about 'not avoiding injury to others, not avoiding injury to myself.'[26] Eloquence was all Lowell had, his first and last resort, and he knew it, the quality that could make him a proper inheritor of the Winslow-Lowell eminence; yet he increasingly deployed it in a way that seems desperate. In 'Identification in Belfast', it deserted him entirely.

---

25 Elizabeth Bishop, 'One Art', *Poems, Prose and Letters*, 166–167.
26 Adrienne Rich, 'Caryatid: A Column', *American Poetry Review* 2 (September–October 1973): 42–43.

LUCY COLLINS

Lost Connections: Reading Family in the Poetry of Eavan Boland and Robert Lowell

The relationship between individual experience and national identity has been formative of Eavan Boland's creative work and its critical reception. In this she has both responded to the cultural conditions of her time and helped to shape its critical debates. As a reader of poetry, Boland is conscious of the many ways in which the intersection between personal and political has found expression in language, and of the specific cultural contexts of this representation. Her engagement with American poetry is informed and extensive, and has influenced her own creative development in significant ways. The construction of individual subjectivity in poetry written in the United States since the 1950s has been especially important for Boland, offering insights into the challenges of self-representation that she herself faced as an Irish woman. Among these poets Robert Lowell was a formative figure for Boland, not only in his range and ambition, but because of the extent of his influence. This authority waned somewhat after his death and, in 1995, Boland felt the need to restate his importance for the general reader, and to suggest that critical fashion was to blame in keeping his reputation 'currently far below what it ought to be'.[1] Boland learned much from Lowell's work, but it was his representation of family, and of the spaces of private encounter, that had the greatest impact on her writing. In this essay I will explore *Life Studies* (1959) as a pivotal volume for the exploration of familial relationships, and examine the ways in which it prompted Boland to move to a new creative phase.

1   Eavan Boland, review of Paul Mariani, *The Lost Puritan: A Life of Robert Lowell* in *The Irish Times*, 21 January 1995.

Lowell published his first collection in 1944 – a fallow time in Irish poetry, coming between the death of W.B. Yeats and the emergence, a decade later, of the 'Dolmen Poets', which included John Montague, Thomas Kinsella and Richard Murphy. The renaissance in Irish poetry that took place in the 1950s also rejuvenated poetry criticism and brought an attention to American work that offered new stimulus for a rising generation in Ireland. Among American poets Lowell was already establishing a reputation: Austin Clarke, in his *Irish Times* review of the Faber edition of Lowell's *Poems 1938–49*, remarked on the poet's 'rapid recognition', marked by a Pulitzer Prize in 1947.[2] In 1955, the 'Irishman's Diary' column in the same newspaper recorded Karl Shapiro's identification of Lowell as the heir to Robert Frost. Despite Shapiro's assertion that American poets were not as well known internationally as writers in other genres, their work was regularly reviewed in Ireland and Seamus Heaney, Michael Longley and Derek Mahon all engaged deeply with Lowell's work.

In the course of the 1970s, Eavan Boland reviewed all Lowell's major volumes of poetry published, reflecting in particular on the relationship between private and public modes in his work. *Life Studies*, though it appeared before Boland had herself begun publishing poems, is a book to which she returns when reflecting on the representation of personal material in poetry. Other work by Lowell also draws her attention: in her review of Richard Ellmann's *New Oxford Book of American Verse* (1976), she distinguishes between nineteenth-century work, which she reads as a 'casualty to transcendentalist sentiment or fundamentalist religion', and the achievement of twentieth-century American poetry.[3] The tensions between tradition and modernity are highlighted in her exploration of Lowell's 'For the Union Dead', one of the two poems she draws on directly in this review. In her own work this opposition was already becoming evident in her juxtaposition of poems such as 'Ode to Suburbia' and 'The Hanging Judge' in *The War Horse* (1975), and this conjunction would be intensified in the sustained engagement with history that has shaped Boland's

---

2 Austin Clarke, review of Robert Lowell, *Poems 1938–49* in *The Irish Times*, 30 September 1950.
3 Eavan Boland, 'American Poetry', *The Irish Times*, 3 December 1976, 12.

work from the late 1980s onwards. Her reflection on the shaping force of private experience is seen as early as 1970, however. Even public poetry is rooted in the private and familial, she argues: 'It begins and grows, not in received truths or rituals of the day, but in [...] private neighbourhoods [...] filial pieties'.[4]

The increasingly vexed relationship between the private and public in Lowell's work would yield to controversy in his use of personal letters from his estranged wife – writer Elizabeth Hardwick – in *The Dolphin* (1973). Before that, *Life Studies* had set new terms by which larger patterns of history could be read through generations of a single family. Lowell recalls the book as a 'windfall', after 'six or seven years' ineptitude – a slack of eternity'.[5] It was written in two years, 'in two lunges' and, after this, Lowell found that 'continuous autobiography was impossible'.[6] As well as marking a radical change in formal approach, the book represents a tonal shift from earlier poems. Lowell has noted the ways in which this evolving style was shaped by public reading: 'I hoped to write poems as pliant as conversation, so clear a listener might get every word'.[7] This clarity and openness also yielded a more tolerant approach to the lives of others. Marjorie Perloff describes the speaker as a 'quietly meditative, delicately humorous and humble self who would rather *see* than *judge*'.[8] This new capacity to release his family stories into a larger interpretative context is later picked up by Boland when she tests the boundaries between private and public narratives in both poetry and prose. From Lowell she would have learned much about the expression of grief and loss, and how this can be focused through the dynamics of intimate life. For Boland, however, this process offers a unique opportunity to place woman at the centre of the experience. It is by opening Irish poetry to the significance of domestic environments as spaces where consciousness is formed and relationships negotiated, that Boland is able to integrate the

4   Eavan Boland, 'Poetry and Theory', *The Irish Times*, 12 November 1970, 10.
5   Robert Lowell, 'A Conversation with Ian Hamilton' in *Collected Prose* (New York: Farrar, Straus and Giroux, 1987), 269.
6   Ibid. 269.
7   Ibid. 284.
8   Marjorie Perloff, 'Death By Water: The Winslow Elegies of Robert Lowell', *ELH* 34.1 (March 1967): 117.

reality of women's lives into larger political narratives. Like Lowell, Boland faces criticism concerning the socially privileged perspective from which she speaks, but her awareness of the responsibilities of this representation have shaped critical debate in far-reaching ways.

Spaces of Childhood

Lowell's sense of history is closely linked to the significance of his forebears in early New England society. He was born into a prominent Boston family that counted poets James Russell Lowell and Amy Lowell, and General Charles Russell Lowell III, among its members. His mother's heritage could reputedly be traced to the *Mayflower*; her ancestor, theologian Jonathan Edwards, would be the subject of several poems by Lowell. '91 Revere Street', a section of *Life Studies* written in prose, explores this background in depth. Lowell's repeated return to spaces of childhood, and the innovative ways he chose to accomplish this – was a way of deepening engagement with the self that had been inherited from the Romantic poets. Yet Lowell's approach was more radical still. Abrupt transitions and elliptical phrasing emphasize process rather than resolution, and the elegiac mood of *Life Studies* evokes the end of an era of social confidence and economic privilege in provocative ways. Boland acknowledges the originality of this strategy: 'One would not have thought the Devereux and Winslows, with their feuds and eccentricities, their trust funds and sense of civic service, a likely theme for poetry. Gradually, however, the sanity of Lowell's obsession emerged'.[9] His strategy, as William Doreski has observed, was as much a response to public discourse in Eisenhower's America, as it was to the poet's private or aesthetic challenges.[10] Elizabeth Bishop's response to the book also acknowledges the reach of the poems,

---

9   Boland, 'Poetry and Theory', 10.
10 William Doreski, *Robert Lowell's Shifting Colors: The Poetics of the Public and the Personal* (Athens: Ohio University Press, 1999), 73.

noting a tonal shift between the opening group of texts and the 'Life Studies' sequence:

> In these poems, heart-breaking, shocking, grotesque and gentle, the unhesitant attack, the imagery and construction, are as brilliant as ever, but the mood is nostalgic and the meter is refined. A poem like 'My Last Afternoon with Uncle Devereux Winslow,' or 'Skunk Hour,' can tell us as much about the state of society as a volume of Henry James at his best. Whenever I read a poem by Robert Lowell I have a chilling sensation of here-and-now, of exact contemporaneity: more aware of those 'ironies of American history,' grimmer about them, and yet hopeful.[11]

Though Bishop was not living in America at the time, she recognized the ethical significance of this work. The debasement of language in a politically conformist and media-saturated culture necessitated a heightened sense of history, and Boland notes the conflict between Lowell's subject matter and the 'new and dangerous world' from which he writes.[12] For her, this is more than a theme, but becomes instead a governing symbol of Lowell's imagination,[13] and one that makes future art possible. This conclusion is significant, because what Boland learns from Lowell is that repeated attention to the particularity of these familial relationships can create a sustaining personal myth. These poems were written while Lowell was on the edge of mental collapse, and the heightened energy that made them possible reflects the movement from self-possession to despair that traces the passage of Lowell's manic episodes. The passivity and isolation of the drifting speaker of 'Skunk Hour' – 'I myself am hell, / nobody's here'[14] – is profound, but it is also part of a larger pattern of continuous movement between past and present, illness and recovery, that shaped Lowell's life and work.

Boland's understanding of the relationship between traumatic experience and the space of the family is somewhat different. *In Her Own Image*,

---

11   Elizabeth Bishop, comments enclosed in a letter to Robert Lowell, February 1959, in Thomas Travisano with Saskia Hamilton, eds, *Words in Air: The Complete Correspondence between Elizabeth Bishop and Robert Lowell* (New York: Farrar, Straus and Giroux, 2008), 289–290.
12   Boland, 'Poetry and Theory', 10.
13   Ibid. 10.
14   Robert Lowell, *Life Studies* (London: Faber and Faber, 2001), 98.

Boland's third major collection, sought to disrupt the lyric containment of her earlier poems with its unflinching attention to the female body. Only when she has gone through this process of self-exposure can she situate the experience of Irish women within a longer *durée* – one that makes clear the restricted potential of women, as citizens and as artists. As Boland's engagement with family history deepens, so do her claims for the larger critical significance of this work. Lowell's radical experiment with form and sequence in *Life Studies* informs Boland's creation in *Object Lessons: The Life of the Woman and the Poet in Our Time* (1995) of a prose form that renders autobiography and critical reflection as entwined and mutually dependent forms. In this work, and in the many poems that engage with family history, Boland explicitly addresses the construction of her own poetic subjectivity. In terms of generational influence, Boland's situation is somewhat different from that of Lowell: with a father a diplomat and a mother an artist, her access to privilege, education and artistic empowerment was clear. It is her grandparents' generation that is marked by the challenges of a country in political and social turmoil, where lives are compromised by limited choices and challenging economic conditions. The upward trajectory of Boland's family circumstances reverses the diminishing social fortunes of the Lowell clan, though both poets are attuned to these periods of significant social transition.

These transitions are often understood in material terms, and Martin Heidegger's representation of the home not as the result of building, but as a necessary precursor to it, affirms the home's foundational importance to the creative act.[15] It facilitates the interrelationship of past and present, foregrounds issues of enclosure and freedom, and allows kinship and sexual relationships to be interrogated. Though *Life Studies* is a volume in which processes of change and transition are figured both formally and thematically, modes of containment are also important. Lowell often figures his mental condition in spatial form, and a poem such as 'Waking in the Blue' addresses the experience of breakdown through the competing subjectivities found within the space of the mental hospital. In this essay

---

15   Martin Heidegger, 'Building Dwelling Thinking' in *Basic Writings*, ed. David Farrell Krell (Oxford: Routledge, 1993), 348.

'Near the Unbalanced Aquarium' the poet figures his recovery from a manic episode in terms of an environment at once sterile and in flux:

> What I saw were the blind white bricks of other parts of the hospital rising in my window. Down the corridor, almost a city block away, I heard the elevator jar shut and hum like a kettle as it soared to the top floor … In my distraction, the walls of the hospital seemed to change shape like limp white clouds. I thought I saw a hard enameled wedding cake, and beside it, holding the blunt silver knife of the ritual, stood the tall white stone bride – my mother.[16]

Here the boundaries of the hospital space alter to accommodate the speaker's adjusting perspective; all that is solid melts into air. What remains immutable is the wedding scene, with the mother as bride – its generative potential given a Freudian twist and rendered in a coldly monumental image. The tensions in *Life Studies* between freedom of movement through space and time, and figures of constraint and diminution, exert a shaping force on the book as a whole, in which transitions between countries (Italy and France, Italy and America) are set against images of containment. More significantly, the representations of the institution – prison and hospital – become interchangeable with those of the home. The reduced freedoms of recovery prove sustained, and the poet loiters with his baby daughter in the bathroom, much as 'Stanley' soaked in his long tub in 'Waking in the Blue'. These overlapping images of restraint and security raise issues recognized by Boland in her investigation of the comfort and estrangement of domestic space. Her fellow Irish poet Medbh McGuckian has called the house 'a place of safety that is also a prison',[17] and the implications of this duality for Irish women can hardly be over-emphasized. If Lowell's subjectivity is troubled by difficult family relationships and persistent mental illness, Boland's reflects the pressures on female self-representation that affected generations of Irish women.

The instabilities of childhood experience play an important role in the representation of the past by these poets. For Lowell these uncertainties were focused on his parents' unhappy marriage, but for Boland the space

---

16 Robert Lowell, 'Near the Unbalanced Aquarium' in *Collected Prose*, 347.
17 See Adam Hanna, *Northern Irish Poetry and Domestic Space* (London: Palgrave Macmillan, 2015), loc. 2844 (Kindle Edition).

of the home itself was unfixed. As the daughter of a diplomat she was at once identifiably Irish, yet always living at some distance from home. Her memories of London, where she moved as a young girl, are shaped by the feeling of otherness that permeated her childhood. These experiences also affirm the sense of cultural difference that inflects the perceiving self. Boland has used the physical spaces of the city and the interior of the house to express the dynamics of belonging and exclusion that have shaped her poetic development:

> My childhood, certainly in the London years, wasn't happy. That isn't to say it wasn't a privileged childhood, because it was. But it was fictional and desolate in an odd way ... there was this huge, compartmentalised house. And I felt thoroughly displaced in it. I never believed I belonged there. I never felt it was my home. Some of the feelings I recognise as having migrated into themes I keep going back to – exile, types of estrangement, a relation to objects – began there.[18]

Adrift in a city not her own, the child appears to register the necessary distance from her own experience expected of the nascent artist. Yet this is a construction of the adult poet, whose purpose is to trace continuities between these early memories and her later preoccupations. Our inability, writes Yi-Fu Tuan, 'to recapture the mood of [our] own childhood world, suggests how far the adult's schemata, geared primarily to the world's practical demands, differ from those of the child'.[19] It is telling, then, that Boland's process is expressed through the metaphor of the compartmentalized house – one that represents family life as marked by disconnection rather than intimacy, and suggests the distinct aesthetic and political aims of Boland's later work. This image also powerfully represents the cultural estrangement that the poet experienced and that, for a time, masked the marginalizing forces to which all Irish women of Boland's generation were subject. For her the challenges to integration into the intellectual life of modern Ireland were two-fold, and Lowell's exploration of the competing forces of inherited status and rising social pressures, though distinct from Boland's own experience, would have been resonant for her.

18   Jody Allen Randolph, 'Interview with Eavan Boland', *Irish University Review* 23.1 (Spring/Summer, 1993): 117.
19   Yi-Fu Tuan, *Space and Place: The Perspective of Experience* (Minneapolis: University of Minnesota Press, 1977), 20.

Lowell's creation of a memorable landscape in *Life Studies* revealed the role of both natural and built spaces in the formation of human subjects. Boland was alert to the resonance of these in the context of Irish history, and especially for the woman whose erasure from the narrative of Irish history also rendered her invisible in both public and domestic spaces. Places of origin are therefore important to both poets – in the words of Gaston Bachelard, 'the house we are born in is an inhabited house. In it the values of intimacy are scattered, they are not easily stabilized, they are subjected to dialectics'.[20] Though Lowell's childhood was marked by several changes of address, his grandparents' farm is noted as a place of origin, and as a site where the representation of subjectivity itself can be scrutinised. Setting childhood locations alongside those of adult experience – the summer memories of Mattapoisett and Beverly Farms and the forced confinement of McLeans and West Street Jail – Lowell explores unexpected connections across space and time, in the face of radical personal and social change.

Naming the Ancestors

As Kay Redfield Jamison has remarked, 'the family names of his father and mother represented different things to Lowell at different times in his life'.[21] As well as providing imaginative material for his writing, they offered a way of exploring what was consistent and mutable about his identity. His friend and fellow poet Elizabeth Bishop seems to hint at the limits of this strategy: 'I must confess ... that I am green with envy of your kind of assurance. I feel I could write in as much detail of my Uncle Artie, say – but what would be the significance?'[22] Similarly, the conviction

---

20   Gaston Bachelard, *The Poetics of Space*, trans. Maria Jolas (Boston, MA: Beacon Press, 1969), 14.
21   Kay Redfield Jamison, *Robert Lowell: Setting the River on Fire* (New York: Vintage, 2017), 33.
22   In her essay 'Elizabeth Bishop: An Unromantic American', Boland suggests that Bishop implies here that 'naming the past is not quite the same thing as knowing it'. See Boland, *A Journey With Two Maps: Becoming a Woman Poet* (Manchester: Carcanet, 2011), 141.

of cultural authority that is expressed in Lowell's work is an important point of distinction between his position and Boland's. Her forebears are barely visible within the narrative of Irish history. Her great-grandfather, master of the workhouse in Clonmel, has first-hand knowledge of the deprivation and suffering of famine times, and his life is entangled with the needy. Though a traceable public role makes him more accessible to Boland than her great-grandmother, both figures are expressive of the traumas of Irish history.

In Lowell's poem 'Sailing Home from Rapallo' the misspelling of his mother's name in 'grandiloquent lettering' indicates the triumph of style over substance. The unspoken hierarchies of New England history are compromised by Charlotte Winslow Lowell's death in Europe, but her return home for burial ensures a permanent monument to her life. For Boland, the act of naming is linked to retrieval from obscurity, and this is made difficult by the challenges and discontinuities of Irish history. In the poet's search for her grandmother's gravestone the name is the essential marker: 'I began to search through them for her name, reaching my hand down through the high grass and moss as if into water, trying to feel a lettering.'[23] Later this search will be refigured in a poem, published in *Code* (2001): 'How the Earth and All the Planets Were Created' enacts the search 'among marsh grass and granite/and single headstones/and smashed lettering.'[24] This continued failure of identification is significant – it consigns her grandmother to anonymity and ensures that she, like so many women of her generation, cannot be fully restored to history:

> For once I said
> I will face this landscape
> And look at it as she was looked upon:
>
> Unloved because unknown.
> Unknown because un-named.[25]

---

23 Eavan Boland, *Object Lessons: The Life of the Woman and the Poet in our Time* (London: Vintage, 1995), 22.
24 Eavan Boland, *New Collected Poems* (Manchester: Carcanet, 2005), 303.
25 Ibid. 303.

By the time this poem was written Boland's grandmother had been the subject of repeated representation in both poetry and prose. Boland had noted Lowell's transformation of his family into an imaginative symbol, and her own ancestors undergo a similar transition. Yet it is not their authority but their occlusion that necessitates their return – Boland's failure to place them securely in history exemplifies the unending search for the marginalized figures of history. This is why she chooses to begin *Object Lessons* by retracing the final days in the life of her grandmother. The National Maternity Hospital on Holles Street is still a Dublin landmark, and the juxtaposition of the view towards the hills with the back streets acknowledges the diverse living conditions of the city: 'Fenian Street. Hogan Place. Past the mills. Past the Dodder River on its way to the Liffey … It is not a long drive. But whatever she saw that morning it is lost'.[26] Here spatial continuities allow Boland to bring the experiences of past generations to life, while acknowledging too their inevitable strangeness.

As early as *The Journey*, a pivotal volume from 1987, Boland was situating the lives of generations of Irishwomen in close proximity. Dedicated to her mother, the volume is divided into three parts and represents the poet's own life as a wife and mother in suburban Dublin, alongside memories of her childhood and elements of her ancestor's lives. Her grandmother's entry into the poem 'Fever' is first matter-of-fact: 'My grandmother died in a fever ward, / younger than I am and far from/the sweet chills of a Louth spring', but the focus soon becomes

> Names, shadows, visitations, hints
> and a half-sense of half-lives remain.
> And nothing else, nothing more unless
>
> I re-construct the soaked-through midnights;
> vigils; the histories I never learned
> to predict the lyric of; and re-construct
> risk; as if silence could become rage.[27]

Boland chooses a different route from that followed by Lowell, presenting these figures as part of the tangled skeins of Irish history, present

26 Boland, *Object Lessons*, 4.
27 Boland, *New Collected Poems*, 134.

within the currents of social and political change, rather than standing apart from them.

The role of grandparents – and of an extended family circle – in exploring the interface between the family unit and larger social structures, is a point of connection between these two poets. The childhood encounter with parent and grandparent is an essential part of Lowell's *Life Studies* and the context in which this encounter takes place exerts a shaping force on the family. The relationship between natural and built environments is highlighted early in 'My Last Afternoon with Uncle Devereux Winslow' where house and farm are closely linked, framed by an 'alley of poplars' linking the cultivated rose garden to a stand of virgin pine.[28] The child is on the threshold, and thus focalizes the relationship between indoors and outdoors, past and future, innocence and experience. His view is mediated through the black-grained screen; he is shadowed by death and loss but conscious of his place in the world, and of his relationship with the people and objects that surround him. Lifelessness and vitality are entwined throughout *Life Studies*, in recognition of the energies sustaining creative work in the shadow of Lowell's mental illness. The material legacy of his grandparents – the objects and habits that shape their life together – express a world that is fading from view. The 'pastel-pale Huckleberry Finn' is drained of vibrancy, a clichéd version of the classic American text, itself a unique reflection of a lost world.[29] The 'disproportioned' setting of the farm is also an amalgam of disparate parts, its blended drinks and composite name hinting at the mixed fate even of these privileged lives. Boland shares Lowell's understanding of the fated nature of these precursors, and his awareness of their diminished lives and thwarted expectations.

---

28   Lowell, *Life Studies*, 67.
29   Ibid. 68.

Object Lessons

The relationship between individual subjects and the narrative of history can be meaningfully mapped through material culture. It is especially illuminating where the subjects in question are marginalized ones, or at times when their social capital is changing in significant ways. Daniel Miller has noted our tendency to assume that the truth of our own subjectivity is located within us, rather than on the surface of our lives, thereby diminishing the significance of material objects.[30] This 'depth ontology' is radically revised by Lowell, whose engagement with challenging mental states – and difficult personal relationships – is often framed within a world of objects. In emphasizing the relational dimension of these objects, Lowell explores how the material culture of others shapes our interaction with the world. The space of the house, and the significance its interior has gathered over time, is an important means by which the individual subject's place in history can be negotiated.

The world that Lowell creates in *Life Studies* is shaped by the material world, and by the complex intersection of social expectations and economic circumstances that determined his parents' lives. The 'town house furniture', incongruous in the cottage at Beverly Farms after his father's death, highlights the mismatch of past and present circumstances. Eastern objects – the 'uncomfortable boulder' with its Japanese associations in 'Terminal Days at Beverly Farms', and the kimono and sandals in 'Father's Bedroom', speak to the fashion for oriental objects as well as the specific history of Lowell's family As Frank Kearful has pointed out, this reference points back to an earlier poem – 'Buttercups' from *Lord Weary's Castle* (1946) – that links Lowell ancestry with China: 'On Ancrem Winslow's ponderous blue plate from China.'[31] Western fascination with foreign objects, which soon translates into commercial opportunity, is made meaningful here by

---

30 Daniel Miller, *Stuff* (London: Polity, 2010), 16.
31 Frank J. Kearful, 'Connecting Rooms: Entering "Father's Bedroom" in Robert Lowell's *Life Studies*', *Partial Answers: Journal of Literature and the History of Ideas* 6.1 (January 2008): 111–133; 122.

their specific connection to the experience of a family member, and a hint at ceremonial use.

Inherited objects have a very different significance to those that have been purchased, and Boland also represents these things to question how the past can be apprehended and used. 'The Black Lace Fan My Mother Gave Me' – the opening poem in the 'Object Lessons' section of *Outside History* (1990) – highlights the role of gifts in the transmission of meaning between generations. This object has a double significance: it was given first by the poet's father to her mother and then passed down to the poet herself. It is emblematic of the uncertain progress of relationships, the true importance of which can only be judged retrospectively. An object of beauty and utility, it also tells a story of exploitation, both of natural resources and of women's labour:

> These are wild roses, appliquéd on silk by hand,
> darkly picked, stitched boldly, quickly.
> The rest is tortoiseshell and has the reticent,
> clear patience of its element. It is
>
> a worn-out, underwater bullion and it keeps,
> even now, an inference of its violation.[32]

The object is expressive of its time and place but also serves as a way to question our versions of the past: 'And no way to know what happened then – /none at all – unless, of course, you improvise'.[33] Though the fan is the focus of the poem, it is used to raise questions about the nature of creative inspiration. The blackbird that appears in the final stanza mirrors the fan's shape and movement, but suggests too the power of association that underpins the poem as a whole. The created object mimics nature, though the way the poet frames the observation may reverse this process.

This poem and others by Boland – such as 'Lava Cameo' – use clothing and objects of adornment to explore the ways in which the past may be lost and preserved. The latter poem touches directly on the circumstances of Boland's grandparents' lives but centres on the role of language in opening

---

32   Boland, *New Collected Poems*, 165.
33   Ibid. 165.

imaginative possibilities. In the absence of established histories these objects offer ways of framing the narratives of previous generations. For those whose forebears occupy a more central position in the narrative of history, these elements assume a different kind of significance. Clothing is of particular importance in the expression of status and intention in Lowell's work, both because of its transformative potential and its role in protecting the self. The child speaker's 'formal pearl gray shorts' and 'sailor blouse' privilege propriety over comfort and indicate the boy's co-option into family myths of naval authority and status. Lowell is thus entered into a masculine hierarchy: generations of men in Lowell's family circle are understood through the symbolism of clothing – the 'severe war uniform' in which Uncle Devereux is photographed, the wine-dark coat of the portrait of Edward Winslow and the blue serge jacket and 'numbly cut white ducks' of the father's golf course attire. The strongest link in this leave-taking poem is between the boy and his uncle, whose ensemble is also implausibly neat: 'His blue coat and white trousers/grew sharper and straighter. / His coat was a blue jay's tail,/his trousers were solid cream from the top of the bottle'.[34] As the description becomes more lyrical, so the poet's consciousness moves further from the shocking reality of the young man's impending death, though Devereux' perfected exterior can ultimately neither disguise nor compensate for his terminal illness. If the poet's own malaise shadows the volume as a whole – developed explicitly in 'Home After Three Months Away' and the final meditation of 'Skunk Hour' – this sartorial mimicry of his dying uncle prefigures the subject of suffering and death in resonant ways.

Journeying towards Death

The evolving representation of material culture in *Life Studies* is highlighted by the accelerated modernity of mid-century America, and its implications for the book's larger patterns of mobility and containment.

---

34 Lowell, 'My Last Afternoon with Uncle Devereux Winslow', *Life Studies*, 71.

Even Lowell's grandparents are part of this dynamic modern portrayal: 'champing for their ritual Friday spin/to pharmacist and five-and-ten in Brockton'.[35] These impulses are shadowed by anxiety, however: Lowell's father's response to straitened circumstances is to buy a smarter car, and even in his final phase of ill-health he depends on his black Chevie, 'garaged like a sacrificial steer' to escape to the Maritime Museum. Commander Lowell's naval history, and his continued attraction to the sea, is a resonant aspect of his portrayal, and expresses both continuity and change – an inherited status of national service combined with the spirit of adventure. The father's failure to impress limits the power of his seagoing experience – he retains the 'ivory slide-rule' and 'clipper ship statistics' but is finally reduced to loafing at the museum, only capable of living in the past.[36]

Lowell's maritime heritage – and its shortcomings – has a particular resonance for Boland, for whom journeys by sea carry both a personal and cultural significance. The hardships of a sea voyage for Irish emigrants emerges obliquely in her work but it is the death of her grandfather by drowning in the Bay of Biscay that is the most resonant of these recurring images. By re-engaging with this aspect of family history, Boland constructs the sea not as an empty space between different phases of experience, but as shaped by histories of conquest and migration. As a site of death and burial, it emphasizes the erasure of the past, and the failure to find lasting signifiers for these lost lives. Acts of commemoration are vital to the structure of *Life Studies* too, where funerary rites and burial practices recur. From the mausoleum of 'Inauguration Day, 1953' to the mother's 'black and gold casket' in 'Sailing Home from Rapallo', the dead acquire a monumental significance in this volume. Robert Pogue Harrison has argued that human concern to house the dead – in graves, coffins and urns – is evidence of a desire to ensure their legacy can be retrieved.[37] For this reason there is continuity between Lowell's representation of the living and the dead, which at once sustains past generations through memory

---

35 Lowell, 'Grandparents', *Life Studies*, 75.
36 Lowell, 'Terminal Days at Beverly Farms', *Life Studies*, 81.
37 Robert Pogue Harrison, *The Dominion of the Dead* (London: University of Chicago Press, 2003), 39.

and renders those alive as haunting figures. Uncle Devereux, though 'animated, hierarchical' will soon return to dust, and Lowell's father's end is 'abrupt and unprotesting'.[38] Even the 'get-aways' from Boston the young poet shares with his grandfather are in fact trips to the graveyard. Images of death crowd the larger landscape too: Sumac is 'multiplying like cancer' in 'Terminal Days at Beverly Farms' and the poet returns from his soujourn in hospital to find weeds threatening to overwhelm the imported tulips in 'our coffin's length of soil'.[39] The landscape of the volume is itself a space of containment, where the traces of history are carried in the earth, first covered in leaves and then turning to stone in the unyielding ground of the New England winter. 'Surely no other modern American poet,' writes Perloff, 'has been as obsessed with death and last things as has Lowell.'[40]

Conclusion

Despite its troubled subject matter and unflinching style, *Life Studies* is a generative source for many poets – Boland, in particular, has learned much from Lowell's interweaving of personal and public pasts, and the formal evolution that made this achievement possible. Boland's reflections on American poetry from the 1960s onwards emphasize its range and energy, as well as its attractions for poets and readers who wish to move beyond the limitations of British criticism. She notes in Lowell, John Berryman and Theodore Roethke 'an almost inflexible growth of the self within the poem, until the centre occupied the edges: the painting outgrew the canvas'.[41] The strength of the 'prophetic and doomed voice'[42] of these poets is a revolutionary one and, though Boland's engagement with traumatic experience in her work is self-reflexive rather than revelatory,

---

38 Lowell, 'My Last Afternoon', *Life Studies*, 71–72; 'Terminal Days', *Life Studies*, 81.
39 Lowell, 'Terminal Days', *Life Studies*, 80; 'Home After Three Months Away', *Life Studies*, 91.
40 Perloff, 'Death by Water', 116.
41 Eavan Boland, 'American Scene', *The Irish Times*, 18 May 1985, 15.
42 Ibid. 15.

she understands the importance of these poets for all those writing in the second half of the twentieth century. Boland is especially sensitive to the shape of Lowell's oeuvre, and to the relationship between formal change and the 'intense imaginative growth' she observes in him.[43] This opinion supported her own decision to use transgressive subject matter as a way of breaking with a conservative aesthetic before developing her mature style.

Lowell's achievement also prompted Boland to consider the importance of the individual poetry volume, and its relationship to larger aesthetic and political aims. She read *Life Studies* as a singular work of art, but one that expressed a particular relationship among individual poems and groups of texts. In a 1985 review, she laments the loss of '91 Revere Street' from the Faber edition of Lowell, an observation that chimes with her own sense of the generative relationship between prose memoir and poetry at the time. Repetition would play an important role in Lowell's work from *Life Studies* onward, and these networks of meaning, and the way they acted on his readers, offered new ways for Boland to shape her oeuvre. Her increased commitment to her own experience, and that of her blood relations – especially female precursors – was made with specific political intent. Her repeated return to episodes from her own family history not only keeps this material in the minds of readers but returns to her earlier texts, creating a cyclical act of reading where meanings accumulate over time. This act of creative return functions to disclose the past to present readers – not only the past of Irish history but also the past of her own texts.

The investigation of origins is also a search for self-knowledge, and Lowell's poems of childhood in *Life Studies* are important precursors to his adult meditations at the close of the book. Boland's construction of self from a barely reclaimable past draws attention to the specific challenges that the representation of personal histories may present for the woman artist. In Lowell's work, the creation of a coherent poetic subject is challenged by private instability as well as cultural change. For Boland a key artistic purpose is derived from returning to family and nation as the foundations of the expressive self.

43 Ibid. 15.

ELLEN DILLON

Radical Tensions: Robert Lowell, Charles Altieri and Catherine Walsh

In her essay on the work of contemporary Irish innovative poet Catherine Walsh, Lucy Collins asserts that:

> The dismantling of subjectivity, and the formal and linguistic impact of this, is an important preoccupation of contemporary poetry. [...] The problems of unitary subjectivity are not always expressed in formally innovative ways, however; widely read poets [...] use a range of strategies to challenge assumptions of coherent identity and to problematize the relation between public and private selves in the poetry.[1]

In this essay I will explore this claim by examining the ways in which the public/private relation is problematized in Robert Lowell's 'Skunk Hour' and Walsh's 1996 collection *idir eatortha*. I will begin by considering Charles Altieri's readings of the 'radical tension between public and private realms'[2] in Lowell's work, paying particular attention to the imposition of chronological and psychological boundaries that characterize Altieri's later readings of Lowell. Then I will use Collins's assertion, and Walsh's own poems, to put pressure on the boundaries Altieri imposes on those readings of the American poet.

The reader who has engaged with Charles Altieri's work from the 1970s to the present will have noticed a tendency to return to the same poems, painters and passages from philosophy in an effort to define and refine the terms of his poetics. *Enlarging the Temple*, Altieri's 1979 overview of the poetry of the 1960s, opens by declaring that 'confessional poetry is

---

1   Lucy Collins, *Contemporary Irish Women Poets* (Liverpool: Liverpool University Press, 2017), 170.
2   Charles Altieri, *Enlarging the Temple* (London: Associated University Presses 1979), 69.

essentially a transition between two faiths – one dead, the other desperately trying to be born.'³ This assertion echoes, without naming the source, Antonio Gramsci's oft-quoted dictum on the crisis of authority: 'The crisis consists precisely in the fact that the old is dying and the new cannot be born; in this interregnum a great variety of morbid symptoms appear'.⁴ Altieri's book ends on a note expressing hope of reconciling 'optimism of will with optimism of intelligence' through 'the specific strategies of contemporary poetics – the rejection of high tradition [...] in favour of careful intense attention to the natural and the familiar'.⁵ Once again, a Gramscian aphorism (in this case his citing of Romain Roland's 'we must combine pessimism of the intelligence with optimism of the will')⁶ is reworked to frame the task of contemporary poetry as a dynamic process, deriving its charge from the oppositional interaction of abstract structure and concrete experience united in the gesture of paying 'careful intense attention' to the particular.⁷ In this dynamic reading, Lowell's work is exiled to a static position in the morbid 'interregnum', the place and time of schism and uncertainty. I wish to trace the path taken by Altieri, then, through and around Lowell's 'Skunk Hour', in *Enlarging the Temple* (1979), 'Contingency as Compositional Principle in Fifties Poetics' (1998) and *The Art of Twentieth-Century American Poetry* (2006), attending to his positioning of Lowell at, and as, a boundary within the field of twentieth-century poetry and poetics.

Of these three readings of Lowell, none considers the poem in its entirety. In *Enlarging the Temple*, the chapter entitled 'Robert Lowell and the Difficulties of Escaping Modernism' presents 'Skunk Hour' as the culmination of a series of patterns which Lowell employs in an attempt to 'overcome the intense privacy he associates with the fall into prose'.⁸ Altieri's initial position is polarizing, setting public self against private

3   Ibid. 17–18.
4   Antonio Gramsci, *Selections from the Prison Notebooks*, trans. Q. Hoare and G. Nowell Smith (London: The Electronic Book Company 1999), 556.
5   Altieri, *Enlarging the Temple*, 243.
6   Gramsci, 395.
7   Altieri, *Enlarging the Temple*, 243–244.
8   Ibid. 69.

and poetry against prose, with the equation of privacy and prose (and, indeed, hell) further complicated by incompatibilities in the processes of meaning-making between genres:

> For value to emerge in the prose world, the poet must develop a style that can convey its glimpses of meaning within contingency without the aid of allegorical or paradigmatic structures. Poems must appear to remain faithful to the casual flux of experience …[9]

This suggestion – that a poem should display a fidelity to the flux of experience that can be *perceived* – hints at a performative dimension to confessional poetics and foreshadows Collins's concern with problematizing 'the relation between public and private selves' and how it manifests itself in confessional and experimental modes. Altieri goes on to suggest that Lowell makes his poems *seem* contingent but provides patterns for their interpretation by 'appropriating techniques from the prose tradition'.[10] This claim is based on a close reading of the poem's last three stanzas, preceded by the following gloss on the opening stanzas and particularly the fifth stanza, where the speaker experiences a 'dark night of the soul':

> The poem first of all embodies the ultimate lucidity, the denial of all imaginative evasions […] This then brings him to a dark night of the soul […] There he encounters the ultimate nothingness or absence of meaning, which is perhaps the result of all pursuits of sheer lucidity […] For Lowell the absence is dual – an emptiness he witnesses in the scene of perverted love among the love cars, mirrored by a horrifying sense of his own inner emptiness, 'I myself am hell; / nobody's here.' Hell here is the ultimate prose – a profound sense of the absence of all sources of meaning and value in the public world represented by the landscape and in the private realm where one defines his personal identity.[11]

The engagement with prose, which others, including Marjorie Perloff,[12] have identified as a source of the collection's richness and strength, is cast

---

9   Ibid. 63.
10 Ibid. 64.
11 Ibid. 66.
12 Marjorie Perloff, 'The Return of Robert Lowell', *Parnassus* 27.1 (2004): 76–102.

by Altieri in infernal terms. This is consistent with his mapping of the poem as a site of Gramscian struggle, but not necessarily fully supported by the text where this struggle is sited.

Robert Duncan's introduction to a reading by Lowell at the poetry centre in San Francisco in 1957 suggested that: 'All realizations in Art are [...] dynamic, at once virtuous and vicious, in relation to new necessities which they call into being.'[13] This 'calling into being' of new necessities is central to 'Skunk Hour,' a birth-struggle that takes place in the soul's dark night, brought about by a realization that Altieri depicts as a crushing sense of doubled absence: the emptiness witnessed among the 'love-cars' reflecting and amplifying the soul's own crushed hollowness. However, 'the ultimate prose' seems a wilfully limiting epithet to apply to an intertextual refrain that locates 'Hell' in an 'I myself' that draws in Marlowe's Mephistopheles, Milton's Satan and Sartre's Garcin, anti-hero of *Huis clos*.

The triggering absence, which Altieri depicts as 'emptiness he witnesses in the scene of perverted love among the love cars,' also bears closer scrutiny. The voyeuristic aspect of this stanza has been the subject of much critical attention. Yet what's so intriguing is Lowell's own textual sleight of hand and use of allusion in order to, as Alan Williamson puts it, 'lead away from the exclusively personal, towards a shared world of sophisticated discourse.'[14] Firstly, nothing is 'witnessed' in the stanza: the speaker seeks out 'love cars', protective metal carapaces that provide a synecdoche for the lovers whose antics ('perverted' in Altieri's formulation) they serve to conceal. Secondly, the urge to seek out and spy on lovers can be read as woven into the stanza's intertextual refrain at least as much as it is propelled by the mind's unrightness. St John of the Cross's 'Stanzas of the Soul,'[15]

13   Robert J. Bertholf, 'Duncan's Introductions at the Poetry Centre', *Chicago Review* 45.2 (1999): 74–120; 93.
14   Alan Williamson, *Pity the Monsters: The Political Vision of Robert Lowell* (Westport' CT: Greenwood Press, 1986), 61.
15   The exposition of the text glosses the 'dark night' as 'purgative contemplation' which 'causes passively in the soul the negation of itself,' and the entire poem is explicated as 'the method followed by the soul in its journey upon the spiritual road to the attainment of the perfect union of love with God'. St John of the Cross, *Dark Night of the Soul*, trans. Allison Peerson, available online at: <http://www.catholicspiritualdirection.org/darknight.pdf> (accessed 20 July 2017).

which provides the line 'On a dark night', depicts a soul driven from its home by desire, guided by the night to the arms of a waiting lover. Even the most 'secular, puritan and agnostical'[16] reading of the stanza that follows must find spiritual and psychic – as well as carnal – impetus for its act of thwarted voyeurism. This sense of authorized or prescribed transgression is compounded in the following stanza's accretion of allusion: Milton's Satan, in Book IV of *Paradise Lost*, discovers himself unable to flee the hell that is himself and yet makes his way to Eden, where he is tormented by the sight of Adam and Eve in each other's arms:

> Sight hateful, sight tormenting! Thus these two,
> Imparadised in one another's arms,
> The happier Eden, shall enjoy their fill
> Of bliss on bliss; while I to Hell am thrust[17]

Even the mirror-reversal of Sartre's 'Hell is other people'[18] (*Huis clos*) in the lines 'I myself am hell; / nobody's here –' offers a glimpse of another inferno of tormented, unwilling voyeurs, where Estelle, Inez and the noble pacifist Garcin are forced to watch the lives they have left continue to unfold. Sartre's play climaxes with Inez, compelled to watch the other two's love-making, taunting them: 'I'm watching you, everybody's watching, I'm a crowd all by myself'.[19] So, to read these stanzas as a depiction of Hell as 'the ultimate prose' is to risk misreading, or simply not reading, their dense allusiveness, which David Gewanter has described as a 'free-styling' of prior voices,'[20] through which the poem enacts its gesture of confession.

---

16   Thomas Parkinson, ed., *Robert Lowell: A Collection of Critical Essays* (Upper Saddle River, NJ: Prentice-Hall, 1968) 131.
17   John Milton, *Paradise Lost*, ed. M.Y. Hughes (Indianapolis, IN: Hackett Publishing, 2003) 98–99.
18   Jean-Paul Sartre, *No Exit and Three Other Plays*, trans. I. Abel (New York: Vintage, 1989), 45.
19   Ibid. 45.
20   David Gewanter, 'Lowell's *Collected Poems*: Some Histories', *Harvard Review* 25 (2003): 133–139; 137.

In the conclusion to the chapter on Lowell in *Enlarging the Temple*, the poet's status as exemplary figure of mid-century stasis, condemned to haunt an increasingly untenable middle ground, is underlined by citing Lowell's own allusion (in 'Window-Ledge 2. Gramsci in Prison') to Gramsci's *Notebooks* – 'optimism of will, pessimism of intelligence' – which Altieri reads as a commentary on Lowell's failure to escape the irresolvable contradictions between his confessional urges and his modernist origins.[21] However, Lowell's torqueing of Gramsci's dictum, and dropping of the need to combine the two qualities rather than have one supersede the other, gives rise to what Vereen Bell describes as 'a relentless, reciprocal action that chews experience into fragments and shreds'.[22] This process of creation through destruction is embodied in the shredding and reworking of other texts, which will be further fragmented and recombined in the endless revising and rewriting of Lowell's poetics.

Altieri's *The Art of Twentieth-Century American Poetry* (2006), to which we will return, opens with a quote from Ezra Pound: 'Nine out of every ten Americans have sold their souls for a quotation. They have wrapped themselves about a formula of words instead of about their own centers.'[23] In Lowell's poem, and Altieri's circumscription of it, the centre is itself constructed of a formula of words, forming and marking the territory of a self. Lowell's own richly allusive process undermines all attempts to distinguish between a public, 'outside' realm and a private interior within which identity is formed. Indeed, what is so striking in Lowell's poem is the extent to which identity is composed of found materials, and the process by which so-called 'inner life' seeps out to colour the landscape and the public realm. Nearly twenty years later, in 'Contingency as Compositional Principle in Fifties Poetics' (1998), Altieri sets out once again to name and mark the territorial limits of a poetics that came into being – or attempted to – in the United States during the 1950s and 1960s. By this time, questions of agency have become central to his thinking, casting the elaboration

---

21   Altieri, *Enlarging the Temple*, 243–244.
22   Vereen M. Bell, *Robert Lowell: Nihilist as Hero* (Cambridge, MA: Harvard University Press, 1983), 168.
23   Altieri, *The Art of Twentieth-Century Poetry: Modernism and After* (Oxford: Blackwell, 2006), 11.

of subjectivity as a central concern, and the essay posits a 'logic of contingency' as the defining dynamic of the innovative poetry of the period.[24] Once again, Lowell is cast as the liminal figure straddling, or, more properly, constituting the dividing line between determined and contingent, a stance already assigned to him in *Enlarging the Temple*.

In 'Contingency as Compositional Principle', however, Lowell is not the central focus. Once again, Altieri is considering the 'transitional moment' between modern and contemporary poetry; and, once again Lowell, specifically 'Skunk Hour' and its closing stanza, are located as the site of a standoff between the old order and a new concept to which Altieri will attempt to affix 'the logic of contingency'. His initial delineation of the concept, called into existence by his need to distinguish his thinking from that of Williamson and Longenbach, demonstrates a somewhat cavalier approach to allusion: 'As Sartre never tired of saying,' he writes, 'contingency is the experience of existence preceding essence and hence of particulars deforming or differing from the very terms used to impose categories upon them.'[25] This assertion seems to have been assembled from fragments of *Nausea*, collaged with *Being and Nothingness*'s famous definition of freedom ('Freedom is existence, and in it existence precedes essence'),[26] with neither source containing these exact elements in this precise relation. In *Self and Sensibility*, Altieri confessed that 'My account echoes Sartre and dozens of sloppy literary allusions to Heisenberg,'[27] and the later essay on contingency takes up this refrain, alluding to Sartre while echoing Heisenberg's much abused 'uncertainty principle' in his reframing of Lowell's existential contingency as 'a staged intensity always already controlled by and for observation.'[28]

---

24 Altieri, 'Contingency as Compositional Principle in Fifties Poetics' in *Postmodernisms Now: Essays on Contemporaneity in the Arts* (Philadelphia: Pennsylvania State University Press, 1998), 82–105.
25 Ibid. 88.
26 Sartre, *Being and Nothingness*, trans. H. Barnes (New York: Simon and Schuster, 1992), 567.
27 *Self and Sensibility in Contemporary American Poetry* (Cambridge: Cambridge University Press, 1984), 28.
28 Altieri, 'Contingency as Compositional Principle in Fifties Poetics', 95.

This reading, based entirely on the final stanza of 'Skunk Hour,' briefly deploys a promising reciprocity that frames Lowell as 'playing the roles of both subject and object of analysis,' assigning a priestly function to the 'I' standing on the steps that feeds off a 'self-victimizing identification with the skunk'.[29] The earlier reading had Lowell's poem embody a site where public and private, poetry and prose, grapple to find meaning and value. In *Self and Sensibility*, this grappling is presented as the continual conflict that is the self's only means of manifesting itself. In 'Contingency as Compositional Practice', the 'continual conflict' is reduced to a 'staged intensity' between arbitrarily designated poles of the self put on display for the reader, what Altieri calls the 'psychological trap at the core of confessional poetry'.[30] Over the course of his re-readings, Altieri has whittled away at the 'middle ground' he assigned to Lowell in the late 1970s until it has become a circumscribed and circumscribing trap.

However, by the time Altieri arrives at *The Art of Twentieth-Century American Poetry* some ten years later, Lowell has been restored to his central role in mid-century poetics. Not only that but, where Altieri's earlier work had positioned him at a turning point – and depicted innovative work of the 1950s, 1960s and 1970s as a movement of opposition to, or at least away from, Lowellian poetics – by 2006 he makes up the borderline, along with Creeley, Ashbery, Rich and Bishop, beyond which Altieri will not venture in his overview of the territory of twentieth-century American poetry. These poets are considered exemplary in their 'exhaustion of the possibilities of modernist styles,' and they 'remain part of my story because the sense of exhaustion requires them to engage the force of the imaginary in quite distinctive ways'.[31] The question, however, is not why this group of poets remains part of the story, but why they have now been reframed as the *end* of the story rather than its beginning. Altieri expresses some of the exhaustion he has projected on the poets in his own refusal to speculate on which contemporary poets will continue or oppose this engagement, claiming: 'I have decided to stop where there has emerged a fairly clear

---

29   Ibid.
30   Ibid.
31   *The Art of Twentieth-Century Poetry*, 9.

canon, and where I am fairly confident that the poets are still engaged with the issues posed by the major modernist poets.'[32] It is hard not to read this as a failure of nerve on the part of a critic who, in the 1970s was already identifying the 'exhaustion of modernism' as the point of departure for late century poetry. In this new dispensation, the previously de-canonized Lowell is restored to the congregation and his confessionalism recast, not as a 'psychological trap' but as 'probably the most powerful instrument for rendering this sense of the imaginary as ineffable burden.'[33] 'Skunk Hour,' once 'the ultimate hell,' 'the ultimate emptiness', 'the ultimate prose',[34] can now be viewed as displaying 'the most intricate treatment I know of how the imaginary can pervade every aspect of efforts at self-knowledge.'[35] With this equally hyperbolic claim, Altieri seems to be suggesting an 'imaginary' that is external to the process of self-knowing, permeating it in the way the 'red fox stain covers Blue Hill.' This reading, once again, skirts around the poem's pivotal fifth and sixth stanzas, moving from a close reading of the opening four stanzas to a detailed reworking of his previous 'priest'/ 'skunk' reading of the closing stanza, without so much as a passing mention of the poem's central crisis, as if the 'ineffable burden' of Lowell's imaginary had rendered it *itself* unspeakable, and reduced all efforts to articulate it to gestures towards its absence.

The picture of 'self-knowledge' Altieri presents here is somewhat difficult to grasp. It seems as though the imaginary, the sense of unity yielded by the infant's encounter with his reflection, and an essential first step in his *becoming* a subject,[36] were somehow thwarting the subject's own efforts at self-knowledge. Altieri seems to be positing a self that is capable of taking an external position from which it can perceive and know itself. This self-reflexive, transcendental subject is, for Altieri, always positioned outside the art-work or experience in relation to which its identity (as writer, reader or viewer) defines itself, exiled to a position outside its territory of

32   Ibid. 157.
33   Ibid. 167.
34   *Enlarging the Temple*, 66.
35   *The Art of Twentieth-Century Poetry*, 166.
36   Jacques Lacan, *Écrits: A Selection,* trans. A. Sheridan (London: Routledge, 2005), 503.

origin. Altieri's own reader is implicated in this process, being split into subject, object and viewer of the act of imagining in his identification of 'Skunk Hour''s gift to the reader as the self-reflexive awareness of 'small revolutions in how we imagine ourselves imagining.'[37] If Lowell as end-point leaves the reader trapped in an infinitely recursive loop of imagining and reflecting on imagining, *Self and Sensibility*'s view of Lowell places the self at the fulcrum of this point:

> Lowell's confessional style marks for me the crucial turning point because it makes the self, shorn of intellectual and cultural traditions, the necessary source of authentic lyric feeling. Yet the self can be manifested only in continual conflict [...] with forms of understanding that might interpret the intensity as a means to some sense of transpersonal powers.[38]

Yet, as my earlier reading of 'Skunk Hour' attempted to show, the self, far from being shorn of intellectual and cultural traditions, creates itself through interaction with these traditions. If Altieri's readings of Lowell frame him as either a boundary or a turning point, it is also clear that these are not mutually exclusive terms and that the boundary itself contains or marks a turning point. Further, the kind of radical tension identified between public and private selves can also be discerned within the poem's inhabiting of the 'intellectual and cultural traditions' from which the poem's lyric self constructs itself.[39] These traditions, as we have seen, are not incompatible with, indeed are a necessary source of 'authentic lyric feeling',[40] and the self emerges, if not necessarily from conflict, from the movement between such ostensibly contradictory states as 'public' and 'private,' a position that is ultimately in keeping with that of *Self and Sensibility* if we replace the passive 'can be manifested'[41] with the active and reflexive 'manifests itself.'

The last section of this essay will focus on the 'in-between-ness' of the contemporary poetic subject in Catherine Walsh's 'idir eatortha' to suggest

37 Altieri, *The Art of Twentieth-Century Poetry*, 171.
38 Altieri, *Self and Sensibility in Contemporary American Poetry*, 40.
39 Altieri, *Enlarging the Temple*, 69.
40 Altieri, *Self and Sensibility in Contemporary American Poetry*, 40.
41 Ibid.

the possibility of a dynamic view of the self of 'Skunk Hour' that allows for generative movement between some of the more circumscribing terms and positions of Altieri's readings. While a reading of Lowell's 'Skunk Hour' fully supports Collins's assertion that 'the problems of unitary subjectivity are not always expressed in formally innovative ways',[42] I'm interested in further exploring the spatial dimension of Catherine Walsh's diffuse subjectivity, where boundaries between inside and out, public and personal, are effaced to not only 'problematize the relation between public and private selves in the poetry'[43] but to render the relation one of constant movement between states, positions and terms. While Collins refers to the 'dismantling' of subjectivity as one of the aims of innovative poetry, Walsh's work diffuses the subject into its surroundings while opening it to the kind of linguistic contamination from outside through which a subject can build itself. John Goodby suggests that:

> In Walsh's poetry the autobiographical material (and self) is more radically dispersed across the space of the page, and intercut with other, non-subjective texts. And while she, too, writes out of a domestic scene, all of her books begin with a sense of personal dislocation, of being in transit, and non-belonging, as reflected in a greater interest in the poetics of error, incompletion, and occasional opacity.[44]

These senses of 'personal dislocation, of being in transit, and non-belonging' are, to a remarkable extent, applicable to the subject of Lowell's 'Skunk Hour.' What I wish to explore here is the possibility that, in Walsh's work as in Lowell's, there are no 'other, non-subjective texts.' The self, as it exists in the text and the world, gathers itself out of fragments and snatches of prior texts and found language in which 'autobiographical material' is just one, not necessarily privileged, element.

The poems of 'idir eatortha' make up the first fifty pages of Walsh's 1996 book *idir eatortha and making tents*. These poems are particularly striking for their use of space to modulate the transitions between the

---

42 Collins, *Contemporary Irish Women Poets*, 170.
43 Ibid. 171.
44 '"Repeat the changes, change the repeats": Alternative Irish Poetry', in Fran Brearton and Alan Gillis, eds, *The Oxford Handbook of Modern Irish Poetry* (Oxford: Oxford University Press, 2013), 623.

time-frames, voices and languages in which they build themselves. The title itself signals that in-between-ness will be a structuring formal principle as well as a thematic concern of the work; or better, that the work's concern with in-between-ness will make itself visible in the shapes the poems take in the space of the page. Memories and brief descriptions cluster in dense blocks, sometimes paragraphs, as in the sections beginning 'pigeons the ledge opposite scratching round the roof',[45] 'I really used to feel nauseated hours afterwards …',[46] 'have you ever seen snow …,'[47] 'or as rambling the frozen locks we went on teatrays ….'[48] Outside and around these clustered descriptions and anecdotes, words drift off in the space of the page, spreading freely or marshalling themselves into slightly wobbly columns. In some cases, free-floating snatches of sensing and thinking recall or prefigure the anecdotes, as in the opening page's 'tunnelling down the slope':[49]

> corona of light in the V of the bottlenecked blackened treetops
> fumed   blue
> city   line
> nightly midget rotating feet
> on pedals around
> tracks laid down
> many others intent
> action sound might
> move
> us now
>   tunnelling down the slope
> (but
> wasn't that somewhere else?)[50]

This particular 'somewhere else' won't be revisited until the reminiscences of playing in the snow from page 42 on, but the entire series takes place somewhere where moments of thinking and feeling in the present are also

---

45 Walsh, *idir eatortha and making tents* (Dublin: HardPressed, 1996), 31.
46 Ibid. 34.
47 Ibid. 42.
48 Ibid. 43.
49 Ibid. 7.
50 Ibid.

always permeated with memory, anecdote and voices from the outside. These voices fold the language of children, the classroom, the overheard street, the muttered 'huh!'[51] and 'ah well'[52] of self-talk into the 'somewhere else' of the series' language-scape. The title itself signals at the space in-between as the poems' domain and concern. The phrase '*idir eatortha*' (more usually spelled '*idir eatarthu*') refers to a state of indeterminacy and transition between two worlds or ways of being;[53] it is often translated as 'betwixt and between'.[54] The very form of Walsh's poem embodies this indeterminate state. Collins draws on Eric Falci's analysis of the functions of two distinct types of page in Walsh's work: 'dense ones' featuring 'partial or fractured narratives'[55] and 'sparse ones' where 'words and phrases hang apart on the page.'[56] In the poem or poems of 'idir eatortha', however, very few poems or sections confine themselves to one or other page type. Dispersed text yields to clustered anecdote over the course of one page; on another, dense blocks of overheard language fragment into echolalia. This formal indeterminacy undermines any attempt to distinguish qualitatively between thinking in the present and thinking about the past: these are not two separate domains, Walsh's pages seem to say, rather they are ongoing and mutually generative actions.

In Collins's view, Walsh's use of the page increases the complexity of the process of reading, 'testing the boundaries of poetic language' as 'it presents an experience of radical estrangement to the reader, one that reflects the impact of existential questioning on the textual encounter'.[57] It is undoubtedly true that the encounter with this poem is profoundly estranging, but I would argue that the 'existential questioning' is immanent to the text,

---

51 Ibid. 40.
52 Ibid. 41.
53 'idir eatarthu' translation available online at: <https://www.aistear.ie/popup.php?ID=297> (accessed 20 January 2018). 'idir eatarthu', translation available online at: <http://www.tearma.ie/Search.aspx?term=idir+eatarthu&lang=3116659> (accessed 20 January 2018).
54 'idir eatarthu' translation available online at: <http://www.teanglann.ie/en/fgb/idir_eatarthu> (accessed 20 January 2018).
55 Collins, 172.
56 Ibid.
57 Ibid.

and that the reader's encounter with the text is an active reanimation of this questioning which recreates through the act of reading the in-between space of the poem itself in its *own* ongoing and mutually generative action.

Returning to re-read this poem in light of Lowell's intertextual confessionalism further complicates its already multivalent in-between space. Just as its own pages both anticipate and recall their own foundational memories and anecdotes, they also make room for snatches of productive conversation with Lowell's concerns in the ear of the reader closely attuned to the cadences of both sets of interwoven voices. The 'I' who is the dispersed subject of page 12 shares the 'hell' of 'Skunk Hour's' 'I myself am hell / nobody's here –' among the 'every one' where this darkness originates. The square brackets build a schematic '[symbol]', '[darkness]', '[light]' around which the dissipated subject hovers in its hell of displacement and the impossible erasure of light:

                                      [symbol] to take it away
                                        considerations
every one is

[darkness]   hell!
I think it's gone!   displaced

[light]
                                  an impossible erasure

On page 14, the snatch of love song recalls 'Love, Oh Careless Love' from 'Skunk Hour':

[singing]
love
            they won't
let me   in
                     the named face
                     meaning
            ringing
all over   sky

As in Lowell's poem the love theme weaves itself into the poem's concerns; but whereas 'Careless Love' is easily identifiable in 'Skunk Hour', and identifies itself readily with the poem's theme, it is not so clear what song is being sung in the passage above and what significance it has within the later poem, or even, how it means *in* the poem. The dispersed fragments 'meaning // ringing / all over sky' place meaning outside of the speaking (or singing) subject, diffusing it into the atmosphere with her song. This is typical of the movement of Walsh's poem: meaning doesn't originate with or reside in any one speaking subject or enunciation. It permeates the subject as song or speech from outside, and it is diffused back into the world outside on the same vectors. Language and meaning, too, are the in-between place.

The point where the form and concerns of 'Skunk Hour' can be heard echoing most clearly in this reader's 'idir eatortha' is in a mischievous twist on page 25:

> resting places we all have our favourites
> evening star clear
> nights across car
> park lights waiting
> for joy
> riders

The favourite 'resting places' and 'car / park lights' invoke 'Skunk Hour's 'love cars', and as that locution's 'love' renders the activities taking place within the cars questionable and somehow unsavoury, the appending, after a cheeky pause, of 'riders' to 'joy' turns the object of pursuit from pleasure to car thieves. It is worth remembering that in Irish dialect the verb 'ride' has sexual as well as transportational connotations so that, in the space between 'joy' and 'riders,' both meanings remain possible.

It is a testament to the openness of Walsh's forms and concerns that the reader, while being permeated by the words of 'idir eatortha,' finds their act of reading resonating, in turn, with echoes of their own memories, anecdotes and prior readings. This experience, while it may initially present as one of 'radical estrangement', as Collins put it, is ultimately radically comforting. Once concerns about establishing a stable meaning are stilled, the reader is freed to move among, and be moved by, the poem's unfixable meanings. The dynamics of this process play out in particularly compelling fashion on page 39, to which I will turn before hazarding some conclusions.

The page opens on a collage of overheard speech snippets, with stage directions in square brackets, resolving into what sounds like a well-to-do couple passing judgement on a (possibly drunk) street-sleeper ('*I* don't know George, drunk'). The second half of the page has a stage direction '[sniffing]' and a quotation mark that is opened but never closed:

> doesn't mean. or we only want to feel – are –
> incapable – world happening –
> Johnson adrift. it's all animate
> poetry struggling to contend with
> a lack our socializing instincts gone apeshit
> thinking we *know*
>
> credo inanimatus
>
> green leaf, sound, wheels on pavement –
> no – footpath – contending with space we box it, label it, extend
> language fencing effect to move, ourselves, we extend
> bridges of words – to pass over – instead of ourselves
>
> that's it,   misnomer, space.
> space a misnomer.
> space is.[58]

In this section, spare use of punctuation leaves clauses hovering in the between space, linking to preceding or subsequent thoughts, or both, or neither. Language itself embodies the in-between-ness it is describing: 'it's all animate' could be conferring agency on the world that is 'happening', or it can latch on to 'poetry struggling to contend with / a lack', or it can do both, meaning the poem itself is also animate. The line 'thinking we *know*', with its exasperated italics, isolated in the page's space, seems to be making a metacommentary on illusions of certainty that set boundaries and limitations on poetry and the world. From this position of exasperation, the poem appears to pivot to a profession of faith in *in*animateness ('credo inanimatus') that plays on the Nicene Creed's *Credo in unum Deum*, although the use of the adjective 'inanimatus' opens the possibility

---

58   Walsh, *idir eatortha and making tents*, 39.

that it is the act of believing itself that is inanimate. Thus, these lines reverse habitual associations to suggest that poetry and the world are animate and the act of believing (and by extension, thinking and knowing) is inanimate. Where poetry struggled to contend with lack, *we* are now struggling to contend with space ('contending with space we box it, label it, extend / language fencing effect to move, ourselves').[59]

This locution strikes me as an extraordinarily apt description of the many ways we use language to render the world measurable and controllable. It could also be a coded critique, as Sarah Broom has suggested,[60] of traditional poetic forms and concerns, with their illusion of mastery. But it also pushes the reader to question critical projects such as Altieri's that set out to erect fences, be they spatial or chronological, between and around poets and poems. While such distinctions serve a heuristic function, if they are allowed to settle in place they cut works off from the in-between space that is the only domain in which they can remain in motion and meaning. It is worth noting that Altieri's readings of Lowell have themselves refused to fix on a single position, tending instead to revisit and review their own conclusions. However, his reading of Lowell's work as *constituting* a boundary or turning point deprives it, somewhat paradoxically, of the freedom of movement derived from *occupying* such a liminal or transitional space.

The line 'we extend / bridges of words – to pass over – instead of ourselves' functions as commentary on how 'we' use language, while incidentally furnishing an apt description of the intertextual sleight of hand at play in 'Skunk Hour' where what appears a spontaneous act of confession has been carefully crafted from a collage of prior sources. That poem, like Walsh's, appears to be offering a glimpse of a self, and may well be doing so, but rather than a 'unitary' subject[61] or a self 'shorn of intellectual and cultural traditions'[62] it is a 'bridge of words,' built of language from the inside and the outside to span a space that is always both inside

---

59 Ibid.
60 Broom, *Contemporary British and Irish Poetry: An Introduction* (London: Palgrave McMillan, 2006), 240.
61 Collins, 170.
62 Altieri, *Self and Sensibility in Contemporary American Poetry*, 40.

and outside, public and private. Goodby considers Walsh's 'fascination with unbelonging'[63] to be particularly evident in 'idir eatortha.' I would like to suggest that what he reads as 'unbelonging' could also be read as a radically open kind of belonging, where the closed and private are never privileged over the open and public, and to 'belong' is to move constantly with and in the space between. In this space Lowell, rather than marking an endpoint or a boundary, embodies a dynamic of inhabiting and reanimating poetic traditions that has much in common with contemporary Irish innovative poetry.

---

63 Goodby, 624.

EVE COBAIN

'The way we are living': Robert Lowell and Leontia Flynn

When asked for a rundown of her 'greatest poetic influences' in 2018, Leontia Flynn noted her indebtedness to a number of 'mid-Twentieth Century Americans' citing '(Berryman, Lowell, Bishop – also Plath and Marianne Moore)', and commending these poets for their 'pattern-making and general nuttiness'.[1] 'I don't think influence works the way people think it does', noted Flynn. In Flynn's long list of influences, these American poets sit comfortably alongside a range of Irish poets – such as Medbh McGuckian, Ciaran Carson, Seamus Heaney and Paul Muldoon – who for a long time, notes Flynn, 'seemed too close to home'.[2]

Throughout her career to date, Flynn has repeatedly asserted the importance of these US American poets to her developing idiom. In an earlier interview with Culture Northern Ireland, she also cited Lowell and Berryman as chief among her poetic influences. 'I admire poets who have great overarching structures at work behind their poems which allow them to keep producing', asserts Flynn,

> I particularly like writers of sequences, so Robert Lowell and John Berryman and Shakespeare (of the sonnets). I return to Paul Muldoon's work again and again.

---

[1] Leontia Flynn, 'Radio Signals: An Interview with Leontia Flynn', Wake Forest University Press, available online at: <https://wfupress.wfu.edu/interview/radio-signals-an-interview-with-leontia-flynn> (accessed 20 November 2018).
[2] Ibid.

> Unlikely as it sounds I'm also reading a lot of Catullus at the moment. I basically admire anyone who sounds believable to me.³

Here influence does not run along simply national lines – which may be at least one of the ways that Flynn suggests people 'think it does'.⁴ The only 'Irish' poet named here is Paul Muldoon, who is also a naturalized American citizen. Through writers of different generations, both Flynn and Muldoon have taken the Irish lyric tradition in surprising new directions, and Fran Brearton has hailed Flynn as 'one of the most strikingly original and exciting poetic voices to have emerged from Northern Ireland since the extraordinary debut by Muldoon 35 years ago'.⁵ Their mutually inclusive sense of poetic influence, of course, has played no small part in this. Yet while Muldoon's American inheritance is now a well-worn subject, little has been made of Flynn's recourse to US poetry in the critical response to her work to date.

Of the many American poets that influence (and feature in) Flynn's work, Robert Lowell's is the most pervasive. Of course Flynn is not the only contemporary Irish poet for whom Lowell is of considerable significance. For her, however, Lowell's appeal lies in his 'believability'⁶ and his ability to situate the political within the personal. In many ways the parallel between Lowell and Flynn's work is broadly tonal and thematic. Flynn's whole body of work could be read as a kind of 'life study', and *Life Studies* (1959) provides a touchstone (implicit and explicit) in each of her collections to date. All of Flynn's books feature 'believable' sketches that form part of a larger idea or project, and which centre around personal experience – whether it be the poet's own, the experience of those close to her, or artists and icons who have left an impression. Particularly in her first collection, *These Days* (2004) Flynn's short lyrics form what Steven

---

3 Leontia Flynn, 'My Cultural Life: Leontia Flynn', Culture Northern Ireland, available online at: <http://www.culturenorthernireland.org/features/literature/my-cultural-life-leontia-flynn-0> (accessed 20 November 2018).
4 Flynn, 'Radio Signals'.
5 Fran Brearton, quoted online at: <http://leontiaflynn.com/books/drives/> (accessed 20 November 2018).
6 Flynn, 'My Cultural Life'.

Gould Axelrod, speaking of Lowell's sonnets, has described as an 'epic' of the poet's 'own consciousness'.[7] This book is made up mostly of sonnets, a form to which, like Lowell, Flynn's work feels a gravitational pull. While the sonnet is certainly one of the mainstays of the Irish lyric tradition, Flynn's disobedience regarding the often-rigid structures of this tradition recall the kind of challenges that Lowell posed to the form in works such as *Notebook* (1969) and *History* (1973).

While the nature of Lowell's influence on Flynn's first collection is pervasive and diffuse, it becomes more explicit in her second collection, *Drives* (2008), most noticeably in her double sonnet, entitled 'Robert Lowell'. I want to begin with a discussion of this tribute before elaborating on some further points of poetic connection in Flynn's most recent collections, *Profit and Loss* (2011) and *The Radio* (2017). The latter, I argue, shows the most profound outworking of Flynn's interest in Lowell to date, particularly in its exploration of the relationship between private and public life.

Drives, the collection within which Flynn's double sonnet for Lowell resides, features a number of 'life studies' after various icons (real and fictional) that have left an impression or influenced her in some way. Among the line-up are Alfred Hitchcock, Annie Hall, and Samuel Beckett, as well as a spectrum of American writers including Elizabeth Bishop, who is celebrated as a 'veteran loser', and Sylvia Plath, whose sinus condition is a lesser-known complaint.[8] The double sonnet for Lowell, however, explores at greater length, and much more seriously, some questions at the heart of the collection – particularly the relationship between art and life and the artistic mediation of impulses (or 'drives'). The book is also preoccupied

---

7   Steven Gould Axelrod, *Robert Lowell: Life and Art* (Princeton, NJ: Princeton University Press, 2015), 194.
8   The book is also prefigured by an epigraph from Bishop's 'Arrival at Santos' (*Questions of Travel*, 1965):

> *Oh, tourist,*
> *Is this how this country is going to answer you*
> *And your immodest demands for a different world,*
> *And a better life, and complete comprehension*
> *Of both at last ...*

with the subject of mental illness and suicide – issues that were examined in entirely new (and believable) ways by mid-century writers including Berryman and Lowell.

'Robert Lowell' is biographically and poetically informed, and uses the sonnet as a vehicle to contemplate Lowell's life and legacy:

> The milky light of a lobster town in Maine
> is light thrown by water. Bleak light. Robert Lowell
> in middle age is frizzled stale and sane
> he feels his ill-spirit sob in each blood cell.
> Back in his childhood were parental rows
> really responsible for this big rebellion
> against the line – that twists and tangles now –
> of Protestantism, of literary tradition,
> against the tide of caste marine-blue blood
> and *politics*? This government-made warfare
> could, in its turn, hardly seem less mad
> than mania's 'magical orange grove in a nightmare':
> the murdered boys and their returning shrouds
> spurring his hell-bent poet's un-scared stare.[9]

In the first stanza alone there are at least three gestures to Lowell poems, including 'Home after Three Months Away' ('fizzled, stale and small'), 'Skunk Hour' (the 'ill-spirit sob') and less obviously, in the final line, to the 'The Quaker Graveyard in Nantucket' from which Flynn pulls the term 'hell-bent'.[10] Her appropriation of Lowell's self-descriptors in 'Home after Three Months Away' is playfully irreverent, casting the poet in a grave light, but also altering his reflection by substituting 'sane' for 'small'. In her questions regarding the poet's rebellion (against Protestantism and paternal politics), Flynn adopts an almost mocking tone, yet inadvertently touches on some historical problems particular to her own (Northern Irish) locale. Flynn's mixing of allusions in the final line in fact connects Lowell's political disquietude with his emotional turmoil, binding together the poet's 'Quaker Graveyard' ('where dreadnaughts' confess the

---

9   Leontia Flynn, *Drives* (London: Cape Poetry, 2008), 37–39.
10 Robert Lowell, *Collected Poems*, eds Frank Bidart and David Gewanter (New York: Farrar, Straus and Giroux, 2003), 185–196; 14–18.

'hell-bent deity' of the dead soldier) with the 'un-scared' skunk stare of his most 'existential' poem.[11] Flynn rightly finds both the personal and the historical to be motivating forces in Lowell's poetry; with this she has no quibble. In fact, to Flynn's mind, Lowell's description of his own mania, a 'magical orange grove in a nightmare', is hardly less sane than government-made warfare – a reference to the Vietnam war, in particular, which Lowell strongly opposed.[12]

Still, as she moves into the second sonnet, Flynn begins to put Lowell's character on trial. This sonnet, much looser and less classical in form, probes both poetic method and life choices. This, if you like, is Flynn's real (or personal) response to Lowell, rather than the more traditional tribute of the first. Her style is conversational and open, though Yeatsian by turns, as she begins to probe Lowell's recourse to 'the living details of a living life'. The repeated, almost gossipy, asides – 'But imagine leaving his third and unreal wife / in order to return to his suffering second', 'And imagine using those letters in his sonnets?' – are her somewhat perplexed response to Lowell's rotating marriages and disclosure of personal material. Here Flynn is indirectly offering a broader critique of Lowell's generation – *Berryman's Sonnets* (1967) comes to mind as just one further example of a work that draws from painfully personal sources.[13] These sonnets record the highs and lows of the poet's extramarital affair; yet Berryman's sequence remained unpublished until almost twenty years later. Lowell's sonnet sequence drew liberally and unsympathetically from Elizabeth Hardwick's letters, and was published mere months after their separation. Flynn's difficulty with how Lowell used 'those letters' – was one shared by the women poets of Lowell's own time. In a letter dated 21 March 1972, Bishop cautioned Lowell on publishing *The Dolphin*:

---

11   Ibid. 191–192.
12   Quoted in *Robert Lowell: Essays on the Poetry*, eds Steven Gould Axelrod and Helen Deese (Cambridge: Cambridge University Press, 1989), 8.
13   Despite the fact that almost all of these sonnets, then titled 'Sonnets to Chris', were composed in July 1947, they remained unpublished until 1967, when five Sonnets (107, 112, 113, 114, and 115), with a prefatory poem, were added to the sequence, prior to its publication as *Berryman's Sonnets*.

> It's hell to write this, so please first do believe I think DOLPHIN is magnificent poetry. It is also honest poetry – almost. You probably know already what my reactions are. I have one tremendous and awful BUT [...] Lizzie is not dead, etc – but there is a 'mixture of fact & fiction,' and you have changed her letters. That is 'infinite mischief,' I think. The first one, page 10, is so shocking – well, I don't know what to say. And page 47 ... and a few after that. One can use one's life as material – one does, anyway – but these letters – aren't you violating a trust. IF you were given permission – IF you hadn't changed them ... etc. *But art just isn't worth that much.*[14]

Adrienne Rich was yet more scathing in her review:

> What does one say about a poet who, having left his wife and daughter for another marriage, then titles a book with their names, and goes on to appropriate his ex-wife's letters written under the stress and pain of desertion, into a book of poems nominally addressed to the new wife? ... I think this bullshit eloquence a poor excuse for a cruel and shallow book.[15]

While Flynn may admire Lowell's 'believability', then, her homage is far from unmixed in its praise. It is not Lowell's use of personal experience that Flynn takes issue with here, but rather his ransacking of Hardwick's letters and complete disregard for her 'living life' (echoed by Bishop: 'Lizzie is not dead, etc.'). Like Rich, Flynn also considers *The Dolphin* as a collection of diminished achievement. Lowell's impulse to 'use' and 'reuse' the 'fact of pain' (Hardwick's pain in this instance) is not for Flynn a mark of inventiveness – it is dully repetitive and parasitic.

Flynn's work is consistently occupied with the boundary – that she considers *The Dolphin* to have overstepped – between art and life, poet and poem. Another sonnet in the same collection, 'Personality', takes a characteristically ambivalent view of the age-old debate (or 'old story', as she calls it in the poem after Lowell) regarding the significance of the self in the lyric. 'Poetry', you are saying, 'is nothing but personality', writes Flynn,

---

[14] *Words in Air: The Complete Correspondence between Elizabeth Bishop and Robert Lowell*, eds Thomas Travisano and Saskia Hamilton (Faber and Faber, 2008), 707–708. Emphasis in original.

[15] Quoted in Michelle Dean, 'Love, Actually: Robert Lowell adored intelligent women and treated them terribly', *The New Republic* (4 February 2016), available online at: <https://newrepublic.com/article/128999/robert-lowells-tainted-love> (accessed 20 November 2018).

> and I look out onto the row upon row of grey hills
> and light striking the rooftops, and just at this moment
> there isn't much in my life I'd miss if it were over [...]
> work's meaninglessness – but its opposite, leisure's abyss!
> a snake coiled in the chest morning after morning ...
>
> [...] What you call 'personality'
> seems something heroic; it seems the rictus grin
> on a student's practice corpse – that breathes iambically
> between each line, with their knives parting the skin,
> 'love me, love me, love me, love me, love me ...'[16]

Of course, Flynn's response to her condescending friend is couched in the transformative, if elliptical, language of poetry. The overall tone of the poem is tinged with Lowellian cynicism. Yet a number of other mid-century US American poets emerge here to help frame the debate: note Flynn's final line blending Plath's 'Old brag of the heart. I am I am I am'[17] with Berryman's 'Love me love me love me love me love me / I am in need thereof', from Dream Song 192.[18]

The ending of Flynn's tribute also considers the anatomy of the poet, and how it seems 'as though'

> life and art
> were, for this poet, as minutely clocked
> as his dramatic final taxi journey
> (as his heart
> in his body) when both stopped.[19]

Flynn's own analogy of the poet's life and art being minutely clocked – and the visual experience of the parenthetical heart – self-consciously explores the ways in which human experience (bodily and psychic) is poetically transformed, while the rhyme of 'art' with 'heart' admits the unconscious pull of intimate material.

---

16   Flynn, *Drives*, 10.
17   Sylvia Plath, *The Bell Jar* (London: Faber and Faber, 2013) 152.
18   Berryman, *The Dream Songs* (New York: Farrar, Straus and Giroux, 2007), 211.
19   Leontia Flynn, *Drives*, 39.

While Flynn's most recent collections, *Profit and Loss* (2011) and *The Radio* (2017), demonstrate a turn toward increasingly public concerns, these are invariably examined through the lens of personal history. In a review of *Profit and Loss* for *The Irish Times,* Philip Coleman noted this dual quality in the collection, describing it as 'a book of searing personal and social insight'[20] – insights that could also be considered the markers of the most successful 'confessional' poetry. Indeed, while the first part of the book navigates its way through a series of rooms and properties of personal resonance to the poet, it is clear that Flynn intends these spaces (often redundant or for sale) to have a larger political significance within the context of the economic downturn (post-2008). Flynn's poetic rooms resemble Lowell's interior spaces in *Life Studies*; there's a kind of human detachment (or dwarfing of the self) in these lyrics while the properties themselves are anthropomorphized. Of course, this is also a quality in the work of Irish poets such as Louis MacNeice and McGuckian (who have left their own imprint on Flynn's writing), yet a poem such as 'Father's Bedroom' also forms a kind of blueprint for Flynn's empty resonant space in 'The Dream House', where she contemplates the ghostly marks left behind by previous occupiers, 'watermarks and coffee-rings on worktops'.[21] Together these lyrics create an atmosphere reminiscent of Lowell's 'For Sale' in which the cottage at Beverly Farms is 'Empty, open, intimate', its townhouse furniture having the 'on tip-toe air / of waiting for the mover' (*Life Studies*, 1959).[22]

In *The Radio* (2017), Flynn continues to examine the relationship between interior/domestic spaces and the 'outside world'. The book is broken into three sections (*Life Studies* into four) that test the boundary of these permeable spaces, these are entitled: 'The Child, The Family', '… And the Outside World', and 'Poems Conceived as Dialogues between Two Antagonistic Voices'.[23] Throughout the collection, the radio acts as an

---

20 Philip Coleman, 'No, really: signs of the new sincerity', *The Irish Times*, 26 November 2011, available online at: <https://www.irishtimes.com/culture/books/no-really-signs-of-the-new-sincerity-1.17031> (accessed 20 November 2018).
21 Flynn, *Profit and Loss* (London: Cape Poetry, 2011), 3.
22 Lowell, *Collected Poems*, 178.
23 Flynn, *The Radio* (London: Cape Poetry, 2017).

intermediary between domestic space and the wider world – a ubiquitous, though now nostalgic, object within the home that gives access to something beyond it. Yet the motif of the radio is not repeated *ad nauseam*, it works metonymically, becoming more broadly symbolic of the relationship between the private and the public. Like *Life Studies*, whose opening poem, 'Beyond the Alps', examines a Europe yawning out of the grip of religious institutions and into new relationships with transport and technology, *The Radio* is interested in how the world around is changing rapidly. It enacts a journey from a family home of the 1970s into an age in which 'we zigzag digitally, thrilled, frenetic / but slowly forgetting how we might go *slow*.'[24]

In the first part of *The Radio*, 'The Child, The Family', Flynn formalizes her memory of the nuclear domestic space of childhood, while also navigating the experience of new motherhood. In her interview with Wake Forest University Press Flynn commented on the imaginative structure behind this section:

> The first poems in *The Radio* were written when I was writing pretty intensely, with all the single-mindedness, or selfishness, you need for that. But there was also a baby, so I had the added job of creating what I believe Winnicott calls a 'containing environment'.[25]

Donald Winnicott's *The Child, the Family, and the Outside World* (1964) is also the text that provides the title of the first two sections of the collection. While Lowell's *Life Studies* journeys into this seemingly enfolded space from a much broader view of the social and religious order in Part One, Flynn's book sets out from the nuclear family before venturing into broader and more impersonal spaces – one of her dialogues enacts a conversation between 'Mother of Older Child, Imploded' and 'The Awesome Voice of the Internet', '*The scene is everywhere, nowhere*'. Like Lowell, who experiments with different formal and tonal qualities in *Life Studies* – moving, for example, into prose for Part Two of *Life Studies* ('91 Revere Street') – Flynn also uses the formal quality of her verse to aid in the transition between different spaces and states of mind. The book contains

24 Flynn, 'August 30th 2013', *The Radio*, 22.
25 Flynn, 'Radio Signals'.

poems in rhymed stanzas of various lengths, including sonnets, as well as a concrete poem, and a work for radio. Flynn also displays the same penchant for rewriting and reworking, reshaping repeated ideas into various different forms. Section one of *The Radio* features three variations on the same theme – a triptych that address itself to the title.

In 'The Radio' (#1) Flynn meditates on the radio of her childhood as intermediary between inner and outer world:

> The radio hoots and mutters, hoots and mutters
> out of the dark, each morning of my childhood.
> A kind of plaintive, reedy, oboe note –
> *Deadlock* … it mutters, *firearms* … *Warrenpoint*;
> *Just before two this morning* … *talks between* …
>
> and through its aperture, the outside world
> comes streaming, like a magic lantern show,
> into our bewildered solitude.
> *Unrest* … it hoots now *both sides* … *sources say* …
> My mother stands, like a sentinel, by the sink.[26]

The world exterior to 'The child, The Family', it soon becomes clear, is Northern Ireland during the 'The Troubles'. What the poet as adult recalls of this experience, though, is much more musical and sensual in nature. Unable to fully comprehend the disorder of the outside world, the sound of the radio communicates or transmits this tension not through 'news' traditionally understood, but through its other acoustic qualities. In its muttering, hooting, and static, moreover, the radio's transmissions function as a metaphor for our understanding of events as they occur – partial and occluded – along with recollected experience, which is also, at best, wavering. Like many of the lyrics in the collection, 'The Radio' (#1) calls back to the book's epigraph: '… *there is a music of words which is beyond speech; it is an enduring echo if we know not what in the past and in the abyss*' (Edward Thomas).

As the poem progresses, the memory of the mother becomes fused with the radio, or in this case, the transmitter tower:

---

26 Flynn, *The Radio*, 11.

> She is small, freaked out, pragmatic, vigilant;
> high-pitched and steely – like in human form,
> the RKO transmitter tower, glimpsed
> just before films on Sunday afternoons,
> where we loaf on poufs, or wet bank holidays.
>
> Or perhaps a strangely tiny lightening rod
> snatching the high and wild and worrying words
> out of the air, then running them to ground.[27]

Here the mother both transmits and conducts energy, redirecting and discharging 'worrying words' from the outside world away from her children. The mother and the radio find a further point of connection in operating as prime movers. And this is Flynn's realization at the close of the poem, whose psychoanalytic turn, typical of postwar American poetry, imagines the poet in a therapeutic encounter:

> *– forgive me, doctor, this is hypothesis,*
> *it's conjecture, really, of the weakest kind –*
>
> and even today, beneath our super-smart
> transactions and our tight commercial smiles
> (half-hearted, regretful, at low frequency)
> at the centre of amazed concentric circles,
> the radio plays behind an unmarked door.[28]

In the concrete poem that follows 'The Radio' (#1), Flynn creates a feminist revisionist version of John 1:1's 'In the beginning was the word and the word was with God'. 'Listening to My Mother Listen to the Radio' (let's call it #2) takes on the shape of a radio, and is composed of alternating word pairings: 'The Word The World', reading from left to right, and closing with 'The Word'.[29] The print fades gradually towards the middle before 'The World' is reasserted at the centre of the poem, surrounded by a rectangle of blank space, roughly the proportions of a tape. It is not clear whether the

27 Ibid.
28 Ibid. 14.
29 Ibid. 16.

poem should be read from the outside in or the inside out. Mother is both word and world, and the space explored by the poem is both particular and cosmic. Once again, the experience of the child is indirect and mediated – they listen to the mother as *she* listens to the radio. This layered listening begs the further question of what sound the mother might make (if she is being listened to) and from where exactly the child is listening. Indeed, the poem also suggests itself as a kind of uterine space, in which the world of the child is contained.

The version of 'The Radio' (#3) that follows this concrete poem, however, enacts a kind of psychic rebirth for the mother, who is imaginatively transported by the sounds of the radio, and released from the threats of the outside world:

> In a spill of sunlight by the kitchen sink
> my mother is listening to the radio.
> Foster and Allen are singing 'A Bunch of Thyme'.
> Oh such a lovely song, she thinks – she lifts
> Through the sun-barred window square, and flies away[30]

Through these three central radio poems, Flynn not only examines the relationship between inner (private) and outer (public) spaces in a way that chimes with Lowell's *Life Studies*, she also shows the same impulse to revise and repeat that characterizes Lowell's later work after *Notebook* (1970) – a point which she addresses in the earlier poem for 'Robert Lowell' in *Drives* (2008).

As it ventures into the 'the Outside World' *The Radio* continues to think about the nuclear family, and Flynn's poems about marriage and relationships are particularly Lowellian. 'Flights' considers a relationship defined by '*Excess and melodrama. Constant flight.*', using the metaphor of flying (a staple in Flynn's work) to consider the couple's 'bumpy landings', wishing instead that they could have

> […] stowed away
> a screwball duo, tucked under a tarp,
> between the ship's launch and its anchorage:

---

30 Ibid. 17.

watching the scenes shift, all ozone and brine,
all cortisol-clear along the razor's edge.³¹

The nautical imagery is a clear nod to Lowell, while the phrases 'screwball' and 'razor's edge' have both been plucked from '"To Speak of Woe That Is in Marriage"' (in *Life Studies*), equally a work of excess and fight. Both of these poems are also sonnets, though they refuse to adopt the form too rigidly. Like Lowell, Flynn's general approach to poetry continues to walk the razor's edge between freedom and traditional form that is so pertinent to Lowell's poetry. While her style suggests what reviewer Stephen Knight has described as 'a writer trading the gravitas of Ireland's elder statesmen poets for a looser, American style',³² Flynn remains preoccupied with classical forms – much in the way that Lowell professed an interest in Latin poetry. Neither Lowell nor Flynn considers these paradigms as the conservative forms that they are often perceived to be.

When asked how he came 'to have such a great interest in Roman history and Latin literature' in an interview for *The Paris Review* in 1961, Lowell responded: 'you take almost any really good Roman poet – Juvenal, or Virgil, or Propertius, Catullus – he's much more raw and direct than anything in English, and yet he has this block-like formality. The Roman frankness interests me.'³³ Looking at Lowell's 'To Speak of Woe that Is in Marriage', which originally began as a translation of Catullus, it is possible to see how this Roman's frankness allows the modern poet new linguistic force. 'I don't know what traces are left', comments Lowell, 'but it couldn't have been written without Catullus.'³⁴ *The Radio* contains three, incredibly frank (or 'believable'), versions of Catullus. Of course Flynn's engagement

---

31   Ibid. 34.
32   'Poetry in brief: *Drives* by Leontia Flynn', *The Independent*, 16 November 2008, available online at: <https://www.independent.co.uk/arts-entertainment/books/features/poetry-in-brief-drives-by-leontia-flynn-1017500.html> (accessed 20 November 2018).
33   'Robert Lowell, The Art of Poetry No. 3: interviewed by Frederick Seidel' in *The Paris Review* 25 (Winter–Spring 1961), available online at: <https://www.theparisreview.org/interviews/4664/robert-lowell-the-art-of-poetry-no-3-robert-lowell> (accessed 20 November 2018).
34   Ibid.

with this Roman poet shares much in common with Anne Carson – a writer who Flynn feels she was only beginning to 'read properly' around the time that she was writing *The Radio*.[35] Carson, a classicist, is also poet of wonderful frankness, whose translations of Catullus can be found in *Nox* (2010) – her poem in a box – and elsewhere.[36]

Flynn's 'Give it up, Moron' *'after Catullus 8'*, reflects on infidelity and a relationship gone sour – the subject of many translations by Carson and Lowell (including 'To Speak of Woe That Is in Marriage'). The poem is full of brilliant vitriol tempered, at close, with wistfulness:

> Don't chase after shadows. Don't dwell on your crappy life
> But make up your mind to endure this – ride it out!
> Do you see – Goodbye! Goodbye! – how I'm riding this out,
> Sweetheart? This stiff upper lip? And you'll be sorry
> When I don't come scampering after you again,
> And nobody does, and no one calls you gorgeous …
> You heartless cow. Let me wish you appalling luck
> In future affairs: Who'll love you? Who'll love you back?
> And who'll get to kiss you – God! – whose lips you'll bite …
> While, make no mistake, I'll do *this*! I'll ride it out …[37]

The other two Catullus poems, 'Government Servants' (*'after Catullus 28'*) and 'I Can't Say I Love You' (*'after Catullus 11'*) are not romantic, but the poet's anger – directed in the former, to the state, and in the latter, to self-important poets – is equally fierce and intimate.[38]

In the same section, 'Taking Blood', draws from another of Lowell's poems about marital breakdown. As the narrator watches a nurse fill the vials, she notices 'a tree outside / has coughed its froth of blossoms up the branch',[39] recalling some of Lowell's most potent lines in 'Man and Wife':

---

35 'The writers in the generation below me that I like take fragmentation and elusiveness as their point of departure, so I'm trying to read poetry which provides a touchstone for them. By this I basically mean I'm belatedly reading Anne Carson properly'. Flynn, 'Radio Signals'.
36 Anne Carson, *Nox* (New York: New Directions, 2010).
37 Flynn, *The Radio*, 41.
38 Ibid. 42, 43.
39 Flynn, *The Radio*, 36.

> At last the trees are green on Marlborough Street,
> blossoms on our magnolia ignite
> the morning with their murderous five days' white.[40]

The flower imagery is subverted in both of these settings, in which, we might say, 'the season's ill'.[41] Perhaps Flynn's blood poem also shares something, though more subliminal, with Lowell's 'Skunk Hour', in which 'A car radio bleets "Love, O careless Love ...."' and the poet hears his 'ill-spirit sob in each blood cell'.[42] Like many of Lowell's speakers (though to a lesser degree the speaker of 'Skunk Hour'), Flynn finds a way to prod at her own self-seriousness as she takes leave of the nurse 'who tilts the glass again / as if to show me, really, it is half-*full*'.[43] This kind of self-abasing humour runs through a number of her poems in *The Radio*, and particularly the ones in which she invokes mid-century writers from the United States. In the third section of 'Wives in Mid-Twentieth Century American Fiction', for example, Flynn scolds the self-indulgent 'poet':

> *Poetry is bullshit egotism:*
> *the trite romance of waking up alone,*
> *gradually, in a room where sun*
> *falls on a chair, a bed, four walls – a prism*
> *of –* spare me please! *– 'essential solitude'*
> *that holds some dumb thought till it clarifies.*
> *Pressed on all sides by urgent needs, sharp cries*
> *(*Iced *drinks are melting!) I am clear as mud.*[44]

This passage enacts a dialogue (between the wife and speaker, or the speaker and themselves) which draws from absurdist imagery in Berryman's Dream Song 46 to respond to the supposed quotation above:

> I am, outside. Incredible panic rules.
> People are blowing and beating each other without mercy.

---

40   Lowell, *Collected Poems*, 189.
41   Lowell, 'Skunk Hour', *Collected Poems*, 191.
42   Ibid.
43   *The Radio*, 36.
44   Ibid. 39–40. Emphases in original.

> drinks are boiling. Iced
> drinks are boiling [...]⁴⁵

In her reference to Dream Song 46 Flynn integrates the qualities of anachronism and melodrama that make Berryman's song so humorous. Elsewhere in the poem, Flynn makes explicit the perceived connection between this epoch and her own: 'Yeah, part of us pities and part shares their fates': 'turning, day by day, / inward and downward, thwarted, like the wife // in some grim post-war thing by Richard Yates'.⁴⁶

Flynn's casual use of the phrase 'day by day', of course, alludes to the title of Lowell's last work, *Day by Day* (1977). While Flynn may poke fun at the 'poet' and their egotism, she also remembers to set these works within their 'post-war' environment, providing another context for their 'incredible panic'. Indeed Flynn's work harkens back to mid-century poets such as Lowell, Bishop, Berryman and Plath as writers in the grip of great societal change, at the tipping point between one epoch and another.

The broadly social changes that are experienced in her own time are scrutinized throughout the book, but most pointedly in the final section, 'Poems Conceived as Dialogues between Two Antagonistic Voices'. These mini dramas draw from the example of another mid-century American writer in arriving at their form, translating Plath's radio play, *Three Women* (1962), into a more contemporary context. The first dialogue, which resembles Plath's work more closely, is between a 'Woman, in receipt of infant under two years' and a 'Man, impatient'. Here Flynn uses *Three Women* as a model to think about how heterosexual domestic relationships have changed. 'Woman, in receipt' asserts her sense of frustration: 'You praise "women" while you fail them / like drunks and statesmen', and is batted down by her sardonic partner:

> An active verb and now an activist?
> You're conscious, so you're raising consciousness?
> give me a break, love. None of your cow-kind

---

45   *The Dream Songs*, 50.
46   *The Radio*, 39.

will ever rouse themselves to re-define
the slavery that each wished on herself.[47]

The male figure in this poem seems not to have evolved, as a feminist, but instead has learned to adopt a more insidious approach to keeping women in check. In the two dialogues that follow, Flynn speaks to the alienating experience of late capitalism, in which human subjects are bombarded and effaced by the outside world. The second features 'Man, a former environmental activist turned PR consultant for logging companies' in dialogue with a 'Voice, neither male nor female, impersonal'.[48] In the final episode, we find a 'Mother of older child, imploded', in conversation with 'The awesome voice of the internet' – 'The scene is everywhere/nowhere'. In all of these dialogues one of the voices has a clear historic and social advantage.

The Radio meditates extensively on the challenges posed by new media technology, its decentring impact on the self, and its broader impact on the world of poetry. In 'August 30th 2013', an elegy for Seamus Heaney that opens the second section of *The Radio*, Flynn reflects on how the news of Heaney's death comes to her through 'Two texts [and] an email on my phone', while 'Twitter erupts, it seems, in shards of verse'.[49] This kind of bombardment is something that Flynn's elegy works through, and against. In an essay entitled 'Radically Necessary Heaney',[50] written around the same time as Flynn's elegy for Heaney, she meditates on this problem using both Lowell and Heaney's poetic craft as counterweight.[51]

> The 'liking' is a problem. Social media celebrates popularity: the counting of followers, the holy grail of things going viral, and, implicitly, the possibility of monetizing this. Poetry has not had a mass audience for centuries now, but since it is usually written by people who are socially isolated and prefer the company of books, has survived anyway. John Berryman noted once that Robert Lowell spent

---

47 Ibid. 56.
48 Ibid. 59.
49 Ibid. 21.
50 Leontia Flynn, 'Radically Necessary: Heaney's Defence of Poetry' in *The Irish Review* 49/50 (Winter–Spring 2014/2015): 208–218.
51 'August 30th 2013' was also published in the *Edinburgh Review* in 2015.

maybe 100 hours on the 'Ovid stanza' of 'Beyond the Alps', only to delete it; in the counter-economy represented by obsessive devotion to poetic craft (there is no one to invoice for this time), in the first instance the poet doesn't care whether lots of people 'like' it, only whether they themselves are satisfied. Social media might not stop people wanting to write poetry, but its logic – and this is evident to me every time I log on – will make everyone feel a lot worse about forms of writing with 'minority' followings.[52]

Flynn's elegy for Heaney also brings Lowell into focus, and to similar effect. The poem concludes with a reflection on a line from Heaney's 'Elegy' for Lowell:

> 'The way we're living, timorous or bold';
> you wrote of Lowell, 'will have been our life';
> and all these gripes aside, *I've* not rebelled
> but drifted: campus-bound, prosaic, *staff* –
> so have no moral stick to beat her with
> the Goddess Dullness squatting on our pages
> – her language slack, her mind a monolith –
> and would it make a difference if I tried
> mounting the lectern, arguing Dark Ages?
> Me, not just *timorous*, but *terrified*.[53]

The line from Heaney's poem (directed at Lowell) gives Flynn pause for thought and self-reflection, acting as a kind of anchor in the poem amid a barrage of tangled thoughts. Heaney's 'Elegy' also reflects on the 'role' of the poet, and presents Lowell as a formidable craftsman, yet like Flynn's elegy, a number of other issues also enter the field, and the elegy is highly observational.

> The way we are living,
> timorous or bold,
> will have been our life.
> Robert Lowell,
>
> the sill where the geranium is lit
> by the lamp I write by,

52 'Radically Necessary: Heaney's Defence of Poetry', 211.
53 Ibid. 23–24.

> a wind from the Irish sea
> is shaking it –
>
> here ten days ago, with you,
> the master elegist
> and welder of English.
>
> As you swayed the talk
> and rode on the swaying tiller
> of yourself, ribbing me
> about my fear of water,
>
> what was not within your empery?
> You drank America
> like the heart's
> iron vodka,
>
> promulgating art's
> deliberate, peremptory
> love and arrogance
> [...]⁵⁴

Like Flynn's tribute to 'Robert Lowell' in *Drives*, Heaney's poem is not unmixed in its praise for the American, but presents him in the round (and somewhat duplicitously), as a poet of 'arrogance' that 'bullied out heart hammering sonnets'.⁵⁵ Yet ultimately Lowell's influence is 'opulent and restorative' – 'you found the child in me' admits Heaney, who in Lowell's absence feels newly vulnerable: '*A father's no shield / for his child*'.⁵⁶

'What does it mean to say that poetry is its own autonomous reality?'⁵⁷ – thinking about Heaney and Lowell together helps Flynn to frame this question. She continues, letting Heaney's 'Elegy' for Lowell resonate a second time within her own, dwelling with his words amid 'the multi-platform din and drift'.

---

54   Heaney, 'Elegy' in *Field Work* (London: Faber and Faber, 1979), 31–32.
55   Ibid.
56   Ibid.
57   'Radically Necessary: Heaney's Defence of Poetry', 209

> The way we're living *will have been* our life:
> that steely line – that Future Perfect – cast
> in an impending retrospective light
> our present efforts, not as some rough draft,
> but, mid and the multi-platform din and drift,
> as an instrument and something to get *right*;
> which is another thing you will have left
> (or *have* left – past tense now – those choices made).
> An ethics: which instructs:
>   Now shut up. Write
> *for joy. Be deliberate and unafraid.*[58]

This elegy acts as a stay against confusion. Here Flynn seeks to represent something of her own private response to Heaney's life and work, something slower and more meditative, something akin to 'the most private self from which poetry arises', beyond 'the confused public self of our online profiles'.[59] Flynn's closing remarks – addressed more pointedly toward the self – espouse an ethics borne out of communion with both Heaney and Lowell. The poet is instructed not only to aim toward the perfection of the work, but also to commit herself to life, as 'an instrument and something to get *right*'.[60] The line is further inflected by another 'mid-century' writer, notably Bishop's forceful injunction ('*write* it'), from the closing line of her great villanelle on loss, 'One Art'.[61] This instruction is given amidst great uncertainty regarding the future of poetry, and contemporary life. Amidst all of this, a belief in *writing* (and *right*ing) is radically necessary; and for Flynn, like Heaney, Lowell continues to be a 'night ferry', an example of how to steer 'wilfully across / the ungovernable and dangerous.'[62]

---

58   'August 30th 2013', 24.
59   'Radically Necessary: Heaney's Defence of Poetry', 215.
60   'August 30th 2013', 24.
61   Elizabeth Bishop, 'One Art', *Complete Poems* (Kent: Chatto & Windus, 2004), 178.
62   Heaney, *Field Work*, 32.

JULIE O'CALLAGHAN

Seamus Heaney Introducing Robert Lowell in Kilkenny, 1975

Here is how I remember the Lowell event in Kilkenny ….
    A phone call came during the morning to the pay phone in the hallway outside our flat. I usually answered it during the day since everyone else was at work. It was Dennis on the phone in a very excited state. He said he had just heard that Robert Lowell was reading that very night in Kilkenny and that we were going. He said he'd take a half day off work and we could take a train down to Kilkenny in the afternoon. He'd booked a room in The Town House Hotel.
    It was a warm day and I don't think I'd ever seen Dennis so absolutely thrilled about anything before. He gave me the entire literary lowdown on Robert Lowell during the journey. We had with us a little battery-operated cassette tape recorder that my father had given me and were hoping to get some of Lowell's reading on tape.
    The upstairs room in Kytler's Inn was quite stuffy and warm – but the windows had to be kept closed because of the noise from the street and traffic outside. Robert Lowell mentioned a few times that it was warm but that he knew it would be distracting if the windows were opened. So jackets came off.
    The first part of the evening Derek Mahon and Richard Murphy read. Robert Lowell wasn't shy, sitting in the audience, listening carefully, and when Derek Mahon was shuffling some papers Lowell said, 'Read a sad one'.
    We had front row seats and I've never been to a more incredible poetry event. Lowell read in a mesmerizing voice and everything he said seemed like an oracle speaking. The tape we had was only an hour long so between the introduction of Lowell by Seamus and the very lengthy and interesting comments Lowell made between the poems we didn't get the entire reading on tape. But every once in a while, I put on the headphones and listen to our recording from ancient history …

SEAMUS HEANEY

Introduction to Robert Lowell Reading at Kilkenny Arts Week, Kytler's Inn, Kilkenny, 28 August 1975

Based on a recording made by Dennis O'Driscoll and Julie O'Callaghan. Transcribed by Julie O'Callaghan in 2017.

I am here at the moment to praise Robert Lowell – whose presence in Kilkenny, I think, not only reflects honour on the Arts Week, but reflects honour on the other poets here who have read and the other poet who will read [on] Friday.

Robert Lowell is a man who, I think, in a continuous – relentless indeed – effort to apprehend what his art means and what being a poet means, has comprehended his own life and a great deal of the life of his times. Because, I think, to master the meaning of your art and to master the meaning of the word 'poet' – is a poet's task. He quickly learns – if he *is* a poet – that the private satisfactions of making verses – private vanities – private therapies – private pleasures of technique and so on – that these things are inadequate somehow. He learns that if verses are to be more than harmless vanity or more than a kind of delicious verbal bouquet – then they have to try to bring themselves to the point of some kind of power. The meaning of that power is a search, I think: How You Can Make Language Powerful. Powerful in itself and powerful in the way that it comprehends things beyond yourself.

A poet, in other words, I think, must not only *sound* himself – literally in words – but his work must also be *soundings* of something beyond himself. To be a poet is to be involved in a covenant between living and dead. He stands between the masterpieces of the past – stands between those 'Monuments of unageing intellect' as Yeats called them, those forms of energy and understanding that make us see what it has always meant to be human. What human life could mean. He stands between those ranged in the tradition and the civilization that he comes from and he stands opposite things that aren't formed. He stands opposite the flux of his own life – the flux and chaos of his own terms and his responsibility – his imperative – if he seeks and accepts the word *poet* – is to make that flux of self and reality of the times into forms that will stand beside those other lines of masterpieces.

This, Robert Lowell has done by mastering himself and his art from the beginning. T.S. Eliot once made a distinction between the man who suffers and the man who creates. W.B. Yeats made a distinction between what he called 'the bundle of accident and incoherence who sits down to breakfast' and the man who is born/reborn in his poems as an idea – something intended; something complete. Robert Lowell has suffered for his principles – and in his person, like the rest of us. But unlike the rest of us in his own way. And he created out of that. He has turned accident and incoherence into something intended and complete that is there already and he is still completing work.

It is an honour to introduce him – to introduce a man who has written poems from the beginning such as 'The Quaker Graveyard' that can be mentioned in the same breath as *Lycidas* without embarrassment. Or his recent work – that can be mentioned with a poem like *In Memoriam*, and it's a question – a delicate question – which would come off best. But there's no necessity to answer that question – or indeed ask it!! [Robert Lowell comments: 'Oh ask it!']

His translations have taken on – have – as Auden said that poetry should do – they have 'broken bread with the dead'. His translations re-do and imitate masterpieces. He is a link in that great chain of beings who constitute, in a sense, the canon of modern poetry. A man who's been a friend of Robert Frost, Ezra Pound, Marianne Moore, T.S. Eliot. A man who is the centre of the most brilliant generation of American poets like Randall Jarrell, John Berryman. A man who began his tutelage, I suppose, under those delicate makers such as John Crowe Ransom and Allen Tate. And a man in whose presence we as poets and we as audience are honoured to be this evening.

MARIE HEANEY

Afterword

On the evening of Tuesday, 6 September 1977, we had an unexpected visit to our home in Strand Road, in Dublin, from Robert Lowell and Caroline Blackwood. They were living in Castletown House at that time and had driven, or been driven, into Dublin. In *Stepping Stones*, his 2008 book of interviews with Dennis O'Driscoll, Seamus describes the probable reason for such a visit. He wrote, 'They'd get bored out in Castletown House – a vast Georgian pile near Dublin, where Caroline had rented an apartment from her cousin, Desmond Guinness – and they would hit town and the vodka and us in one single swoop.'[1] We were pleased to see them, unexpected as the visit was, and they both had brought with them their recently published books: *Day by Day*, a collection of poems by Robert, and a novel, *Great Granny Webster*, by Caroline. On this occasion because they were clearly staying for the evening, I rustled up a meal of meatballs and spaghetti in a tomato sauce – hardly the food of the Gods (and I did think of Lowell as one of the gods of contemporary poetry) – but we ate it together happily enough.

Though I had met Lowell on number of occasions – and he and Seamus talked freely to each other – I was slightly overawed by him. The combination of his poetic reputation and his Boston Brahmin reserve made me constrained in his company. But that evening, Caroline and Seamus were talking together so Robert and I became engaged in a genuine conversation. I felt, for the first time, that I had made real contact with him. It was so meaningful that I wrote it up straight away in a journal that I kept

---

[1] See Dennis O'Driscoll, *Stepping Stones: Interviews with Seamus Heaney* (London: Faber and Faber, 2008), 219.

sporadically. It was the early hours of Wednesday morning by the time Seamus drove them back to Castletown House.

At that time literary gossip had it that Robert and Caroline's marriage was coming to an end. We'd heard it from a couple of American participants at the Rotterdam Poetry Festival that we had been to earlier in the year, but I had no sense of that on that evening in Strand Road. I felt they were happy in each other's company. However Seamus sensed something different. In *Stepping Stones* he writes: 'What I did sense, however, with the aid of the gossip then going the rounds, was that the relationship with Caroline was about to end,' and goes on to describe a quick coded exchange with Robert, as they were leaving Strand Road, that seemed to indicate that the marriage was indeed over.[2]

We knew, too, that Robert was about to go back to America, for he had given his phone number to Seamus so that he could contact him when he, Seamus, would be in Stony Brook University in New York a couple of weeks later.

Seamus went to London a day or two after that visit and, late on the night of 12 September, he returned to Dublin. The next morning I drove him to Carysfort College where he was teaching at the time. As he got out of the car, a colleague from the English department told him the news had just come through that Robert Lowell had died. We simply could not believe it. He had been with us, in Strand Road, exactly a week to the day earlier – but it seemed like hours, not days, since we'd been in his company. Because of the intimacy of that evening we felt his death as a very personal loss. I had felt, for the first time, that he was becoming a friend whom we would see from time to time. I must add, however, that though we *did* feel a genuine connection with him, we still addressed him as Robert, not as Cal, which was what his oldest and closest friends called him.

A day or two after that sad news, Seamus and I went back into the room, where we had all had spent the evening together such a short time before, to listen to the eulogies for Robert on BBC Three, including one by Seamus. The books they had brought us were lying on the coffee table where their hands had laid them.

2   Ibid.

Afterword

We looked at the inscription Robert had written in the fly leaf of *Day By Day*, and it was signed 'Cal'.

The news of Lowell's death shocked and saddened both of us profoundly and ten days after his visit Seamus wrote 'Elegy' in his memory.

Our house looks out on the Irish Sea, and from its windows he could see the night ferries coming and going from Britain, so the scene was set for the maritime images that pervade the poem.

> Two a.m., seaboard weather.
> Not the proud sail of your great verse ...
> No. You were our night ferry
> thudding in a big sea,
>
> the whole craft ringing
> with an armourer's music,
> the course set wilfully across
> the ungovernable and dangerous.

I consider 'Elegy' one of Seamus's most passionate poems, a ringing tribute to the work, in its many aspects, of the poet he admired so much. However the poem ends on a gentler note as he remembers his parting from Lowell on an earlier visit at the gate of our cottage in Glanmore, Co. Wicklow:

> you found the child in me
> when you took farewells
> under the full bay tree
> by the gate in Glanmore,
>
> opulent and restorative
> as that lingering summertime,
> the fish-dart of your eyes
> risking, 'I'll pray for you.'[3]

---

3 See Seamus Heaney, 'Elegy' in *Field Work* (London: Faber and Faber, 1979), 25–27.

Notes on Contributors

STEVEN GOULD AXELROD is Distinguished Professor of English at the University of California, Riverside. The founding president of the Robert Lowell Society, he has served as president of PAMLA and is currently on the Advisory Boards of *Pacific Coast Philology*, *College Literature*, *The William Carlos Williams Review*, and *Plath Profiles*. At UC Riverside, he has received the Distinguished Teaching Award, was founding holder of the McCauley Chair in Teaching Excellence and has served on the Academy of Distinguished Teachers. He has helped shape the field of Robert Lowell studies since the 1970s. He is the author of *Robert Lowell: Life and Art* (1978), and *Robert Lowell: A Reference Guide* (1982). He has also written *Sylvia Plath: The Wound and the Cure of Words* (1990). He is the editor of *Robert Lowell: Essays on the Poetry* (1986) and *The Critical Response to Robert Lowell* (1999). He has recently edited (with Grzegorz Kosc) *The Memoirs of Robert Lowell* (forthcoming).

ADAM BEARDSWORTH is Associate Professor of English at Grenfell Campus, Memorial University, where he teaches courses in contemporary literature and critical theory. His primary research focus is on American poetry and the cold war and he has published numerous essays on American and Canadian poetry. He is currently serving as vice president of the Canadian Association for American Studies.

ANNA CHAHOUD studied Classics in Bologna and Pisa, Italy, and worked in Reading and Durham before coming to Ireland in 1999. She joined the Classics Department in Trinity College Dublin in 2006, where she is now Professor of Latin. Her research focuses on fragmentary Republican Latin, Latin linguistics, and the transmission of Latin texts from antiquity to the early modern period. She is especially interested in the study of Latin registers and of the interaction between literary and spoken language. She has long been engaged in the study of early Latin satire, working on a new edition of, and the first English-language commentary on, the fragments of Lucilius. She is also preparing an edition, with English translation, of fragmentary satire, political invective and popular verse for the Loeb Classical Library, which explores the relationship between literary and colloquial, sub-literary and non-literary Latin. She is Public Orator of the University of Dublin.

EVE COBAIN was awarded a PhD from Trinity College Dublin in 2017. Her doctoral research explored the significance of music in the poetry of John Berryman and was funded by the Irish Research Council. She has contributed to volumes including *John Berryman at 100: Centenary Essays* (2017) and *Making Integral: Critical Essays on Richard Murphy* (2019).

PHILIP COLEMAN is an associate professor in the School of English and a Fellow of Trinity College Dublin, Ireland. His most recent books are *John Berryman: Centenary Essays* (co-edited with Peter Campion, 2017) and *George Saunders: Critical Essays* (co-edited with Steve Gronert Ellerhoff, 2017). Other recent publications include *Critical Insights: David Foster Wallace* (2015), *John Berryman's Public Vision* (2014), and *Berryman's Fate: A Centenary Celebration in Verse* (2014). With Calista McRae, he is editing a selection of John Berryman's literary correspondence for Harvard University Press.

LUCY COLLINS is Associate Professor of English at University College Dublin. Educated at Trinity College Dublin and at Harvard University, where she spent a year as a Fulbright Scholar, she teaches and researches in the area of modern poetry and poetics. Recent books include *Poetry by Women in Ireland: A Critical Anthology 1870–1970* (2012) and a monograph, *Contemporary Irish Women Poets: Memory and Estrangement* (2015), both published by Liverpool University Press. She has published widely on contemporary poets from Ireland, Britain and America, and is co-founder of the Irish Poetry Reading Archive, a national digital repository. Her current project is a study of Irish poetry and print culture in the Free State period 1922–49.

GERALD DAWE was born in Belfast, Northern Ireland, in 1952. He attended Orangefield Boys School, Ulster University and the National University of Ireland, Galway. He published his first collection of poems, *Sheltering Places*, in 1978. He moved to Trinity College Dublin in 1988 where he taught until 2017. He has published twenty books of poetry and literary essays, including *The Lundys Letter*, which was awarded the Macaulay Fellowship in Literature, *Lake Geneva, Selected Poems* and *Mickey Finn's Air*. He has been Burns Professor at Boston College, Charles Heimbold Professor at Villanova University Philadelphia and Visiting Scholar at Pembroke College, Cambridge. He lives in Dun Laoghaire, County Dublin.

ELLEN DILLON completed a PhD at the School of English, Dublin City University. She has a BA in French and Italian and an MA in Italian from University College Dublin. She is currently working on a project called 'Dynamic Abstraction in Modern and Contemporary Poetry.' Her research interests include modernist, modern and contemporary poetry in English and French, with a particular focus on the literary criticism of Charles Altieri, the poetry and translation of Peter Manson and the work of Peter Gizzi.

STEPHEN GRACE lives and works in York, where he is a PhD candidate in the Department of English and Related Literature. His poems and reviews have appeared, or are forthcoming, in *The Year's Work in Critical and Cultural Theory*, *The Compass*, *The Honest Ulsterman*, and *The Literateur*.

MARIE HEANEY was born in County Tyrone and began her teaching career in schools in Northern Ireland. She and her family moved to Dublin in 1972 where she still lives. As well as *Over Nine Waves* (1995), she has written *The Names Upon the Harp* and a book of Irish legends for children (Faber, 2000, illustrated by P.J. Lynch). As an editor with Townhouse Publishing in Dublin, she has produced several anthologies, including *Heart Mysteries*, a personal selection of Irish poetry. She has also contributed to newspapers and journals and has written for radio and television.

SEAMUS HEANEY was born in County Derry in Northern Ireland. *Death of a Naturalist*, his first collection of poems, appeared in 1966, and was followed by poetry, criticism and translations, which established him as the leading poet of his generation. In 1995 he was awarded the Nobel Prize in Literature, and twice won the Whitbread Book of the Year, for *The Spirit Level* (1996) and *Beowulf* (1999). *Stepping Stones*, a book of interviews conducted by Dennis O'Driscoll, appeared in 2008; *Human Chain*, his last volume of poems, was awarded the 2010 Forward Prize for Best Collection. He died in 2013. His translation of Virgil's *Aeneid* Book VI was published posthumously in 2016 to critical acclaim.

MICHAEL HINDS is a senior lecturer in the Department of English in Dublin City University, where he is also Director of the MA in Poetry Studies programme. He has taught in Trinity College Dublin, University College Dublin, and the University of Tokyo, and he has co-edited *Rebound: The American Poetry Book* (2007). He edits the poetry studies journal *POST* and directs an annual summer school in Dublin City University devoted to poetry studies. He is completing studies of Randall Jarrell and Johnny Cash.

FRANK J. KEARFUL, Professor Emeritus at the University of Bonn, is vice president of the Robert Lowell Society and has published numerous articles on Lowell. From 2003 to 2014 he also assessed directions in Lowell studies in his annual chapter on American poetry since the 1940s for *American Literary Scholarship*. He is currently completing a book on *Robert Lowell's Signs of Life*.

J.V. LUCE was Professor of Classics and Emeritus Fellow at Trinity College Dublin. He was also the College's Public Orator between 1971 and 2005.

CALISTA MCRAE is an assistant professor of English at the New Jersey Institute of Technology. Her first book, *Lyric as Comedy: The Poetics of Abjection in Postwar America*, explores humour in postwar and contemporary American poetry, and is forthcoming from Cornell University Press. Her work has also appeared in *Modern Philology*, *Arizona Quarterly*, and *Modernism/Modernity*. With Philip Coleman, she is editing a selection of John Berryman's letters for Harvard University Press.

JULIE O'CALLAGHAN was born in Chicago in 1954 and has lived in Ireland since 1974. Her collections of poetry include *Edible Anecdotes* (1983), a Poetry Book Society Recommendation, *What's What* (1991), a Poetry Book Society Choice, *No Can Do* (2000), a Poetry Book Society Recommendation and *Tell Me This Is Normal: New and Selected Poems* (2008), also a Poetry Book Society Recommendation. A chapbook, *Problems*, appeared in 2005. She received the Michael Hartnett Poetry Award in 2001 and was awarded Arts Council of Ireland Bursaries in 1985, 1990 and 1998.

KARL O'HANLON is a lecturer in the Deparment of English at Maynooth University, researching twentieth-century poets who held various public and institutional offices. He has published on Geoffrey Hill, John Berryman, and W.B. Yeats. His poetry pamphlet *And Now They Range* was published by Guillemot Press in 2016.

ALEX RUNCHMAN is Lecturer in Academic English at University College Dublin's Applied Language Centre. He is the author of *Delmore Schwartz: A Critical Reassessment* (2014) and, more recently, articles and book chapters on Ezra Pound, John Berryman, and *BLAST*. With Tom Walker, he has co-edited a special edition of *Modernist Cultures* on 'Poetry and Collaboration in the Age of Modernism.'

Index

A
Abel, I. 215n18
Adams, Henry 41–42, 51, 52n8, 53, 56, 61, 141
Adams, John 53
Adams, John Quincy 53
Adorno, Theodor 186
Ahmed, Sarah 97n35
Alexander, Cecil Frances 172n17
Allen, Michael 107n2
Allison, Robert J. 58
Althusser, Louis 101
Altieri, Charles 211–28
Alvarez, A. 38n64, 175
Ambrose, St 12
Arendt, Hannah 24, 27–28, 38, 47
Armstrong, Neil 7
Arnold, Matthew 12
Ashbery, John 218
Auden, W.H. 62, 93, 123, 125–26
Austenfeld, Thomas 3, 6n9
Axelrod, Rise B. 23n1
Axelrod, Steven Gould 4, 5, 75, 94, 107n2, 160, 231, 233n12

B
Bach, Johann Sebastian 117–19
Bachelard, Gaston 201
Bartók, Béla 34
Bayley, Isabel 135n36
Beardsworth, Adam 4, 83–105
Beatty, Jack 54n14
Beatty, Paul 80
Beckett, Samuel 124, 128, 129, 231
Bell, Vereen 216
Bellow, Saul 7, 170n13

Benjamin, Walter 46, 185
Berlant, Lauren 99, 104
Berryman, John 3, 38, 77, 85–86, 127, 190, 209, 229, 235, 243–44, 252
Bertholf, Robert J. 214
Bidart, Frank 76, 133n30
Biddle, Katherine 130, 142
Bishop, Elizabeth 26, 29, 59n23, 71, 77–78, 83, 107, 116–17, 123, 142, 177, 179, 190, 196, 201, 218, 229, 231, 233, 244, 248
Blackwood, Caroline 1, 2, 175, 253
Boland, Eavan 4, 7, 193–210
Boland, Frederick Henry 7
Boru, Brian 63n34
Bossidy, John Collins 49–50
Boyers, Robert 126
Brearton, Fran 221, 230
Breton, André 124
Brewer, Sam Pope 138
Brewster, Kingman 7
British Army 188
Brooks, Cleanth 131, 139n46
Broom, Sarah 227
Brown, Michael 185
Brown, Terence 112
Buffington, Robert 135
Burke, Edmund 72
Bush, Laura 38

C
Calder, Alex 69
Calley, William 179
'Careless Love' (traditional song) 180, 224, 243
Carson, Anne 242

Carson, Ciaran 229
Cato the Elder 12
Catsam, Derek C. 79
Catullus 241–42
Chahoud, Anna 1, 7–15
Chapin, Marguerite (Princess Caetani) 142, 144–45
Char, René 143
Chaucer, Geoffrey 180
Cicero 12–13, 15
Clarke, Aidan 7
Clarke, Austin 4, 124, 194
Cobain, Eve 5, 23n1, 229–48
Cocteau, Jean 134
Coffey, Brian 124, 128, 129, 138n41, 141
Cohen, Israel 52
Coleman, Philip 23n1, 85, 86n6, 236
Collins, Lucy 4, 193–210, 211, 213
Collins, Patrick 53
Congleton, James Edmund 59n24
Cooke, Alistair 72n22, 74
Corcoran, Neil 107n2, 150, 161
Corns, Thomas N. 137n40
Cosgrave, Patrick 29
Crane, Hart 108, 124, 129, 131
Creeley, Robert 218
Cromwell, Oliver 62
Cummings, E.E. 123
Curley, James Michael 51, 53–54
Curley, Walter 7

D
Daniels, Conky 56
Dante 14, 189
Davidson, Peter 181
Davis, Alex 124n5, 127n14
Dawe, Gerald 4, 5, 167–76
Dean, Michelle 234n15
Deese, Helen 233n12
Deutsch, Babette 139
Devine, Kathleen 107n2

Devlin, Denis 4, 123–46
Dickens, Charles 180
Diggle, James 14
Diggory, Terence 3
Dillon, Ellen 5, 211–28
Dillon, John 11
Donne, John 59n24
Doreski, William 196
Drayton, Michael 126
Du Plessis, Rachel Blau 80
Duncan, Robert 214
Dworkin, Craig 190
Dylan, Bob 173

E
Eisenhower, Dwight D. 98
Eliot, T.S. 36, 80, 85, 94, 107, 108, 118, 119, 120, 124, 130, 131, 134–35, 179, 252
Elizabeth I 9
Ellmann, Richard 194
Eluard, Paul 124
Emerson, Ralph Waldo 261
Empson, William 137
Erasmus 126
Erskine, Albert 131
Eyerman, Ron 70n13, 71

F
Falci, Eric 223
Ferguson, Frances 103
Flynn, Leontia 4, 5, 229–48
Ford, Ford Madox 142
Foster, Roy 25n13
Foucault, Michel 28, 69
Frances, Allen 23
Frost, Robert 94, 111, 120, 194, 252
Fulbright, William J. 38

G
Gardner, Isabel 61
Genet, Jean 144

Index 265

George I 47
Gewanter, David 76, 133n30, 215
Ghandi, Mahatma 73
Gilbert and Sullivan 61
Gillis, Alan 221
Gilman, Richard 37n62, 41n83
Giroux, Robert 143–45
Glover, Ann 57–58
Godwin, Martha 57
Goldman, Eric 39
Goldsmith, Kenneth 178, 184
Gonne, Maud 26
Goodby, John 221, 228
Gordon, Caroline 132
Grace, Stephen 5, 147–66
Gramsci, Antonio 212–16
Guevara, Ernesto (Che) 41
Guinness, Desmond 253

H
Hall, Donald 168
Halpern, Nick 151
Hamilton, Ian 35n56, 41n84,
    78, 195n5
Hamilton, Saskia 25n18, 66n44,
    71n14, 123n3, 141n51, 177n1,
    197n11, 234n14
Hancock, John 52
Händel, Georg Friedrich 52
Hanna, Adam 199n17
Hardin, Richard F. 65n40
Harding, Jason 135n34
Hardwick, Elizabeth 41, 82, 141, 188,
    195, 233
Hardy, Thomas 81
Harrison, Robert Pogue 208
Harrison, Victoria 59n23
Hart, Henry 87, 92, 150, 154
Hawthorne, Nathaniel 180
Hayley, Alex 79n56
Heaney, Marie 1, 253–55

Heaney, Seamus 1, 2, 4, 5, 141, 147–66,
    189, 194, 229, 245, 249
Heidegger, Martin 198
Henry IV 67–68
Henry V 44, 67, 69
Henry VIII 9
Hercules 63, 69
Higgins, F.R. 137
Hinds, Michael 23n1, 177–91
Hirohito, Michinomiya 91
Hitchcock, Alfred 231
Hitler, Adolf 91, 93
    Mein Kampf 37
Hofmann, Michael 188
Holdridge, Jefferson 3
Holmes, Oliver Wendell, Sr 49, 55n17
Homer 14
Hopkins, Gerard Manley 138–39
Hone, Joseph 128
Howard, Jane 24n11
Hughes, M.Y. 215n17

I
Ignatius of Loyola, St 136
IRA (Official) 187
IRA (Provisional) 187
Irvine, Kenneth 171n15
Isserman, Maurice 74n31

J
Jacobs, Jane 23
James, Stephen 150, 154
Jamison, Kay Redfield 27n26, 29,
    33n53, 201
Jarrell, Randall 28, 76, 123, 177, 190, 252
Jefferson, Thomas 76
Jesus 64
Joan of Arc 67
John of the Cross, St 27, 214
Johnson, Lyndon 37–39, 44, 72, 83
Joyce, James 62, 125, 127, 128, 139

Joyce, Trevor 141
Juster, A.M. 50n3
Juvenal 14, 17n1, 18n2, 241

K
Kant, Immanuel 62
Kazin, Michael 74n31
Kearful, Frank J. 4, 49–66, 205
Keats, John 46, 65
Kennedy, Jacqueline 41, 62, 69n8, 71
Kennedy, John F. 38, 45, 60, 71
Kennedy, Joseph 68
Kennedy, Robert F. 37, 41–46, 62, 64, 67–82
Kenney, E.J. 14
King, Martin Luther 41, 67–82
Kinsella, Thomas 194
Kirsch, Adam 152
Klein, Bernhard 149–50
Knight, Stephen 241
Kość, Grzegorz 23n1, 31
Kunitz, Stanley 28n32, 30n46, 38, 133n28

L
Lacan, Jacques 219n36
Leonard, John 137
Levertov, Denise 40
Lewis, Wyndham 107, 115, 123
Liberace, Władziu Valentino 35
Lifton, Robert J. 95
Lippmann, Walter 39n71
Little, Roger 144, 146n66
London, Michael 126
Longenbach, James 217
Longley, Michael 107n2, 141, 189, 194
Lowell, Amy 196
Lowell, Charles Russell III 196
Lowell, Charlotte Winslow 30, 202
Lowell, Francis Cabot 53
Lowell, James Russell 196

Lowell, Robert, works by
BOOKS
Collected Poems 46
Day by Day 63, 244, 253
The Dolphin 179, 188, 191, 195, 233–34
For the Union Dead 168–69, 194
History 62, 65, 69–70, 73, 76–77, 81, 107, 117, 179, 184, 188, 190, 230
Imitations 145
Land of Unlikeness 56, 86, 108–09, 125, 132, 133, 140
Life Studies 14, 18, 27, 36, 55, 60, 84, 94, 95, 112–13, 115, 118–19, 133, 140, 147, 168, 179–80, 193, 195–96, 198–99, 201, 204, 205, 207–10, 230, 236–37, 240
Lord Weary's Castle 58, 86, 140, 177, 205
The Mills of the Kavanaughs 76, 86
Near the Ocean 70, 168, 175
Notebook (1970) 62, 64, 69, 115, 119, 184, 190, 240
Notebook 1967–68 41, 62, 69, 107, 116, 121, 188, 230
Poems 1938–49 194
Selected Poems (1976) 46, 48
PLAYS
Benito Cereno 78
POEMS
'Another Circle' 65, 69
'Another June' 69
'At the Indian Killer's Grave' 58
'Beyond the Alps' 180, 237
'Colloquy in Black Rock, Connecticut' 133, 138
'The Drinker' 170
'Epilogue' 63–64, 153, 179
'The Exile's Return' 58
'Eye and Tooth' 100

'Fall 1961' 25, 83, 96–98, 104, 153, 159, 161–62
'Father's Bedroom' 205
'For Robert Kennedy 1925–68' 36, 46, 62–63, 66, 69
'For Robert Kennedy 2' 62–63, 65, 73, 81
'For Sale' 236
'For the Union Dead' 24, 29, 37, 76–77, 94, 101, 162–63, 165, 194
'George III' 47
'The Ghost (after Sextus Propertius)' 145
'Grass Fires' 108
'Hedgehog' 14, 18, 19
'Home' 29
'Home After Three Months Away' 207, 232
'The House Party' 107, 117
'Identification in Belfast' 65, 177–91
'Inauguration Day: January 1953' 37, 83, 97–98, 104, 208
'In Memory of Arthur Winslow' 59
'Louis MacNeice, 1907–1963' 120–22
'Man and Wife' 82
'Memories of West Street and Lepke' 139
'Mr Edwards and the Spider' 58
'My Last Afternoon with Uncle Devereux Winslow' 204
'Night Sweat' 100
'Returning' 174
'Sailing Home from Rapallo' 202, 208
'Skunk Hour' 27, 36, 100, 197, 207, 211–12, 214, 218–20, 224–27, 232, 243

'Terminal Days at Beverly Farms' 114, 205, 209
'The Park Street Cemetery' 56
'The Quaker Graveyard in Nantucket' 84, 88, 92, 97, 151–54, 156, 160, 162, 232, 252
'To Peter Taylor on the Feast of the Epiphany' 84, 91–92
' "To Speak of the Woe That Is in Marriage" ' 180, 241
'To Summer' 107
'Two Walls' 37
'Waking Early Sunday Morning' 24, 26, 36, 39, 40, 46, 83, 101
'Waking in the Blue' 28, 33, 60–62, 199
'Water' 167
'Women Children, Babies, Cows, Cats' 179, 188
PROSE
'91 Revere Street' 55, 168, 196, 237
'Acceptance Speech, National Book Award' (1960) 94
'After Enjoying Six or Seven Essays on Me' 47
'Art and Evil' 93
'The Balanced Aquarium' 34–36, 41
'Current Poetry' 109
'Judgment Deferred on Lieutenant Calley' 25
'Near the Unbalanced Aquarium' 199
'New England and Further' 56
'Sylvia Plath' 47n107
[Unpublished Memoir] 31–32
'Yeats Memorial Lecture' 26
Lowell, Robert III (the poet's father) 30
Luce, J.V. 1, 2n3, 5, 7–15, 17–19

Luke, St 12
Lyons, Francis Steward Leland 7

M
McCarthy, Eugene 37, 41, 42, 107
MacDonagh, Donagh 129
McDonagh, Francis 186
McDonald, Peter 120
McDowell, David 144–45
McGinniskin, Barney 51
McGough, Roger 182
MacGreevy, Thomas 124, 125
McGuckian, Medbh 199, 229, 236
Mackenthun, Gesa 149
MacLeish, Archibald 130
McLeod, James Richard 142
MacLeod, Norman 128, 134
MacNeice, Louis 4, 107–22, 125, 236
McRae, Calista 4, 107–22
Mahon, Derek 1, 2, 141, 172n16, 194, 249
Maier, Thomas 60n27, 63
Mailer, Norman 40
Malcolm X 79
Malraux, André 71
Manahan, Ernest 31
Mariani, Paul 33n51, 37n61, 132n26, 135n35, 139, 193n1
Maritain, Jacques 134
Marlowe, Christopher 59n24, 214
Martin, Jay 121
Marx, Harpo 107
Mary, the Virgin 136
Massumi, Brian 95
Mather, Cotton 57–58
Mather, Increase 57
Mathews, Jackson 143, 145
Matterson, Stephen 23n1
Matthews, Steven 127n13
Maxwell, C. 8n1
Mazzaro, Jerome 37
Melville, Herman 78, 88, 151, 171, 180
Mentz, Steve 147–48, 160, 165

Meyers, Jeffrey 24n10, 133n28, 181n12
Miller, Daniel 205
Milton, John 65–66, 137, 152, 180–81, 214–15, 252
Mitchell, Gregory 95
Mitchell, T.N. 11n8, 12
Monroe, Marilyn 40
Montague, John 124, 194
Montgomery, Niall 129
Moore, Marianne 115, 134, 229, 252
Moynihan, Daniel Patrick 45n103
Mozart, Wolfgang Amadeus 24
Muir, Kenneth 65n39
Muldoon, Paul 4, 21–22, 229–30
Mullally, Una 2
Murphy, Richard 194, 249
Mussolini, Benito 91

N
Nessus 63
Nixon, Richard 42, 47

O
Ó Conchubhair, Brian 3
O'Brien, Hugh 53
O'Callaghan, Julie 1, 249, 251
O'Connor, Edwin 51
O'Connor, Thomas H. 50
O'Donoghue, Bernard 163
O'Driscoll, Dennis 1, 150n12, 249, 251, 253
Ogden, C.K. 62
O'Hanlon, Karl 4, 123–46
Oswald, Lee Harvey 72

P
Palfrey, John Gorham 50
Palmer, Arthur 10
Parker, Joseph 181, 185
Parker, Stephen 182, 184, 186
Parkinson, Thomas 215n16
Pasternak, Boris 145
Paulin, Tom 2, 3, 5

Peacock, Alan J. 107n2
Peerson, Allison 214
Perloff, Marjorie 176, 177–79, 190, 195, 213
Perse, Saint-John 130, 133, 135, 145
Pethica, James 90
Phipps, C.B. 9n5, 10n7
Plath, Sylvia 3, 28, 47, 61, 168, 229, 231, 235, 244
Plimpton, George 41n85
Plutarch 69
Poirier, Richard 24
Porter, Katherine Anne 130–31, 134–35
Pound, Ezra 41, 84, 107, 111, 118, 120, 142, 179, 252
Propertius, Sextus 241
Puleo, Stephen 51n6
Purser, Louis Claude 10
Pyle, William Fitzroy 7

Q
Queen, Victoria 93
Quinn, Antoinette 124n4
Quinn, Charles 68

R
Randolph, Jody Allen 200n18
Ransom, John Crowe 85–86, 105, 108, 132, 134, 252
Rich, Adrienne 191, 218, 234
Richards, I.A. 62
Ricks, Christopher 66, 73, 190
Rimbaud, Arthur 14
Roberts, Michael 168
Roethke, Theodore 27–28, 107, 120, 142, 209
Rogers, W.R. 125
Roland, Romain 211
Roosevelt, Theodore 91
Rosen, Charles 7
Rosenthal, M.L. 27n28
Roth, Philip 38
Rubinstein, Arthur 34
Runchman, Alex 5, 67–82

S
Salkeld, Blanaid 128
Salvagni, Lorenzo 143, 144
Sandburg, Carl 134
Santayana, George 25, 28, 141
Sartre, Jean-Paul 27, 214–15
Schwartz, Delmore 77, 80
Scott, Evelyn 135
Seidel, Frederick 126n12
Sexton, Anne 61
Shakespeare, William 14, 65, 67, 75
Shapiro, Karl 194
Shaw, George Bernard 125
Shaw, Robert Gould 162
Silone, Ignazio 141, 142n52
Simmons, James 189
Sirhan, Sirhan 73–74
Skillman, Nikki 27
Smith, Michael 141
Snodgrass, W.D. 38
Snyder, Timothy 23
Spender, Stephen 112, 123
Spock, Benjamin 41
Staël, Madame de 142
Stafford, Jean 135
Stalin, Joseph 93, 107
Stallworthy, Jon 112
Stanford, W. Bedell 10
Stein, Jean 41n85, 67n2
Stephen, St 139
Stevens, Wallace 131, 134
Stevenson, Adlai 37
Stubbs, J.W. 9n3

T
Tate, Allen 3, 33, 85–87, 105, 123, 129, 130, 135, 136, 137, 141, 146, 252
Tate, Robert William 10
Taylor, Peter 33, 141, 141n51
Temple, William 9
Tennyson, Alfred 74, 252
Teuber, Andreas 43
Theresa of Avila, St 136

Thomas, Edward 238
Tracy, Spencer 51
Travisano, Thomas 25n18, 71n14, 83n1, 177n1, 197n11, 234n14, 234n14
Truman, Harry 54
Trump, Donald J. 5, 23
Tuan, Yi-Fu 200
Tyrrell, Robert Yelverton 10

U
Underwood, Thomas A. 131
Untermeyer, Louis 85
Uris, Jill 182, 185
Uris, Leon 182, 185
Ussher, James 9
Ussher, Percy 128

V
Varro, Marcus Terentius 13n14
Vendler, Helen 115, 162–63
Vermeer, Johannes 153
Virgil 241
Voznesensky, Andrei 40

W
Walcott, Derek 149
Walker, Tom 107n2
Walsh, Ann 51n7
Walsh, Catherine 4, 5, 211–28
Warren, Robert Penn 38, 130–31, 137, 141
Weaver, Richard M. 125
Webb, Thomas E. 10
Wescott, Glenway 135n36
White, H.O. 5, 23n1
Wilkinson, Alec 178n5
Williams, William Carlos 84, 94, 111, 115, 120, 123
Williamson, Alan 214, 217
Winnicott, Donald 237
Winslow, Marcella Comès 130
Winslow, Mary 61
Winslow, Warren 151
Winthrop, John 52
Wordsworth, William 59, 139
Workell, Donald 10

Y
Yeats, W.B. 3, 4, 25–29, 37, 39, 45, 47, 74, 83–105, 108, 125, 127, 131, 194, 235, 251–52
York, Richard 107n2

Z
Žižek, Slavoj 187

Lightning Source UK Ltd.
Milton Keynes UK
UKHW051607090322
399808UK00020B/123